COMPLETE GUIDE *to* SLOWPITCH SOFTBALL

RAINER MARTENS
JULIE S. MARTENS

Human Kinetics

Library of Congress Cataloging-in-Publication Data

Martens, Rainer, 1942-
  Complete guide to slowpitch softball / Rainer Martens, Julie S.
Martens.
    p. cm.
  Includes index.
  ISBN-13: 978-0-7360-9406-1 (soft cover)
  ISBN-10: 0-7360-9406-7 (soft cover)
  1. Slow pitch softball. I. Martens, Julie S., 1949- II. Title. III.
Title: Complete guide to slow pitch softball.
  GV881.M36 2010
  796.357'8--dc22

                              2010014230

ISBN-10: 0-7360-9406-7 (print)
ISBN-13: 978-0-7360-9406-1 (print)

The Web addresses cited in this text were current as of September 2010, unless otherwise noted.

Acquisitions Editor: Justin Klug; **Developmental Editor:** Julie Marx Goodreau; **Assistant Editors:** Elizabeth Evans, Casey A. Gentis; **Copyeditor:** Bob Replinger; **Indexer:** Katy Balcer; **Permission Manager:** Martha Gullo; **Graphic Designer:** Bob Reuther; **Graphic Artist:** Tara Welsch; **Cover Designer:** Keith Blomberg; **DVD Face Designer:** Susan Rothermel Allen; **DVD Producer:** Doug Fink; **Video Production Coordinator:** Amy Rose; **Photo Production Manager:** Jason Allen; **Art Manager:** Kelly Hendren; **Associate Art Manager:** Alan L. Wilborn; **Illustrators:** Alan L. Wilborn and TwoJay!; **Printer:** McNaughton & Gunn

We thank the Sarasota County Parks and Recreation Department in Sarasota, Florida, for assistance in providing the location for the photo shoot for this book.

Human Kinetics books are available at special discounts for bulk purchase. Special editions or book excerpts can also be created to specification. For details, contact the Special Sales Manager at Human Kinetics.

The contents of this DVD are licensed for private home use and traditional, face-to-face classroom instruction only. For public performance licensing, please contact a sales representative at www.HumanKinetics.com/SalesRepresentatives.

Printed in the United States of America   10 9 8 7 6 5 4 3 2 1

The paper in this book is certified under a sustainable forestry program.

Human Kinetics
Web site: www.HumanKinetics.com

United States: Human Kinetics
P.O. Box 5076
Champaign, IL 61825-5076
800-747-4457
e-mail: humank@hkusa.com

Canada: Human Kinetics
475 Devonshire Road Unit 100
Windsor, ON N8Y 2L5
800-465-7301 (in Canada only)
e-mail: info@hkcanada.com

Europe: Human Kinetics
107 Bradford Road
Stanningley
Leeds LS28 6AT, United Kingdom
+44 (0) 113 255 5665
e-mail: hk@hkeurope.com

Australia: Human Kinetics
57A Price Avenue
Lower Mitcham, South Australia 5062
08 8372 0999
e-mail: info@hkaustralia.com

New Zealand: Human Kinetics
P.O. Box 80
Torrens Park, South Australia 5062
0800 222 062
e-mail: info@hknewzealand.com

E5123

COMPLETE GUIDE
GUIDE
to
SLOWPITCH
SOFTBALL

CONTENTS

PART III PREPARATION 205

PART IV COACHING 271

DVD CONTENTS

OFFENSE

DEFENSE

Pitching

Delivery Methods

Types of Pitches

    Vertical Topspin

    Vertical Backspin

    Left Curve

    Right Curve

    Knuckleball

Defensive Setup

Covering the Bases

Pitcher-Initiated Double Plays

Infielder Skills

Fielding Ground Balls

Fielding on the Move

Diving, Bloopers,
  and Pop-Ups

Types of Throws

    Overhand Throw

    Sidearm Throw

    Dart Throw

    Underhand Toss

    Backhand Flip

Difficult Throws

    Throwing on the Run

    Throwing to a Running Fielder

    Relaying Throws From the Outfield

Tagging Runners

Receiving Throws at First

Fielding Plays at First

Plays at Catcher

Second-to-First Double Plays

Rundowns

Outfielder Skills

Catching Fly Balls

Fielding Ground Balls

Overhand Throws

Defensive Strategies and Tactics

Relays and Cutoffs

    Single, No One on Base

    Double, No One on Base

    Triple, No One on Base

    Single, Runner on First Base

    Double, Runner on First Base

    Fly Out, Runner on First Base,
      Less Than Two Outs

    Single, Runners on First
      and Second Base

    Fly Out, Runners on First
      and Second Base,
      Less Than Two Outs

    Single, Bases Loaded

    Fly Out, Bases Loaded,
      Less Than Two Outs

Less Common Double Plays

    With Runner on First Base

    With Runners in Other Locations

Two More Special Plays

Infield Hits With 11 Defensive Players

Outfield Hits With 11 Defensive Players

Total running time: 69 minutes

PREFACE

We're addicted to slowpitch* softball. If one must have addictions, this is a good one to have. We love the game so much that in our senior years we've organized our work lives to fit around our softball lives. The game has been good to us, and we want to be good to the game by writing the most comprehensive book available on the sport. We not only want to help you play and coach the game better but also want to infect you with the passion that we have for slowpitch softball. Being passionate about a recreational activity is cathartic, and playing slowpitch softball can add both years to your life and life to your years.

All players, regardless of skill level, share the objective of having fun. Why else would we play? But have you noticed the strong relationship between playing the game well and having fun? We didn't say winning and having fun, although you've probably learned that winning is more fun than losing. But personally playing the game well is intrinsically rewarding because it makes us feel competent, and we each have a basic need to feel competent. So we hope that this book will help you become a more competent player and therefore have more fun playing slowpitch softball.

If you're a recreational slowpitch softball player somewhere between the ages of 16 and 92, you'll find this book loaded with useful information to help you play better and enjoy the game more. If you're a competitive slowpitch softball player striving to improve your game, to come closer to your potential as a player, you'll find this book essential.

This book is both a basic and advanced analysis of how to play slowpitch softball. The technical skills (hitting, fielding, and so forth) that we cover are equally applicable to young and old, novice and elite, and women and men players. The tactics of the sport, however, differ for some versions of the sport. We have not covered elite adult slowpitch softball, a version of the game played by a small number of outstanding players who do much of their scoring by hitting home runs. We also do not cover the specifics of 16-inch slowpitch softball, although much of what we discuss in this book is applicable to the 16-inch game. What we have covered are the tactics of slowpitch softball played in recreational leagues during weeknights and in competitive tournaments on weekends by millions of players, what we think of as mainstream slowpitch softball.

If you coach this wonderful sport, your first step to coaching greatness is to buy a dozen copies of this book and hand them out to your players. (Isn't that shameful self-promotion!) And because you have the book in your hands, you'll especially want to read and reread part IV, "Coaching," to learn how you can be more effective in your role.

*Is it *slow pitch*, *slowpitch*, or *slow-pitch* softball? Usage is inconsistent in the skimpy literature available on the sport, and slowpitch organizations are inconsistent in their use of the term. Thus, the Human Kinetics editorial team decided to use *slowpitch* as one word when used as a noun or adjective, just as it does with *fastpitch* softball. We encourage others to use *slowpitch* as the preferred usage to standardize the reference to this sport.

We do not dwell on basic skills such as catching, fielding, and throwing, skills that you likely learned by playing baseball or fastpitch softball and that you perform the same way in slowpitch softball. Many books and videos are available if you need help with these fundamentals. Instead we focus on the skills unique to slowpitch softball. Although words and pictures are our tools for this book, video can demonstrate offensive and defensive skills more effectively. Thus you'll find the DVD packaged with this book to be a vital instructional supplement to the text. The technical skills covered on the DVD are highlighted with this icon in the margin.

In chapters 1 and 2 of part I you'll learn about the art and science of hitting. With better hitting you'll be running the bases a lot more, and we'll show you how to speed around them in chapter 3. You'll want to deploy your improved hitting and baserunning skills intelligently, so in chapter 4 you'll learn about the strategies and tactics of offensive play.

Common lore is that slowpitch softball is a hitter's game, and it is, but equally so—not more or less—it is a defensive game. It's the increased offense and defense that makes this game so much fun. So in part II we'll help you improve your defensive skills. Chapter 5 is an extensive look at slowpitch pitching, including a section on fielding the pitching position. In chapter 6 we examine infielder skills, and in chapter 7 we analyze outfielder skills. The final chapter in part II, chapter 8, describes defensive strategies and tactics to give your team the winning edge.

Part III of the book is about preparation, and it logically could have been part I. But we thought that you'd prefer to dig into offensive and defensive skills first and then look at preparing yourself to play. In chapter 9 you'll find essential information about the playing field and the equipment used in slowpitch softball. In chapters 10 and 11 we help you prepare to play better by training physically and mentally, and in chapter 12 we cover some basic sports medicine to help you prevent and treat those annoying minor injuries that occur when playing the game and provide you with guidelines about when you should seek medical care.

Part IV is for those courageous people who are willing to take on the role of coach, whether it's for a team of teenage girls or 75-year-old seniors. Coaching is challenging and, when done well, rewarding. In chapters 13 and 14 we provide guidelines about how to conduct effective practices and manage game-day activities.

This book is not like a novel; you don't need to read it from beginning to end in that order. We suggest that you read the introduction, jump around the 14 chapters based on your interests, and then use the supplemental DVD when we suggest doing so in the appropriate chapters.

Two more things: first a warning. The United States is blessed with nine major national slowpitch softball associations, all playing the game in the same general way but each having some minor rule variations. And then there are hundreds of local and regional organizations that usually adopt the rules of one of the national associations but then modify them for local preferences or conditions. So we will reference what we believe comes closest to being the consensus rule by national associations and then note major variations to those rules when we think that they significantly change the game. Because not everyone plays by the same set of rules, be sure to find out the applicable rules in the league or tournament in which you play.

Second: a request. We welcome your comments about this book and DVD package. Tell us what's missing or what we could cover better. And, of course, we are eager to hear what you think we got right. You can e-mail us at Juliem@ hkusa.com or send your comments to Julie Martens, Slowpitch Softball, 2190 John Anderson Drive, Ormond Beach, FL 32176.

ACKNOWLEDGMENTS

To the teams who taught me humility through their superior play, I now appreciate those lessons.

To my teammates throughout the years who let me share in their successes, thank you for the memories.

To my wife, Julie, who shares my passion for the game and has helped me so much as a player and coach, my heartfelt thanks.

—Rainer Martens

To my parents for their support through every aspect of my life.

To my high school and college coaches who helped me develop my sport skills and enabled me to experience the joys of competition.

To the Florida Legends, especially the Legendary Ladies, for being such good friends and for making my job of managing all the details that much easier.

To Rainer, who continues to teach me about the game of softball and challenges me to reach a little further for the things that aren't easy to achieve, thanks for being a great mentor and husband.

—Julie Martens

To the many people who helped us create this book and the companion DVD, our sincere thanks. Foremost, we would like to acknowledge our friends and teammates who are members of the Florida Legends senior softball team who participated in the video, served as models for the photos in this book, and provided logistical support. They are Patrick Bidelman and Bonnie Catalano, Bill Brotherton, Matt and Bev Callahan, Zeb and Susan Carter, Bob Conrad, Tom Dabbs, Dave and Nancy Decker, Derry Dedmon, Bob Koss, Jeff MacDonald, Vince Melograno, and Mike Pickett. We also wish to thank our younger models who played with such skill and grace: Ashley Bodi, Consuelo Flickinger, Bill Crieslar, Shawn Harville, David Phillips, Gabe Preece, and especially Jerry Hoffer, who recruited and performed with this group. We also wish to thank Hansel Faulkner, Cliff Stratton, Walt Taylor, Dave Foltz, Dick Kanyan, Al Mahar, and Joe McWhertor for serving as photo models.

We offer a big thank-you to Lou Giovanini, Patrick Bidelman, and Derry Dedmon for providing comments about the first draft of this manuscript. Thanks also to those staff members at Human Kinetics who contributed in many ways to the development of both the book and the DVD. We especially appreciate the guidance of Doug Fink in developing the companion DVD. And we owe a big debt of gratitude to Julie Marx Goodreau, our editor at Human Kinetics. Not only is Julie a superior editor, she's also a veteran slowpitch softball player whose knowledge of the game made this book much better.

And finally, we'd like to express our gratitude to the many players, spouses, umpires, and administrators who have made the game so enjoyable for us.

—Rainer and Julie Martens

ABOUT THE AUTHORS

We wrote this book together not only because we're married and because the game is a big part of our lives but also because we each have a unique perspective about the game that we wanted to share. Rainer is the player and coach; Julie is a former player, now manager, scorekeeper, and tactician. Together, we're students of the sport and are eager to share our knowledge about the game.

When you read a book about how to do something, you should rightfully know whether the authors are credible. So permit us to introduce ourselves to you.

Rainer's Background

Like many young boys, Rainer grew up playing sandlot baseball with the neighborhood gang and then played in organized youth leagues from 8 to 16 years of age. Many wax eloquently about the virtues of sandlot play and the vices of highly competitive, adult-organized youth sports, but Rainer loved them both. American Legion and college baseball followed, and at the end of his senior year he pondered his dream of becoming a professional baseball player. The Kansas City A's had offered him an opportunity to play minor league baseball. Meanwhile, the University of Montana had admitted him to graduate school and had an assistantship waiting for him. Having developed a chronic sore arm from training improperly and pitching way too much, and having considerable doubt that he had the ability to be successful professionally, he decided on graduate school. It was the right choice for him.

After Rainer completed his master's degree at the University of Montana, he returned to his hometown of Hutchinson, Kansas, in the summer of 1966 to manage a swimming pool before beginning his doctorate degree in the fall at the University of Illinois. Upon his arrival in Hutch, his former American Legion baseball coach, Bob Swanson, asked him to play on his slowpitch softball team. Until then Rainer hadn't heard of the game and, in fact, like many devout baseball and fastpitch softball players, thought that the game looked silly when he first saw it. But after playing only a few games he was hooked and played the game for the next 20 years.

Rainer quit playing at age 45 when his wife, Marilyn, needed continual care as she fought the insidious disease of diabetes. The small publishing company that he founded in 1974, Human Kinetics, began to prosper and took what remaining time he had available. Marilyn lost that fight in 1991.

Like many others, Rainer figured that he would never play again. He was now too old, but then the husband of an employee at Human Kinetics invited him to play in a 55-year-plus senior softball league in Champaign, Illinois. Rainer initially declined, believing that he was too busy and was traveling too frequently to be a good team member. But one day Rainer was asked again to play because the team was short one player. So he played. And like the on-the-wagon alcoholic who takes one drink, he was addicted again. He has been playing ever since.

Rainer, with his second wife, Julie, began spending winters in Florida, partly, or perhaps mostly, to play softball. Known as God's waiting room, Florida is where millions of seniors retire to be away from the cold. Consequently, the state has many outstanding senior softball players. Rainer was able to play in a local league twice a week and then played once a month in the Florida Half Century League, arguably the best competitive senior softball program in the country.

He played in his first national tournament in 1999 and won a 55-year-plus national championship in 2000 with a Daytona Beach team that Human Kinetics sponsored. In 2002 Rainer was asked by Lou Giovanini to join the 60-year-plus Florida Legends, a team that he hadn't heard of but should have. Since the 1990s the team had won more than 50 national championships, and in 2002 the team played in seven national tournaments, winning six of them and placing second in the other one. Playing with the Florida Legends taught Rainer much about how the game should be played. Seven years later he continues to play with the Florida Legends in the 65-year-plus age category and now coaches the team as well. In 2009 Rainer was inducted into the Senior Softball Hall of Fame.

Having played the game over many years is only part of Rainer's credentials to write this book. He also has been a student of the sport sciences. He spent 16 years as a sport psychology professor at the University of Illinois, during which time he worked with college and Olympic athletes. For 6 years he served as the sport psychologist for the U.S. ski team, working with the team through the 1984 Olympic Games in Sarajevo.

In 1973 Rainer hosted a sport psychology conference at the University of Illinois. After several publishers turned down his request to publish the papers presented at that conference, he and his wife, Marilyn, published them, which was the start of Human Kinetics. Today the publishing company is the largest publisher of sports books, journals, and coaching courses in the world. So Rainer spent much of his adult life not only learning about sport psychology but also reading manuscripts on sport biomechanics, sport physiology, sport nutrition, motor skill learning, and other sport sciences.

He's written 15 books over the years and hundreds of articles. Rainer's book *Successful Coaching* has sold over a million copies and is the best-selling coaching book ever published. But according to Rainer, the book that he's enjoyed writing most is this book because of his passion for the game.

Julie's Background

Like Rainer, Julie grew up playing sandlot baseball with the neighborhood gang, but then her youth experiences took a different turn. Organized youth baseball was only a dream for Julie because girls were not permitted to play alongside the boys. It didn't matter that the young tomboy was better than many of the boys; what mattered was that she was a girl and baseball leagues were for boys only. She continued to play alongside the boys at the vacant lot down the street and participated in all the weekly sports and games competitions in the local park and recreation program, winning her fair share of events. Then the summer before eighth grade, Julie and her best friend, Sharon Noodell, discovered a fastpitch girls softball team that was looking for players. Both girls jumped at the opportunity to play on the team. They began their softball careers with Sharon playing second base and Julie playing the outfield or infield if needed. This continued for several years until other teenage activities began conflicting with their weekly practice and twice weekly evening games.

With interscholastic girls sports programs in Omaha being limited only to tennis, Julie figured that she better learn to play if she wanted to experience the joys of higher-level competition. She took many lessons and spent her afternoons at the local tennis center playing against anyone willing to step out on the court with her. She began entering age-group tournaments and won a number of them around the state, and she competed in both singles and doubles competition for her high school tennis team.

Julie went on to Purdue University and majored in physical education. In those pre–Title IX days, sports competition was limited to club-level play between universities, but Julie's urge to participate in competitive sports was still very much alive. During her 4 years at Purdue she had the opportunity to play basketball, field hockey, fastpitch softball, and tennis against other universities in the Midwest.

Following graduation from Purdue, Julie went on to graduate school at the University of Washington, where she set aside competitive sports because of studies. She then came to the University of Illinois to study sport psychology under the tutelage of Professor Rainer Martens, who later became husband Rainer Martens. While at Illinois Julie taught lifetime sports classes to undergraduates and continued to play a variety of sports, including tennis and racquetball, the latter of which she coached at the collegiate club level. During her time at Illinois she was introduced to slowpitch softball, a game that would become a major part of her life.

After completing her doctorate at the University of Illinois, Julie went to work for Human Kinetics, becoming the first full-time employee of the young publishing company. Besides working, she enjoyed playing on a women's slowpitch team for several years. She then decided that playing coed softball was more fun for her, and she played for the Human Kinetics team for many years.

But then a new chapter in slowpitch softball began for her—only not as a player, but as a supportive wife and fan. For the last several years Julie has been the team manager, scorekeeper, and statistician for the Florida Legends Senior Softball team and loves traveling with Rainer to tournaments around the country and talking softball with him. They also both enjoy biking, walking, traveling, and photography. *Complete Guide to Slowpitch Softball* is the first book that she has coauthored.

INTRODUCTION

Welcome to slowpitch softball, an exciting team sport played by 13 million people in the United States and 2 million in other countries. Why is slowpitch softball the most popular participant team sport in the United States? To answer that question, we first look at how slowpitch softball differs from baseball and fastpitch softball and follow that with a brief look at the origin of the sport. Then we'll share with you many reasons for the popularity of this sport. We end the introduction with a section on terminology to help you understand the remainder of the book.

UNIQUENESS OF SLOWPITCH SOFTBALL

Obviously, slowpitch differs from fastpitch softball in that the ball is pitched s–l–o–w–l–y, making it easy for the batter to hit the ball. The consequence is a remarkable transformation between the two sports. Pitchers dominate fastpitch softball. The consequence is little hitting and thus little fielding. Batters dominate slowpitch softball, and the consequence is lots of hitting, lots of baserunning, lots of defensive play, and most of all lots of fun. Here's a brief description of additional differences between the two games:

- **Number of players.** Slowpitch teams have 10 defensive players rather than 9. Usually the 10th player is an additional outfielder. Some senior leagues have 11 defensive players on a team, and the 11th player is usually positioned behind second base. In many leagues, teams can bat more than 10 players, which allows coaches to let every player on the team bat.

- **Pitching and the strike zone.** The ball must be pitched underhand with an arc. Most leagues require the ball to reach a minimum height of 6 feet (1.8 m) and a maximum height of 12 feet (3.7 m). Strikes are called in one of two ways: (1) by the pitch passing through a strike zone as in baseball, or (2) by the ball hitting the plate or a mat that is placed behind it. You'll learn about both of these methods of determining a strike in chapter 1.

- **Balls and strikes.** Many leagues and tournaments begin with a 1 ball, 1 strike count on the batter. In many tournaments, however, the game is played with the conventional 4 ball, 3 strike count. Usually, the batter is out when hitting a foul ball on the third strike.

- **Baserunning.** As we'll cover in chapter 3, because the pitch is thrown slowly batters cannot bunt. In most leagues, base runners can advance only when the ball is hit, so there is no base stealing. Some local leagues do allow runners to advance after the pitch hits the ground, although that variation of the sport is not common.

- **Safety base.** Many leagues and tournaments use a double, or safety, base at first to reduce the chances of collision. The safety base is an extra first base placed immediately adjacent to the regular one but outside the foul line and usually colored orange or red. When a play occurs at first base the runner must touch the safety base and the fielder must touch the regular first base.

- **Scoring plate.** In some recreational leagues and tournaments and in all senior slowpitch softball, a separate scoring plate is used, which is located 8 feet (2.4 m) away from the regular home plate as shown on page 52 in chapter 3. To avoid collisions, the runner from third must run to the scoring plate, not the regular home plate. To learn more about this play at home, see page 52 in chapter 3.

- **Coed game.** A popular form of slowpitch softball is played by men and women together. Although the usual 10 defensive players are used, up to 12 players can bat, alternating between women and men. Most leagues require an equal split of male and female infielders and outfielders, and a male pitcher and female catcher (or vice versa). Some leagues even require that men and women alternate positions in the infield and outfield so that two men or two women aren't playing adjacent positions. Most coed leagues allow more female than male players; for example, a team could play with 7 women and 5 men.

HISTORY OF SLOWPITCH SOFTBALL

Whether you're new to slowpitch softball or a veteran, we thought that you would appreciate a brief account of the evolution of the sport. Here's the story.

Origins of the Sport

On Thanksgiving Day, November 24, 1887, Harvard and Yale alumni met at a Chicago boat club to hear the score of the annual football game between the two schools. When it was announced that Yale won 17-8, someone picked up a boxing glove that was lying around and threw it at a Harvard alumnus. After a few more tosses, someone grabbed a pole and hit the glove. Observing the action, George Hancock yelled, "Let's play ball!" He took the boxing glove laces and tied the glove into a ball. Someone broke off a broom handle, and they marked off a diamond in the boathouse. Voilà—softball was born.

The game may have died the day of its birth, but George was smitten with the game, and so within a week he created a 16-inch (41 cm) ball and a narrow, rubber-tipped bat. He developed a set of rules and called the game indoor baseball. In 1888 the game began to be played outdoors as well as indoors and became known as indoor–outdoor.

The game's popularity spread across Chicago and the Midwest like the raging Great Chicago Fire of 1871. As the game grew in popularity, Hancock published the first set of rules in 1889.

The Chicago indoor–outdoor team of 1897. This photo is thought to be the first of a softball team.

Copyright by X.O. Howe, 1897. From Library of Congress Prints and Photographs Division, Washington, DC.

In 1895, apparently without knowledge of Hancock's invention, Lewis Rober, a Minneapolis fire department officer who was looking for an activity to keep his firemen in shape, developed a version of softball that they played in a vacant lot next to the firehouse. Called kitten ball, this version of the sport was played with a 12-inch (30 cm) ball and a bat that was 2 inches (5 cm) in diameter.

The 1920s Through the 1940s

From the turn of the 20th century to the 1930s, the game flourished across America. The name *softball* began to be promoted as the name for the sport in 1926 and became the official name in 1934 when the Joint Rules Committee on Softball christened the name and standardized the rules of the sport.

Softball became much more visible when Leo Fischer and Michael J. Pauley invited 55 teams from around the coun-

A player demonstrating hitting a 16-inch softball in 1907.

SDN-005372, Chicago Daily News negatives collection, Chicago Historical Society.

try to play in the 1933 World's Fair in Chicago. Single-elimination tournaments were held for men's fastpitch, men's slowpitch, and women's fastpitch. All teams used a 14-inch (36 cm) ball. On opening day of the tournament, 70,000 people attended the games. The *Chicago American* newspaper wrote, "It is the largest and most comprehensive tournament ever held in the sport which has swept the country like wildfire." And it resulted in teams and leagues springing up across the country and eventually the founding of the Amateur Softball Association (ASA). Over the next decade it was estimated that five million people played softball.

Sixteen-inch softball thrived in Chicago in the 1930s and continues to be played by a small but avid group of players today, as witnessed by a drive around Grant Park in Chicago any summer weekend. In the 1940s 12-inch fastpitch was the prevailing version of the game. As pitchers began to dominate the fastpitch game, resulting in little action, slowpitch emerged as an alternative recreational version of softball.

In 1937 the ASA published the first rules of 16-inch slowpitch softball in the same publication as the rules for fastpitch. In introducing the slowpitch rules the ASA stated

> *Although the fastpitching game of softball is equal to any sport for thrills and skillful play, the Amateur Softball Association also is endeavoring to stress the advantages of the slow-pitching type of softball, which likewise has attained immense popularity in many sections of the country. In the slow-pitching game, emphasis is taken off pitching and placed on hitting and fielding with amazing results.* (1937 Official Softball Guide and Rule Book, *Amateur Softball Association*)

No rules were published during World War II. As the standardized rules were forgotten or rulebooks were lost and destroyed, new rules were developed and adopted by various leagues throughout the country. This circumstance caused considerable confusion when teams from various regions competed against each other. Consequently, in 1947 a uniform set of rules was again published in the *ASA Rulebook*.

Modern-Day 12-Inch Slowpitch

The 12-inch slowpitch game of today is thought to have its roots in Ohio, Indiana, and Kentucky. It appears that the Not So Good softball league in Cleveland, Ohio, consisting of men mostly past 30 years of age, was the first 12-inch slowpitch softball league. Over the next several years the game spread across those three states, and in 1953 the ASA officially recognized 12-inch slowpitch softball and held the first world championships in Cincinnati, Ohio. Twelve teams participated, and Shields Contractor of Newport, Kentucky, won the title. In 1957 the first annual women's national invitational slowpitch tournament was held.

From the 1960s to the 1990s participation in slowpitch softball exploded, although good estimates of the actual growth nationally are not available. In the 1960s the Amateur Softball Association was the only organization conducting slowpitch tournaments, but its leaders were primarily interested in fastpitch because most had been fastpitch players. Neglecting the call for more opportunities to play slowpitch softball by youth, women, and seniors, the ASA saw other organizations respond to the interest. Today, besides the ASA, no fewer than eight national associations conduct slowpitch softball tournaments, and unknown numbers of state and local organizations do the same. See appendix B for a list of the national and international associations and their contact information.

Dave Reed, a National Hall of Fame Player, demonstrates how to hit with power.

During the late 1970s three professional softball leagues started but all collapsed by 1982 for lack of financial viability. We believe that one reason the sport has been unsuccessful at the professional level and has received almost no television coverage nationally is that its greatest appeal is to play it, not to watch it.

Since our society has gotten beyond the silly belief that women could not engage in physically demanding sports, participation by girls and women in slowpitch softball has increased substantially. From local girls' leagues to highly competitive women's national tournament teams to senior women's leagues, estimates are that more than 6 million girls and women play slowpitch softball today.

The biggest changes to the game in the modern era are the result of technology. The bats are no longer wooden but are made of exotic composite materials that propel the ball much farther. In the 1970s metal barrels and wooden-handled bats were introduced, but they were short-lived because they were dangerous when the bat broke where the wood and metal were pinned together. That led to all-metal bats made of aluminum. Beginning in the late 1990s bats made of exotic composite materials were introduced and are widely used today, the Miken Ultra II being by far the most popular bat. As bats improved, the risk of injury to players, especially pitchers, increased, and some bats were banned. See chapter 9 for more information about the evolution of bats.

As bats and balls improved, players hit the ball farther and thus playing fields expanded. In the 1960s and 70s the outfield fences were often 275 feet (84 m) from home plate. Today, most are at a minimum of 300 feet (91 m) and some are even farther. As the sport grew in popularity many communities constructed softball complexes that have four or five diamonds in a circle with a tower in the middle used for scorekeeping, concessions, restrooms, and maintenance equipment and supply storage. These wonderful facilities stimulate local economies by bringing teams to their communities for weekend tournaments.

A well-designed softball field in Salem, Virginia, with fences at 300 feet, a groomed infield and outfield, and stadium seating for spectators.

POPULARITY OF THE GAME

So why has this sport become so popular in the last 50 years? The reasons are several, and if you've been playing the game, you'll likely know them.

- It's an easy sport to begin playing without a lot of practice compared with baseball or fastpitch softball.

- The game includes a lot of action because it's easy to hit the ball, and consequently it creates lots of baserunning and defensive play.

- The game has a quick pace compared with fastpitch softball, which is dominated by the pitchers.

- It can be played by young and old alike and by females and males separately or together in coed leagues.

- The game is relatively safe, and few serious injuries occur.

- Although building playing facilities is costly, after those are established it's inexpensive to play because little equipment is required.

- When lights were added to the playing fields, participation expanded because working adults could play in the evening during the workweek.

- The sport can be played at many different levels, and most communities offer both recreational and competitive leagues.

- The sport lends itself to social interactions. Just hang around the bench of various teams and you'll see what we mean.

SLOWPITCH TERMINOLOGY

Throughout the next 14 chapters we'll be making reference to the slowpitch softball playing field, the positions of the players on the field, and the holes or lanes between those positions. In figure 1 you'll see the position names and numbers assigned to each position on the defensive team that we'll refer to throughout the book. We've placed the players in their typical positions on the diamond. We've also shown the 11th player as the middle infielder. Men's teams 65 and older and women's teams 50 and older often use this position.

The number assigned to each position is used primarily for scorekeeping. For example, a player hits a ground ball to the third baseperson (5), who fields it and throws it to the first baseperson (3) for the out. In the scorebook that out would be recorded 5-3. The number does not refer to the number on the player's uniform.

Let's assume that you're a Martian who has landed on earth and has never seen or heard of baseball, softball, and particularly slowpitch softball. As we get into the intricacies of playing the sport, we'll make frequent reference to

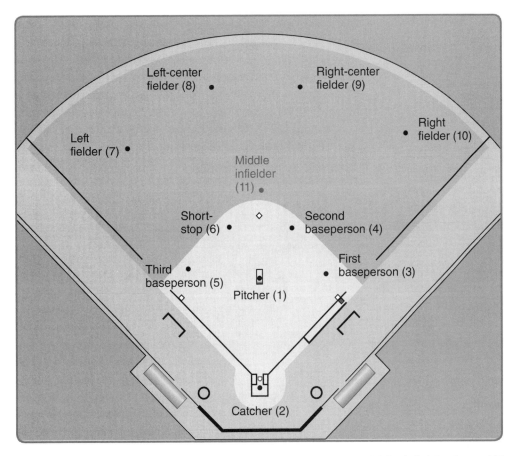

FIGURE 1 Defensive position names and numbers. The middle infielder is an 11th fielding position adopted by many senior leagues.

locations on the playing field. Figure 2 will help you with the terms that we'll use to reference locations on the softball field:

- **Infield**: The space encompassing the four bases (referred to as the diamond) and the dirt area from the diamond to where the outfield grass begins
- **Outfield**: The space shown in grey from the edge of the infield to the fences
- **Left field**: The third of the outfield area that is to the left side when a player is standing at home plate looking toward the outfield
- **Center field**: The third of the outfield area that is located in the center of the outfield
- **Right field**: The third of the outfield area that is to the right side when a player is standing at home plate looking toward the outfield

In figure 2 we show the typical defensive positions by number. When we need to refer to the spaces or lanes between those positions, we'll do so by hyphenating the two numbers. For example, we may say that the ball was hit in the 5-6 hole. That means that the ball was hit in the lane between the third baseperson and the shortstop. Or we might say the ball was hit in the 8-9 hole, which would refer to a ball hit to center field between the left-center fielder and the right-center fielder.

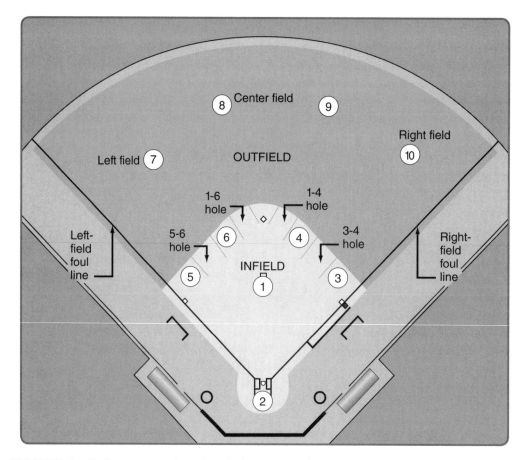

FIGURE 2 Reference system for defensive positions and locations.

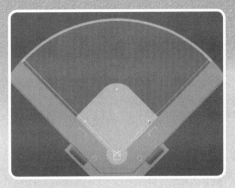

PART I
OFFENSE

The inventors of slowpitch softball gave birth to an exciting offensive sport. Players of all skill levels hit the ball almost all the time, although it's not always easy to get a base hit.

In part I you'll learn the offensive skills of hitting and baserunning and ways to apply those skills tactically during the game. In chapter 1 we'll cover the basics of hitting by helping you select a bat, determine whether you're a power hitter or place hitter, and learn the mechanics of an effective bat swing. And for your entertainment we'll give you a short quiz about how far the ball travels under various atmospheric conditions.

Chapter 2 will extend your knowledge by showing you how to hit with more power and precision. You'll also learn about the most common mistakes made in hitting and ways to avoid them. We conclude the chapter with knowledge from the field of sports vision, sport pedagogy, and sport psychology. Combining science with our experience, we'll help you see the ball better when hitting, practice more efficiently, and think more constructively when you're batting.

Now that you're hitting the ball well, you have the opportunity to run the bases regularly. So in chapter 3 you'll learn how to be an excellent base runner. First we'll cover the rules that apply to baserunning (remember that you can't steal a base!). We briefly discuss correct running technique and explain our four principles of good baserunning. Next you'll learn how to slide feetfirst, not headfirst because it's too dangerous. Then we take you on a tour around the bases to guide you in your decision making as you run from base to base, pointing out along the way mistakes to avoid. We close the chapter with guidelines for coaching first and third base.

Chapters 1, 2, and 3 are primarily about the technical aspects of offensive play. In chapter 4 we look at the tactical side of offense. We first examine the offensive strategies that teams may adopt in any particular game. Do you play cautiously or aggressively? Do you focus on power or place hitting? Do you exploit a weakness in the defense? Next our attention turns to your individual tactics when batting. We'll look at hitting tactics with different ball–strike counts and in various game situations.

If you're new to slowpitch softball, you'll find a lot of useful information in part I. And if you're an experienced player, you'll find it helpful to review what you may already know—perhaps you'll find a few points that will help you improve your game.

CHAPTER 1

Hitting Basics

Hitting in slowpitch is *about* the same as hitting in baseball and fastpitch softball. You hold the bat *about* the same way; your stance, forward stride, and swing are all *about* the same. But if you talk to accomplished veterans of the slowpitch game, they will tell you that hitting in slowpitch is considerably different from hitting in baseball and fastpitch softball, although they are *about* the same. And they will also tell you stories about accomplished baseball hitters who couldn't adapt to slowpitch.

The good news in slowpitch hitting is that you have much more time to hit the ball. The bad news in slowpitch hitting is that you have much more time to hit the ball . . . and thus to swing incorrectly.

If you're relatively new to slowpitch, studying this chapter and the companion DVD will provide you with a solid foundation to become a successful hitter. If you've been playing slowpitch softball for several years and are an accomplished hitter, you may choose to skip this chapter, although you'll miss a point or two that may help you become an even better hitter. Or if you're currently unsatisfied with your hitting, a careful review of the basics will be a good foundation before you go to chapter 2, "Advanced Hitting."

Although no single way of hitting is correct for every player, following the basic principles covered in this chapter can increase the odds of your hitting well.

As you read this chapter, have the DVD loaded in your DVD player. We'll shuttle back and forth between the content in this chapter and the video clips on the DVD to help you really understand these hitting basics. Also, have a bat handy and enough space to swing it so that you can try out what is being discussed.

PRELIMINARIES

Before you start swinging away, you should know several nontechnique aspects of slowpitch softball hitting to help you gain the most from this chapter and the next one on advanced hitting:

- Strike zone
- Power versus place hitters
- Hitting and power zones
- Ball flight
- Batting average

Strike Zone

In baseball and fastpitch the strike zone is a vertical rectangle that is 17 inches (43 cm) wide (the width of home plate) and has its upper boundary at the midpoint between the top of the shoulder and top of the uniform pants and its lower boundary at the hollow beneath the kneecap of the batter as shown in figure 1.1.

In slowpitch softball two methods of determining a strike are in use today. The first method, called the strike zone, has been in use since slowpitch originated. The strike zone is defined as a legal pitch that passes through an imaginary cube rising above home plate, the top of the cube being the top of the batter's back shoulder and the bottom being even with the batter's front knee when in a natural batting stance as shown in figure 1.2.

FIGURE 1.1 Baseball and fastpitch softball strike zone.

FIGURE 1.2 Slowpitch strike zone using home plate and no strike mat.

The strike zone in slowpitch softball has always been difficult for umpires to interpret with consistency, and it has been the source of many arguments between batters and umpires. So someone got the bright idea to put a mat behind home plate to help define the strike zone; a pitched ball that hit the plate or the mat when thrown with a legal arc would be a strike. This innovation made the work of the home-plate umpire easier and eliminated much bickering on the field.

Think of the strike mat in slowpitch this way: We take the baseball and fastpitch softball strike zone and place it on the ground as shown in figure 1.3. A strike is any legal pitch thrown with a minimum arc of 4 (1.2 m) to 6 feet (1.8 m) and maximum arc of 10 (3 m) to 12 feet (3.7 m) (or other arc limits as specified in the rules of various associations) that hits the plate or mat. Increasingly, leagues and tournaments are replacing the notched mat behind the plate with a single mat that fits over the plate. And some softball associations are now using a single mat that is wider by 2 inches (5 cm) on each side and an inch (2.5 cm) longer as shown in figure 1.4.

Today both the cube and strike mat are used to determine strikes, although many recreational leagues, women, and senior slowpitch organizations use the strike mat as the strike zone. (See table 5.1, Major Pitching Rules for the Leading Slowpitch Softball Associations, on page 114, for specific strike zone rules by association.) Hereafter we'll use the term *strike zone* to include both the cube and the strike mat to avoid having to reference both methods continually.

Power Versus Place Hitters

Most hitters quickly become either power hitters, hitting the ball as hard as they can and having a home run as their ultimate goal, or place hitters, seeking to hit the ball to a certain location in the field. Some talented players are able to be both power and place hitters, choosing one or the other depending on game circumstances.

So what type of hitter are you? What type of hitter do you want to be? How you apply the basic principles of slowpitch hitting discussed in this chapter and chapter 2 will depend to some extent on whether you're a power hitter or a place hitter.

Hitting and Power Zones

Batters have a preferred hitting zone. All of us prefer to hit pitches that are located in a zone where we can swing the bat with good bat control and reasonable bat speed regardless of whether we are power hitters or place hitters. Your hitting zone is where you hit pitches on the nose more consistently. That zone varies from batter to batter, of course, and some batters have a larger hitting zone than others, which makes them a more difficult out. For most batters the hitting zone is most if not all of the strike zone because they position themselves in the batter's box and stride into the pitch so that they can hit balls that would otherwise be called strikes.

Good hitters patiently wait for pitches to come into their hitting zone. Some batters, lacking patience, will swing at most any pitch they can reach. Such hitters

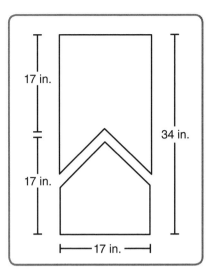

FIGURE 1.3 Slowpitch strike zone using a notched mat behind home plate.

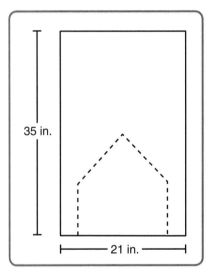

FIGURE 1.4 Slowpitch strike zone using a one-piece strike mat that covers the plate.

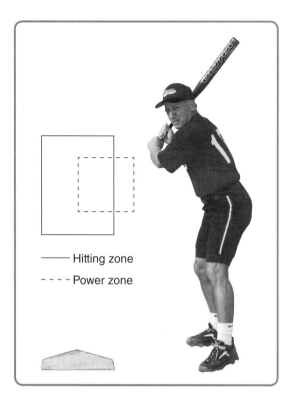

FIGURE 1.5 The hitting zone and power zone for a right-handed batter.

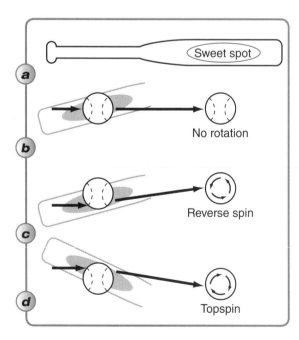

FIGURE 1.6 *(a)* Sweet spot on a bat. *(b)* Ball hit dead center, resulting in no rotation of the ball. *(c)* Ball hit slightly below the center so that it leaves the bat with reverse spin. *(d)* Ball hit slightly above the center, creating topspin on the ball.

do not have a large hitting zone; rather, they are undisciplined batters who need to discover their hitting zone.

Within the hitting zone many batters have a power zone, which refers to the area in which they can generate their maximum bat speed and thus hit the long ball (see figure 1.5). Typically, the power zone is the inside half of the plate and between the waist and armpit so that a right-handed batter can pull the ball to left field and a left-handed batter to right field. If the ball is outside the power zone, the smart batter will "go with the pitch," driving the ball up the middle or to the opposite field.

Ball Flight

As we dig into the complex skill of hitting, understanding the physics of ball flight is helpful. The direction and speed of the ball when you hit it is determined by the point of impact on the bat and the ball, the angle or plane of the swing, and the weight and speed of the bat. That explanation is common sense.

Let's assume that you hit the ball dead center on what is called the sweet spot of the bat. The sweet spot is the part of the bat barrel usually located a few inches down from the top end and as large as 6 inches (15 cm) or more (see figure 1.6a). When you hit the ball on the sweet spot, the bat doesn't wobble or vibrate and all the power of the swing is transferred to the ball. You get that good feeling when hitting.

When you hit the ball dead center on the barrel of the bat (see figure 1.6b), it will have no rotation and will behave like a knuckleball, fluttering in flight. If you hit the ball slightly below the center, it leaves the bat with a reverse spin (see figure 1.6c). And if you hit the ball slightly above the center, it leaves the bat with topspin (see figure 1.6d). What's the best location to hit the ball? It depends on your hitting objective.

When the ball is hit dead center and does not rotate, which happens infrequently, it leaves the bat with the greatest momentum, but because it is not spinning it encounters greater air resistance, moves erratically, and travels less distance. The ball hit very slightly below dead center spins counter-clockwise, with what is called reverse spin, and leaves the bat with slightly less speed but travels farther because the reverse spin aids its flight in the air (see sidebar, chapter 5, pages 92–94, "Softball Aerodynamics"). This spot on the bat is where home-run hitters aim to hit the ball.

A ball hit slightly above dead center has topspin (spinning clockwise), which causes the ball to dive downward sooner than a ball without spin or reverse spin. Line drives with topspin are often good hits.

Atmospheric Conditions and Ball Flight

What are the ideal atmospheric conditions for hitting home runs? The easiest part of the answer to that question is to have a gale wind blowing straight out to your favorite hitting field, but what do we know about conditions beyond a favorable wind? Let's consider what effects humidity, temperature, barometric pressure, and altitude have on the distance that a ball travels when hit with a given momentum.

Does a ball travel farther in dry or humid air?

If you said dry air, as we did, you would be wrong. We've always believed that balls travel farther in dry air because humid air (air with high water vapor) is denser than dry air, thus creating more friction on the ball. Surprisingly, physicists tell us that the opposite is true. When humidity increases, the heavier oxygen and nitrogen molecules in the air are replaced by the lighter water molecules, creating less dense air. The difference in density between 20% humidity and 80% humidity, however, is only about 1%. So if you hit a ball 300 feet (91.4 m) in dry air, it will travel about 303 feet (92.4 m) in humid air, just enough to clear that 300-foot fence.

Will a ball travel farther in colder or warmer temperatures?

We've always observed that when temperatures are cooler the ball seems to jump off the bat more so than when it's warmer. Well, our observations are wrong again. As air warms it becomes less dense (that's why warm air rises) and thus provides less resistance to a hit ball. Meteorologists tell us that air is 8% less dense at 95 °F (35 °C) than it is at 50° F (10 °C). Now if you hit a ball that would travel 300 feet (91.4 m) on a 50 °F day, it would travel 324 feet (98.8 m) on a 95 °F day.

Will the ball travel farther when the barometric pressure is lower or higher?

First, let's consider a little information about barometric pressure: It's the weight of the atmosphere above us. When the weather woman tells us that a low-pressure system is moving in, we know that bad weather is coming, and when we're in a high-pressure zone, we'll have good weather. So what's the answer? The ball will travel farther with less pressure than with more pressure, about 2% farther when the barometric pressure is 29.50 inches (999 mb) of mercury than when it is 30.50 inches (1033 mb). So that 300-foot (91.4 m) hit on a beautiful high-pressure day will travel 306 feet (93.3 m) on a stormy low-pressure day, other things being equal.

What's the effect of different altitudes on the distance that the ball will travel?

We bet that you know the answer to this one. At higher elevations the atmospheric pressure and the density of the air decrease about 3% for every 1,000 feet (305 m) of elevation. Thus the ball will travel farther with less resistance in higher elevations. A 300-foot (91.4 m) hit in Florida at sea level would travel 45 feet (13.7 m) farther in Denver, which is located at an elevation of 5,000 feet (1,500 m).

So you've never been a home-run hitter but would like to experience the thrill of seeing the ball sail off your bat over a 300-foot (91.4 m) fence. Then here's our prescription for you: Go to Leadville, Colorado (the highest city in the United States), which is located 10,000 feet (3,000 m) above sea level. Wait for a hot, humid, stormy day with the wind blowing straight out to your hitting field and swing away!

Hitting the ball above its center by more than a few millimeters results in a ground ball, and the more the ball is hit above its center, the slower the ball travels. Hitting the ball below its center by very much produces a pop fly.

The plane at which you swing the bat combines with the point of contact between ball and bat to determine the angle at which the ball travels. Home-run hitters use a slight upward swing, and line-drive hitters swing level.

Batting Average

What is a good batting average to aim for in slowpitch softball? Before answering that question, we'd like to make a case for not using the conventional batting average used in baseball and fastpitch softball. The conventional batting average dismisses walks as not being a time at bat, and getting on base with a fielding error goes against your batting average.

In slowpitch we think that on-base percentage (OBP) is a much better metric than the conventional batting average to measure success as a batter. Walks are rewarded because they are the safest way to get on base; the defense has no opportunity to get the batter out. OBP also rewards batters who get on base by fielding errors based on the premise that if you're hitting the ball hard, fielders are more likely to make errors. Using OBP also eliminates the problem of requiring a scorekeeper to judge whether a hit ball was a base hit or an error.

So what benchmarks do we have to determine successful hitting using OBP to measure hitting performance? In baseball and fastpitch softball .300 is a widely recognized standard for good hitting using conventional batting averages. We propose that in slowpitch a good average is .600 because hitting is much easier in slowpitch and we are using OBP as the performance measure. A few exceptional players consistently hit .750 to .800, and some of the great power hitters in the game bat .900 in tournaments. Our Florida Legends team played in nine national tournaments in 2009 and compiled a team OBP of .699. Our goal for each of our players is to have an OBP of at least .700.

In the absence of a comprehensive study of hitting records in slowpitch among all levels of play, we propose the following guidelines for adults who strive to play the game well.

.500	.600	.700	.800
Rookie	Pro	Star	MVP

PREPARATION

In this section you'll learn how to select the right bat, how to grip the bat, where to stand in the batter's box, and how to assume your stance or ready position. Each of these factors will help prepare you for success as a hitter.

Bat Selection

If you're not familiar with slowpitch softball bats, read pages 209–213 in chapter 9 and then return to this section. Because all slowpitch bats are about the same size (34 inches [86 cm] in length, 2.25 inches [5.7 cm] in diameter), the key differences are their weight and composition. With weight your choice is limited to between 26 (737 g) and 30 ounces (850 g) in increments of 1 ounce (28 g), although the rules permit bats to weigh as much as 38 ounces (1,077 g). So what is the right weight for you? You'll be able to answer that question better after a quick biomechanics lesson.

If you are a power hitter you want to hit the ball as hard as you can. The speed with which the ball travels when it leaves your bat is a product of the weight of your bat and the velocity or speed of the bat at the point of impact (assuming that the impact is dead center between the ball and the bat). Biomechanists calculate the power that you generate with a swing using this formula:

Mass (weight of the bat) × velocity (speed of the bat at the point of impact) = momentum (the speed of the ball after being hit)

Power is the amount of work (swinging the bat) done in a given time. So here is the critical conclusion: The faster the bat is swung for the same weight bat, the greater the power is; and the heavier the bat is swung at the same speed, the greater the power is.

To hit the ball as hard as you can, you want to select the heaviest bat that you can swing with the greatest speed that you can achieve. One way we could scientifically determine the optimal weight bat for you would be to use high-speed video to see how fast you swing bats of various weights. That type of analysis is expensive, and thus players simply try bats of various weights and make a subjective decision about which one represents the best combination of weight and speed.

So you ask, is it better to swing a heavier bat slower or swing a lighter bat faster? Based on what has happened over the last 30 years, hitters have dramatically shifted from swinging heavier bats to much lighter bats. The first slowpitch aluminum bats weighed up to 38 ounces (1,077 g). Today the heaviest bat you can buy for slowpitch softball weighs 30 ounces (850 g). Greater bat speed, combined with bats that flex, which add more whip to the bat at the point of contact, are two of the major reasons that batters are hitting the ball farther. (Another reason is that athletes are stronger and more powerful.)

Conclusion: To find the bat of the right weight for you, keep in mind that if the bat is too heavy, you'll not be able to generate the greatest bat speed possible. And if the bat is too light, you'll sacrifice mass, which will decrease your power and thus reduce the momentum applied to the ball.

Another factor to consider is your ability to control the bat. If the bat is too heavy for you to control the swing, you will be less likely to hit the ball squarely. If you're a place hitter, generating maximum power is less important than having bat control. So you're likely to select a bat that is lighter than one that a power hitter would use.

Obviously, your strength is also important in determining the weight of the bat that you select. If you're not happy with the power that you can generate, then you may need to build strength and improve the mechanics of your swing, a topic that we'll discuss later.

Other factors that influence bat selection include whether the bat is balanced versus end loaded (more weight toward the end of the barrel of the bat), the thickness of the handle and the grip, and bat composition. We discuss these bat differences in chapter 9, but here are just a few things to consider:

- Power hitters are more likely to prefer end-loaded bats, and place hitters usually prefer balanced bats.

- Some players prefer thin-handled bats, and others prefer thicker-handled bats. The issue here is personal comfort.
- Bats today are made from a variety of materials. If you're relatively new to the game, attend a league or tournament and look at the bats that good players are using. They search out the best tools of the trade.

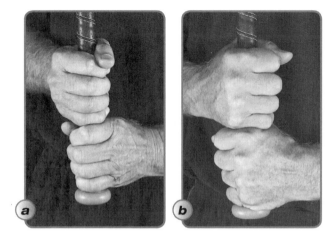

FIGURE 1.7 *(a)* The correct way to apply the standard grip with the middle knuckles of both hands approximately in line; *(b)* the incorrect way to grip the bat with the major knuckles of both hands aligning.

Grip

You want the grip to be comfortable, but you also want to have complete control of the bat as you swing and be able to generate as much bat velocity as you desire. We've seen players successfully use many different grips, but most grips follow some basics. Foremost, if you're a right-handed batter, you place your left hand on the bottom just above the knob of the bat and place your right hand above the left. For left-handed batters, of course, the opposite is true.

Most hitting instructors recommend that the middle knuckles of the two hands on the bat be in line as shown in figure 1.7a. This is a good standard grip. Avoid the grip shown in figure 1.7b. As you can see, the major knuckles of the top hand are lined up with the major knuckles of the bottom hand.

When using the standard grip, begin by placing the bat in the crease of your two hands where your fingers are joined to your palms as shown in figure 1.8. Wrap your fingers around the bat loosely and then hold the bat up to see whether the middle knuckles line up as shown in figure 1.7a. If they do not, rotate your top hand slightly so that the knuckles are in line. Don't fret if they are not exactly lined up as long as you feel that you have a comfortable grip in which you can accurately control the plane of the swing.

Don't hold the bat deep in the palm of your hand as illustrated in figure 1.9. Although this position provides you with a firm grip, it doesn't let the wrists move as freely as needed when executing the swing. Also, don't put a death grip on the bat. Remind your teammates and yourself to "swing with loose hands" because with a tight grip you lose bat speed and control. Don't worry about the bat flying out of your hands. As you begin the swing, your grip will automatically tighten.

The standard grip has many variations. Some batters place the small finger of the lower hand below the knob of the bat as shown in figure 1.10. They do this to have a longer extension of the bat to gain greater bat speed. Some batters also use the golf grip. In this grip the little finger of the top hand interlocks with the index finger of the bottom hand on the bat as you can see in figure 1.11. We don't see any clear advantage to the golf grip.

Location and Stance

Location refers to where you stand in the batter's box in relation to the plate. Stance refers to your body's orientation or position in space as you prepare to hit; it's the ready position before you initiate your swing. The objective with location is to position yourself so that you can hit the ball with maximum power

FIGURE 1.8 Apply the standard grip by placing the bat in the crease of both hands where the fingers are joined to the palms.

FIGURE 1.9 Don't hold the bat deep in the palm of your hand; it doesn't let the wrists move as freely as needed when executing the swing.

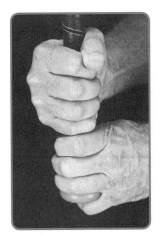

FIGURE 1.10 Place the little finger underneath the knob to have a slightly longer extension of the bat.

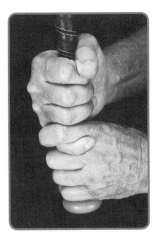

FIGURE 1.11 The golf grip, a personal preference of some players.

or place the ball where you want it. The purpose of a good stance is to orient yourself so that you are ready to execute an optimal swing.

Before digging into the specifics of location and the stance, we need to consider the difference in the speed of the pitch between slowpitch compared with baseball and fastpitch softball and the impact that difference has on location and stance. Professional baseball pitchers throw pitches between 80 and 95 miles per hour (between 130 and 155 kph). Women fastpitch pitchers throw near 70 miles per hour (115 kph), and men throw about 80 mph (129 kph). From the point of release in those sports, batters have less than 0.4 seconds not only to decide to swing but also to execute the swing. In contrast, it takes between 1.5 and 2.0 seconds for a slow-pitched ball to travel from the pitcher's hand to the strike mat, giving batters plenty of time to decide to swing, to adjust their location in the batter's box, and to adjust their stance or ready position to initiate the swing. Consequently, the initial location and stance of the batter are of less importance. What is critical, however, is what we'll call the *ready position* (a combination of location and stance) at the moment the batter initiates the swing.

Squatters and Nomads

Many slowpitch batters assume a location and stance in the batter's box without moving their feet until they initiate their swing. We refer to these batters as *squatters*. If that is the way you prefer to hit, then your initial location and stance are important and you should follow the recommendations for a good ready position, which we'll present in the next sections.

In contrast to squatters are *nomads*, a less common breed of batters. They often take a position in the batter's box farther back and away from the plate. When the pitch is thrown, nomads roam around the batter's box in search of the ideal location from which to hit the pitch. Well, they don't actually roam, but they do move quickly into a location in the batter's box that they judge is the optimal position from which to hit the pitch. Some nomads roam a lot, moving

Hitting Terminology

As we discuss hitting we'll constantly refer to the type of hitter and the batter's position and movements in the batter's box.

○ **Pull hitter:** A right-handed batter who hits the ball to left field or a left-handed batter who hits the ball to right field.

○ **Opposite-field hitter:** A left-handed batter who hits to left field or a right-handed batter who hits to right field.

○ **Location of batter in the box:** We'll describe the location of the batter in the batter's box by the terms shown in figure 1.12. Batters can be located in front or in back of the box, and they can be close to the plate or away from it.

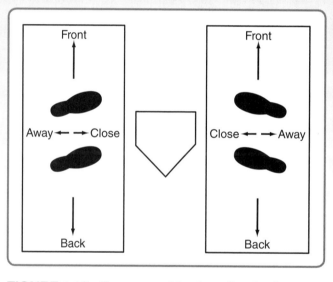

FIGURE 1.12 Terms used to describe the location of the batter in the batter's box.

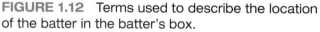

quickly from the back of the batter's box to hit the pitch. Others make only small adjustments in their position. (See Offense→Hitting Basics→Squatters and Nomads on the DVD)

An advantage of being a nomad is that you are not waiting for the pitch to be in your hitting or power zone (refer back to figure 1.5 on page 14). Instead, you position yourself into those zones. The disadvantage of being a nomad is that your movement about the batter's box is another component of hitting that you must time and execute correctly, adding complexity to hitting. And you've probably noticed some batter's boxes have uneven surfaces created by previous hitters that make it difficult to maintain good balance when moving about.

So is it better to be a nomad or a squatter? We can't answer that question; it's something that you need to discover for yourself.

Given that you have plenty of time to make adjustments when the pitch is made, your initial stance in the batter's box is unimportant but your ready position as you begin the swing is important. So let's first look at your location in the batter's box, and then we'll consider the ready position to hit.

Location in the Batter's Box

So what's the best location in the batter's box? It's the location where you can hit any strike, especially when you have two strikes on you, and hit the ball on the sweet spot of the bat. The exact location that you take in the batter's box depends on

- whether you're a squatter or a nomad,
- whether you're a power hitter or a place hitter,
- your anatomy, and
- the location of the pitches.

If you're a squatter, you want to position yourself so that you can hit any strike and so that you have the best chance of seeing a pitch in your hitting or power zone. If you're a nomad, the initial location is less important. Most nomads stand either back in the box or away from the plate and then move forward and closer to the plate to prepare to hit the ball.

If you're a power hitter and you like to hit the ball chest high, you'll want to locate yourself just slightly in front of the plate or strike mat as shown in figure 1.13*a*. If you're a place hitter, you'll position yourself differently depending on where you want to hit the ball. If you want to pull the ball, you'll likely stand closer to the plate with a square or more open ready position (figure 1.13*b*). If you want to hit to the opposite field, you'll likely stand farther away from the plate with a closed ready position and then step toward the opposite field as you swing (figure 1.13*c*). See also Offense→Hitting Basics→Location in the Batter's Box on the DVD for a demonstration of these locations.

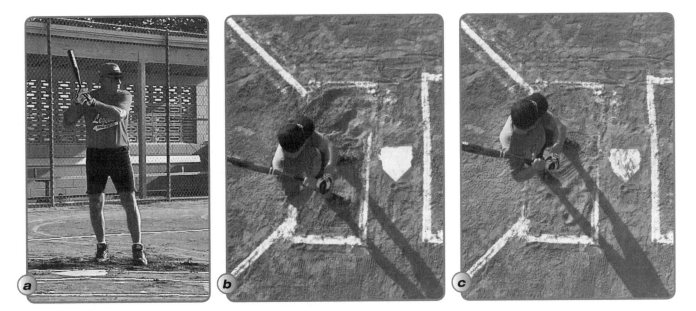

FIGURE 1.13 *(a)* The batter standing toward the front of the box, a common position when the strike mat is being used. *(b)* The batter standing close to the plate, a position often taken to pull the ball. *(c)* The batter standing away from the plate, a common position taken to stride into the ball to hit to the opposite field.

FIGURE 1.14 The ready position for initiating the swing.

Your body size will make a small difference. If you're 5 feet (152 cm) tall with relatively short arms, you'll need to stand closer to the strike zone than a 6-foot-8-inch (203 cm) long-armed batter would.

You'll also want to consider how the pitcher is pitching in determining your location in the batter's box. If the pitcher is pitching with a low arc, and especially if he or she is trying to hit the front part of the strike zone or mat, you'll want to be located at the front of the batter's box so that you can hit the ball above your knees or waist. If the pitcher is throwing a high arc and trying to hit the back of the strike zone or mat, you'll want to move back in the box.

Ready Position

Whether you're a squatter or a nomad, at the moment when you are ready to initiate your swing, as in baseball and fastpitch softball, you'll want to be in what we call the ready position (see figure 1.14).

- Stand comfortably with your feet spread about the width of your shoulders.
- Be well balanced, have your weight mostly on the balls of your feet, and have the ankles and knees flexed and relaxed.
- Hold the bat a few inches off the back shoulder ready to initiate the load phase of the swing (we'll cover that in the next section).
- Turn your head toward the pitcher so that you can see the ball well with both eyes.

For squatters, ready positions are commonly described as open, closed, or square, which describes the position of the feet and body in relation to the plate. In an open position, as shown in figure 1.15*a*, the batter's front foot (closest to the pitcher) is farther away from the plate than the back foot so that the batter faces the pitcher more directly. The closed position is just the opposite; the front foot is closer to the plate than the back foot so that the batter's shoulder is facing the pitcher (see figure 1.15*b*). The square position has both feet equidistant from the plate (see figure 1.15*c*). See Offense→Hitting Basics→Ready Position for a demonstration of the ready position.

So what's the best ready position? No one position is best for everyone. Place hitters tend to prefer a slightly open position so that they can face the pitcher and see the ball with both eyes without straining their necks. If you're a power hitter you may find that a square or slightly closed position makes it easier for you to move into the load phase of your swing (we'll discuss this shortly).

EXECUTION

OK, you're now in the batter's box prepared to swing, and the ball is being pitched. Your first task is to decide whether to swing. If you decide to swing, you want to execute the swing with good mechanics, which involves three

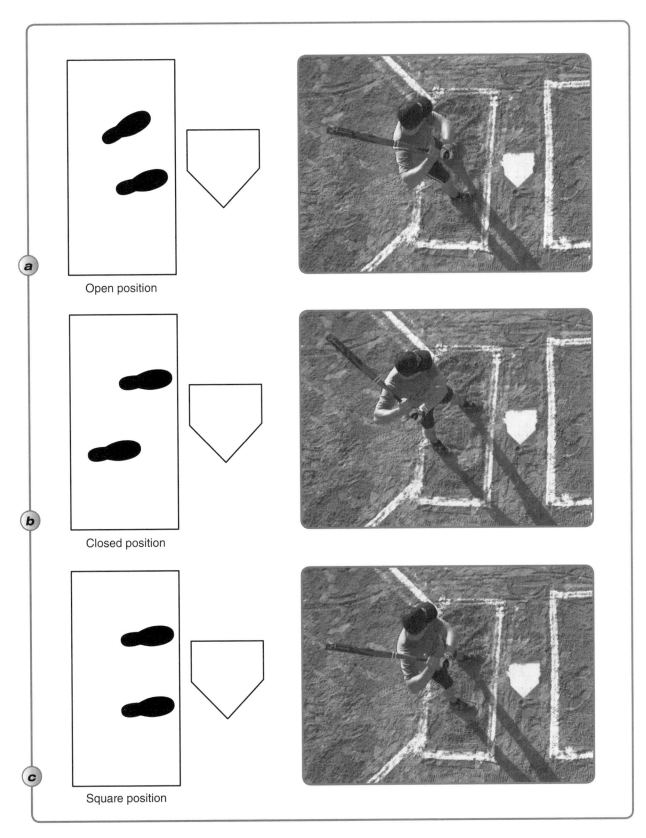

a Open position

b Closed position

c Square position

FIGURE 1.15 The three ready positions showing a right-handed batter's feet position and orientation to the pitcher.

phases—the load phase, the swing phase, and the follow-through phase. At the same time you want to employ excellent timing in executing the swing. In this section you'll learn the basics about decision making, swing mechanics, and timing when batting.

Decision Making

All too often when teaching hitting, instructors focus entirely on the mechanics and ignore the decision-making process involved in hitting. In baseball and fastpitch you must make a split-second decision to swing or not to swing; in slowpitch you have much more time.

The first major decision to be made occurs before you step into the batter's box. You should decide what you want to accomplish this time at bat. Do you want to hit a home run, hit a sacrifice fly, or hit the ball to a certain location? This decision is about offensive tactics, and we'll consider those tactics in chapter 4. Here we'll consider the decisions that you need to make about any one pitch.

When the ball is pitched you will first decide whether to swing at the pitch. As you begin the load phase of your swing you will have time to reverse your decision and decide not to swing. For example, if the pitch changes its trajectory to one that you don't like, or you see it is going to be short of the strike zone, you can decide to stop your swing up to the point when the bat starts to move forward.

Your thinking process may go something like this:

- The pitch leaves the pitcher's hand and as it approaches the apex of its arc, your inner voice says, "Yes, it's going to be a good pitch to hit."
- As it continues toward you, you continue to monitor the pitch saying, "Yes, yes, yes."
- As the ball descends, you realize that it's going to be outside and not in a good position for you to hit. At the last moment you say, "No," and stop the load phase of your swing.

If you are a nomad and decide to swing, you also will make a decision about where you want to locate yourself in the batter's box to be in the best position to hit the ball. Then you will make a decision about when to begin your swing, that is, the initiation of the timing mechanism to hit the ball. Finally, to be a good hitter you can't have just one swing in your repertoire. You must have several, and thus you must decide which swing you will use for the approaching pitch. For example, you start to swing but see that the ball is going to be short of the strike zone, so you modify your swing to be more like a golfer's swing. Or, as the ball curves away from you, you quickly decide to hit to the opposite field, not swinging with power but taking a short "punch" swing.

Good hitting is as much about good decision making as it is about good technique. If the novice batter tries to make each of these decisions in a thoughtful way, the catcher will have caught the ball and thrown it back to the pitcher before the batter completes his or her decision making. What happens with practice is that those decisions become automated; you make them without being aware that you're making each of them. Automating these decisions is part of learning the motor skill of hitting and is a result of considerable practice. Through correct practice you will automate the decision-making skills correctly, and through incorrect practice you will develop poor decision-making skills.

Now note this point carefully: A common mistake that players make in batting practice is swinging at any pitch they can reach. Although your teammates may not appreciate your being selective about which pitches you hit because you'll take more time, you'll make better decisions about which pitches to hit in the game by practicing good decision making in batting practice.

Hitting Mechanics

The term *mechanics* refers to the coordination of your muscles to execute the movement of swinging the bat to hit the ball. The mechanics of the swing start with a load phase, which consists of shifting your weight back so that you can then drive forward, analogous to pushing a spring down (loading it) so that it springs up. The load phase is followed by the swing phase and the follow-through. Let's look at each phase more closely.

Load Phase

You begin the load phase by shifting your weight from a balanced ready position to the back foot, accomplished by pushing the weight back with the front foot. Some batters then lift the front foot up and bring it back as far as the back leg as they prepare to drive their weight forward (see figure 1.16*a*). Other batters only shift their weight to the back foot, keeping the front foot on the ground balanced on the ball of the foot (see figure 1.16*b*). Then they stride forward. Still other hitters use variations between these two approaches. See Offense→Hitting Basics→Hitting Mechanics→Load Phase on the DVD for demonstrations of the load phase.

Power hitters turn their hips inward or away from the pitcher in the load phase before driving forward (see figure 1.16*a*). This coiling action gives them greater rotation through the hips when they stride forward and swing, which generates greater power if correctly timed and executed. Power hitters usually have greater movement backward than place hitters do, and they tend to take

FIGURE 1.16 *(a)* Loading for the swing by lifting the front foot and bringing it back to the back leg and coiling the hips inward. *(b)* Loading for the swing by transferring the weight from the front foot to the back foot without lifting the front foot completely off the ground.

FIGURE 1.17 Power hitter taking a large stride.

bigger strides forward than place hitters in order to generate greater power (see figure 1.17).

The last part of the load phase is the stride, a controlled step forward with your front foot to begin the weight transfer. Power hitters tend to take a big stride forward to achieve a powerful position to initiate the swing. The weight remains mostly on the back foot, and the front foot touches the ground to stabilize the batter through the swing phase. Place hitters tend to take a much smaller stride forward.

A critical part of the swing, the stride has the following purposes.

- It initiates the timing of the swing.
- It puts you in the position to contact the ball with the sweet spot of the bat.
- It makes it possible to rotate the hips when swinging to generate power.
- And if you are a place hitter, the stride positions you to direct the ball where you want it to go.

The exact location of the stride forward depends on your hitting objective and the location of the pitch. For example, if the pitch is on the inside part of the strike zone and you want to hit the ball as hard as you can, you'll step toward the shortstop or third baseperson if you're a right-handed batter (see figure 1.18a) and toward the second baseperson or first baseperson if you're a left-handed batter. If the pitch is on the outer half of the strike mat and you want to hit to the opposite field, you'll step toward the second baseperson if you're a right-handed batter (see figure 1.18b) and toward the shortstop if you're a left-handed batter.

FIGURE 1.18 (a) Place hitter striding to pull the ball to left field. (b) Place hitter striding to hit to right field.

Swing Phase

The swing phase also can be divided into three parts. These three parts are shown and described in figure 1.19 and then demonstrated on the DVD (Offense→Hitting Basics→Hitting Mechanics→Swing Phase) in normal and slow motion speed.

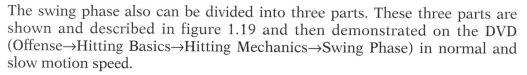

FIGURE 1.19 *(a-b)* As the batter initiates the forward stride, the hands move into position near the back shoulder to launch the swing. The hands stay in this position as the body begins to move forward, coiling inward slightly; the front arm (closer to the pitcher), called the power arm, is pulled back nearly straight. *(c-d)* Next, the batter begins to rotate the hips, or open up, toward the pitcher to create more rotational force or torque. *(e-f)* The hands stay back, but only momentarily, before the swing forward begins with the power arm pulling the bat through. The top hand pushes on the bat as it moves forward, and at the same time it guides the bat to be in the correct plane to contact the ball.

Follow-Through Phase

The follow-through phase of the swing, which is shown in figure 1.20 and on the DVD (Offense→Hitting Basics→Hitting Mechanics→Follow-Through Phase), is about decelerating the bat efficiently. Two methods are used to decelerate the bat momentum—the one-arm and the two-arm follow-through. In the two-arm follow-through, right-handed batters bring both hands next to their left shoulder as the bat comes around; left handers will bring both hands next to the right shoulder. The bat decelerates from the pull of the stretched right arm and from both hands being blocked from moving farther by the left (or right, for left-handers) shoulder, as shown in figure 1.20a.

More frequently in slowpitch, batters use the one-arm follow-through. Rather than ending up by the shoulder after the swing, the arms stay fully extended. For right-handed batters, as the body continues to rotate from the swing, the right hand lets go of the bat when the batter's body is facing the third-base bench, and the left hand continues to decelerate the bat as shown in figure 1.20b.

When you execute the sequence of movements in hitting correctly, the ball seems to jump off the bat effortlessly and you have a real sense of satisfaction from hitting the ball. One of the reasons that great hitters make it look effortless is that they minimize extraneous movements just before executing the swing. They avoid extra movements during the loading phase and swing phase. Although they may drop their hands during the early part of the loading phase, as they begin the swing phase the hands are just off the back shoulder ready to execute the swing. Their heads are still, and their eyes are intently focused on the ball. Each movement is purposeful and precise.

FIGURE 1.20   *(a)* The two-arm follow-through with the batter pulling the arms in next to the rotating front shoulder. *(b)* The one-arm follow-through with the top hand releasing after the swing phase and the bottom hand decelerating the bat.

Timing

Great hitters in slowpitch also have exquisite timing. After the decision to swing is made, the initiation of the sequence of movements described earlier must be timed with perfection to hit the ball optimally. The stride forward is the key timing mechanism in the swing. See Offense→Hitting Basics→Timing on the DVD to learn more about timing.

Although in baseball and fastpitch softball the batter often initiates the swing too late, in slowpitch the batter often starts the swing too early, usually causing him or her to slow the bat precipitously to avoid missing the ball entirely. The result is a very weak swing.

Although swinging too early is the more common problem, swinging too late also occurs, resulting in a weak hit. When the batter swings too late, the ball is closer to the plate and is contacted by the bat head before the bat reaches its maximum acceleration. Most batters reach maximum acceleration of the bat head about a foot in front of the front shoulder, so that is the best place to make contact with the ball if you're hitting for power.

A well-coordinated swing—that beautiful sequence of movements—has a rhythm to it not unlike the rhythm to a dance step. The rhythm comes from the linking of one movement with the next, appropriately timed. When hitters are in that rhythm every part of the swing flows together almost effortlessly. Hitting becomes an art form, an exquisite skill, appreciated by those who play the game.

That rhythm, however, can be elusive and ephemeral. One of the objectives of a pitcher is to disrupt the batter's timing by pitching the ball to different locations and with different trajectories (see chapter 5). As a batter, you can win the pitcher–batter duel by making good decisions about the pitches that you swing at and by concentrating intensely on the pitched ball.

Rhythm may also be disrupted by stress, which is manifested in the form of muscle tension and may disrupt concentration. A prepared but relaxed body can time the sequence of movements much better than a tight-muscled body can. The reminder to "swing with loose hands" helps us stay tension free.

SUMMARY

- For maximum power select the heaviest bat that you can swing with maximum speed.
- Select a bat that feels comfortable, that you can swing with precise control, and that lets you generate as much power as you want (within the limits of your ability) for the type of hitter that you are.
- Adopt a grip that is comfortable, gives you good bat control, and lets you execute a powerful swing.
- Your location in the batter's box should position you to cover the strike zone and to hit the ball in your hitting or power zone. Whether you're a squatter or a nomad is a matter of personal preference.
- The initial stance is unimportant, but you want to be in a good ready position when you initiate your swing.
- Practicing good decision making in determining what pitches to swing at is as important as practicing the technique or mechanics of the swing.
- The load phase of the swing is a sequence of timed movements that prepares you to initiate the forward movement of the swing. Good hitting requires good timing in initiating the load phase.
- The forward stride should be adjusted to the location of the pitch to position the swing so that the ball is contacted on the sweet spot of the bat.

• The swing is initiated when the hips rotate toward the pitcher. Closely thereafter, the front arm pulls the bat forward, and the back arm pushes the bat and guides it through its rotational plane.

• Skillful hitting has a rhythm to the swing that is initiated by correctly timing the launch of the load phase of the swing. The rhythm of a swing may be disrupted by the pitcher's action, the batter's lack of concentration, or stress that affects the batter.

CHAPTER 2

Advanced Hitting

In the pitcher–batter duel, skillful pitchers try to get you to hit pitches that you don't want to hit, or they seek to disrupt your timing by varying the location and speed of the pitch. You, on the other hand, want to make good judgments about which pitches are best to hit and then execute a skillful swing to hit the ball where you want. In this chapter we'll help you win that pitcher–batter duel by showing you how to hit with more power through strength training and by increasing the speed of your bat swing. You'll learn how to place hit more precisely, how to see the ball better, how to practice better to improve your hitting, and how to think better as a hitter. We'll also cover common hitting mistakes and ways of avoiding them.

POWER AND PRECISION

You've learned the basics of hitting, have experienced some success, and have begun to enjoy playing slowpitch softball. Now you're motivated to become an even better hitter. In this section we'll show you how to improve your power and precision as a hitter.

Improving Power

Hitting a home run, especially a game-winning home run, is a memorable moment for any player. Many batters try to hit the ball as hard as they can each time they bat, hoping for a home run or at least a long ball, and to do that they need power. Recall from chapter 1 that power is strength and speed combined. So you can improve power in two ways:

1. Increase the strength of your muscles so that you can increase the velocity of the bat or swing a heavier bat with the same velocity as you swing a lighter bat.
2. Increase bat speed through a modified grip and improved swing mechanics.

Increasing Strength

The great home-run hitters of slowpitch are invariably strong, and they train to become strong and stay that way. The amazing improvement in women's slowpitch hitting is a direct result of women becoming stronger. If you feel that your strength is insufficient and you want to be a home-run hitter or hit the ball with more power, then a good strength-training program will help, and you'll be amazed at how fast you can improve your strength. Begin by reviewing chapter 10, "Physical Preparation," to understand the basics of fitness training. Then go to appendix A for a listing of strength-training resources.

Increasing Bat Speed

Do you remember from your physics class that the longer a lever is from the fulcrum, the faster it moves, other things being equal? You can see this principle in figure 2.1.

So why are we discussing physics 101? One way to improve bat speed is to use a unique grip shown in figure 2.2, what we call the power grip. Here the index fingers interlock, the little finger of the lower hand is below the knob, and the two hands overlap, thus extending the arm–bat lever farther than in a conventional grip. As long as the batter has the strength to swing the bat with the same force, the result is greater bat speed. The challenge with this grip, however, is retaining good control. Yet if you can master it, science says that you'll hit the ball farther.

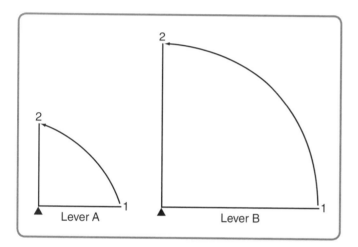

FIGURE 2.1 Lever B is twice as long as lever A, and if both move from point 1 to point 2 in the same time, lever B has to travel twice as fast as lever A.

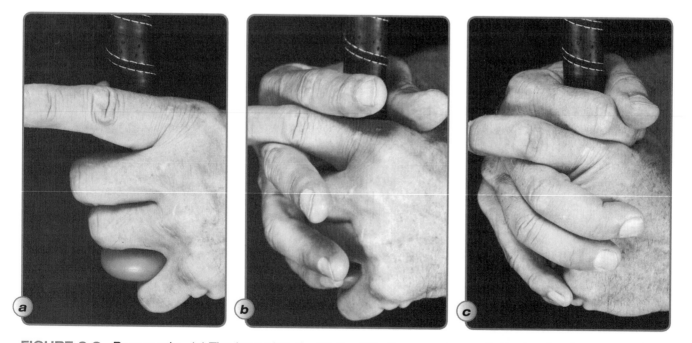

FIGURE 2.2 Power grip. *(a)* The lower hand with the little finger underneath the knob, *(b)* the top hand wrapped over the lower hand with the index fingers interlocking, and *(c)* the complete grip.

One common mistake that batters make is not getting their arms extended when they swing. The result is that the lever is substantially shortened, with the consequence being much slower bat speed. So, in our opinion, hitting the ball with the arms extended is more important than a longer grip in optimizing the length of the lever.

Another way to improve bat speed is to improve the mechanics and timing of each part of the swing, from the load phase, to the stride, the swing, and the follow-through. We can demonstrate these technical improvements better by video, so go now to Offense→Advanced Hitting→Power Hitting on the DVD.

Here are seven key points for executing the power swing, which is unique to slowpitch softball because batters have time to load up as they prepare to swing, something that usually can't be done in baseball or fastpitch softball.

1. Start from a good ready position (see figure 2.3*a*).

2. The load phase begins by bringing the front foot back to the back leg, which causes the hips to curl in. The shoulders, however, stay parallel to the plate (see figure 2.3*b*).

3. With precise timing, the batter shifts his weight from moving backward to moving forward. The front leg strides out and the back leg pushes forward at the same time (see figure 2.3*c*).

4. As the lower body moves forward, the upper body remains in the same relative location. The hands come up in a good ready position to launch the swing (see figure 2.3*d*).

5. As the front foot hits the ground, the batter launches the swing by beginning to uncoil. The hips rotate powerfully away from the plate, the back leg pushes forward, and the weight transfers to the front foot (see figure 2.3*e*).

6. A critical component of this skill is that the arms and hands remain back for just a split second as the stride forward takes place. Then the batter "throws" the knob of the bat at the ball, with the hands leading the way and the bat barrel remaining behind the hands (see figure 2.3*f*).

7. The batter now pulls the bat hard toward the pitcher. The batter's arms are almost straight as the bat barrel catches up with the hands and contacts the bat in what feels and looks like a whipping action (see figure 2.3*g*).

Three other points to keep in mind:

1. As you master the mechanics of the power swing, you'll learn to adjust your stride to position yourself to hit the ball with the sweet spot of the bat. If the pitch is on the inside part of the plate, you'll step a little more to the outside of the box, and if the pitch is on the outside of the plate, you'll step toward the inside of the batter's box.

2. Timing is absolutely critical to executing the power swing successfully. Swing slightly too early or late and you'll lose bat speed.

3. You may increase your strength and bat speed, but if you don't hit the ball squarely you'll likely pop up or ground out. So along with improving your power and timing, don't forget to work on your eye–hand coordination to hit the ball on the nose.

FIGURE 2.3 The power swing.

Improving Precision

Place hitting is more about accuracy than power. As you develop your hitting skills, you'll want to decide whether you want to be a power hitter, a place hitter, or both. In doing so you should know about Fitt's law. This well-established scientific principle of motor behavior is about the speed–accuracy tradeoff. In hitting terms, it means that the faster you swing the bat, the less accurate you'll be. Thus you need to decide whether you want to swing the bat with greater speed or give up some of that speed so that you can hit the ball more accurately. It may be a decision to hit .500 with occasional home runs or hit singles three out of four times to hit .750.

Here are the key things that place hitters do differently compared with power hitters.

- They more often use a conventional grip to maximize bat control.
- They tend to use a more open stance or ready position.
- They are modestly nomadic, making minor location adjustments with their feet in the batter's box as the pitch approaches to position themselves to hit to the location they have targeted.
- The load phase involves less movement. The hands may reach back only a short distance before starting forward in the swing phase.
- The stride is shorter; it's a smooth, soft step that adjusts the position of the batter to the location of the ball to hit it in the direction desired.
- The swing is less powerful (slower speed), and the emphasis is on timing the swing to hit the ball to the desired location.

A less powerful swing doesn't mean a weak swing. Place hitters want to hit the ball sharply too so that fielders have less time to catch the ball. As Fitt's law states, they trade off some speed in the swing to swing more accurately.

Hitting to the Near Field

If you're batting right-handed, the near field is the left side of the field, and if you're batting left-handed, the near field is the right side of the field. Most players learn to hit to the near field when they first learn the game; that is, they learn to pull the ball toward third base if hitting right-handed and toward first base if hitting left-handed. This swing seems to come more naturally, with greater accuracy and more power.

Right-handed batters like to hit the 5-6 hole between the third baseperson and shortstop; left-handed batters may try the 3-4 hole between the first and second basepersons (see figure 2 on page 8 for a review of the holes). If the third baseperson moves away from the foul line into the 5-6 hole, right-handed hitters may choose to hit the ball down the third-base line. Likewise, left-handed hitters may try to hit the ball down the first-base line if the first baseperson moves into the 3-4 hole.

To hit the ball to the near side, you want a pitch on the inside half of the strike zone that is waist to shoulder high at the point of contact. Hitting an outside pitch with accuracy to the near side is difficult, especially if you're trying to hit just inside the foul line. Another pitch to avoid is the low, inside pitch, which if hit will likely go foul or to the third baseperson if you're a right-handed batter and to the first baseperson if you are a left-handed batter. Also avoid deep, inside

pitches. Those you'll likely pop up or foul, and they are definitely difficult to hit to a desired location. See Offense→Advanced Hitting→Near- and Opposite-Field Hitting on the DVD to master these skills.

Hitting to the Opposite Field

Hitting to the opposite field (right-handed hitters to right field and left-handed hitters to left field) is a valuable skill not only for place hitters but for power hitters as well. If your opponents discover that you can hit only to the near side, they may shift more fielders to that side of the field. When you hit at least occasionally to the opposite field, defenses must play you straight away.

The key difference between hitting to the near-side field and the opposite field is that in the second case you let the ball come farther into the strike zone when hitting it (see figure 2.4a-b). Therefore, to hit the ball between your shoulder and waist, you'll want to stand forward in the batter's box. If you stand back in the box, the ball will more likely be low in the strike zone and more difficult to control.

The best pitch to hit to the opposite field is one on the outside half of the strike zone at shoulder to waist height. One common mistake when hitting to the opposite field is trying to hit pitches that are too far outside, resulting in your reaching too much and losing bat control (see figure 2.5a). Reaching could also cause you to step on the plate or strike mat as you're swinging, which is an automatic out. Another common mistake is dipping the back shoulder when positioning yourself to hit (see figure 2.5b). Although you want to rotate inwardly to align your body to hit toward the opposite field, keep the shoulders level. A third common mistake made when hitting to the opposite field (although it can occur when hitting to any field) is pushing the bat in that direction rather than swinging the bat. Pushing the bat refers to batters pushing the bat forward with the back arm (top hand on the bat) rather than pulling forcefully with the front arm (bottom hand on the bat) to get good velocity on the bat head. Consequently, the bat head is farther back when contacting the ball, resulting

FIGURE 2.4 *(a)* To hit to the near-side field, contact the ball farther forward in the strike zone. *(b)* To hit to the opposite-side field, contact the ball farther back in the strike zone.

FIGURE 2.5 Two common mistakes when trying to hit to the opposite field: *(a)* reaching too far for an outside pitch and *(b)* dipping the back shoulder.

in little momentum being imparted to the ball. In hitting to the opposite field, you want to maintain good swing mechanics. The adjustments are positioning the body to swing comfortably to the opposite field and delaying the swing slightly. Watch Offense→Advanced Hitting→Near- and Opposite-Field Hitting on the DVD to see these incorrect swings.

Some skilled place hitters are squatters, making only a slight adjustment in the forward stride by stepping in the direction that they intend to hit the ball. They commonly take a position in the batter's box farther away from the plate and then stride toward the opposite field. Most of their adjustment comes in the timing of their swing. They wait longer to make contact, hitting the ball not in front of the body as when they pull the ball, but even with the body. Thus, the defense has more difficulty determining where a squatter will hit the ball.

Other place hitters are nomads. They'll take almost any position in the batter's box, but when the pitch is coming they adjust their position to align themselves to hit to the opposite field. A common approach for nomad place hitters is to take a comfortable stance for hitting to the near-side field but, as the ball is pitched, to step away from the plate with the back foot and to step slightly toward the opposite field with the front foot.

Hitting up the Middle

After the ball is past the pitcher, the holes on either side of the pitcher (the 1-4 and 1-6 holes) are often wide open. And line drives over the pitcher will find the grass between the left-center and right-center fielders. But this kind of hitting calls for precision. If the ball is hit to the pitcher, it's an easy out, and if a runner is on first, it's an easy double play. If the shortstop or second baseperson is playing closer to second base, especially if the fielder knows that you like to hit up the middle, then you should look to hit the 3-4 or 5-6 hole. The best pitches for squatters to hit up the middle are those in the middle of the strike zone from waist to shoulder height. Nomads, on the other hand, will adjust their position in the batter's box to align themselves to hit the pitch wherever it's located, except that they will avoid reaching for outside pitches.

Going With the Pitch

When you step into the batter's box, you should have a plan for what you want to do. We'll discuss those tactical plans in chapter 4, but let's consider one example here. You are a right-handed hitter, you have runners on second and third, and so you decide to hit to right field behind the runners, hoping to score them both. The pitcher, knowing that you're a place hitter, thinks that you will likely want to hit to right field, so you see nothing but pitches on the inside half of the strike zone, ones that are difficult to hit to right. If you're a nomad place hitter you may be able to step back and position yourself to hit to right with good bat control. If not, you now have two strikes on you, so what do you do?

You go with the pitch, which means you hit it into the holes or lanes based on the location of the pitch. As a right-hander, if the ball is on the inside third of the plate, you drive it into the 5-6 hole. If it's down the middle of the strike zone you hit it slightly to either side of the pitcher, assuming that the shortstop and second basepersons are in their normal positions, and if it's on the outside third of the plate you hit it into the 3-4 hole.

Some place hitters follow this approach to hitting regardless of the offensive situation. As they come to bat, they see how the defensive players are positioned and then go with the pitch to hit the holes.

Place hitters not only hit ground balls and line drives through the infield but also hit the gaps between the outfielders. Also, if you consistently hit singles, outfielders will play in closer to the infield in hopes of catching your line drives. So occasionally it's valuable for you to be able to drive the ball deep over the outfielders.

HITTING MISTAKES TO AVOID

In this section we'll examine the most common and serious mistakes made in slowpitch hitting. If you don't make any mistakes in hitting, then don't read this section because it may put bad ideas in your head. But if you're not perfect yet, then review these ailments and see what medicine we offer. We've mentioned most of these mistakes briefly before, but now we'll examine them more closely.

Not Having a Plan

Some batters step into the batter's box thinking only that they want to hit the ball hard. That's a good plan if you're a consistent home-run hitter or if you crush the ball so ferociously that even when you hit it at someone he or she is unlikely to catch it.

But for most of us mere mortal souls, it's helpful to have a hitting plan. That plan is based on the game situation, and we'll review offensive tactics in chapter 4 that will help you know when it's good to swing for the fence or hit that 3-4 lane. You want to have a plan not only for getting a hit but also so that if you make an out it is a productive out for the team, which means that at least you advance the runners or avoid a double play. The best thing you can do when batting is to hit a home run over the fence; the safest thing you can do is walk. After that you need to know how to weigh the risk of hitting to certain locations.

Some players assert that they don't hit well when they come to bat with a plan. They do better with an empty mind, they say, focusing only on hitting the ball. That may be the case, but those players are much more likely to hit into a double play, fail to hit a sacrifice fly when needed, and fail to take a tactical walk. Those mistakes can really hurt an offensive effort.

As a batter you should have a plan for each offensive situation you will face. That plan should take into account your strengths and weaknesses as a hitter, and perhaps what your coach is asking you to do. Then when you step in to hit you look for the opportunity to execute that plan. As noted before for place hitters, when you get two strikes, your flexibility to execute a certain plan diminishes and you need to focus on hitting any pitch that will be a strike.

Formulate a plan based on the game situation and defensive player positions.

Selecting Poor Pitches

Some batters usually swing at the first pitch thrown to them if it is anywhere near being a strike. You hear players talking about these batters by saying, "They've never seen a pitch they didn't like." The goal of good pitching is to try to get batters to swing at pitches in locations that are not easy to hit. Pitches on the edges of the strike zone can be more difficult to hit. Short inside, short outside, deep inside, and deep outside pitches are all more difficult to hit well than pitches waist to shoulder high in the middle of the strike zone.

Batters who fail to select good pitches to hit are usually more inconsistent hitters. They'll hit well one game and then hit poorly the next, with the difference being the pitches that they choose to swing at. A lack of discipline in the batter's box also means that batters are less likely to execute the right offensive tactic or plan. If runners are on first and second or the bases are loaded and less than two are out, a batter does not want to hit to the pitcher or third baseperson. Those hits turn into easy double plays.

The lack of discipline or impatience when batting may be a result of anxiety. Anxiety comes about when batters have doubts about being successful in getting a base hit or are concerned that they may even strike out. Thus they jump at the first pitch near the strike zone. We briefly discuss how to reduce stress and anxiety in chapter 11.

Hitting discipline begins in practice. Without good pitching, batters in practice often swing at any pitch they can reach. That's not a good idea. Batting practice is the time to practice not only your technique of swinging but also your decision-making skills about what you want to swing at. Batting practice is the best time to learn your strengths and weaknesses as a hitter, which means knowing what pitches you hit well and what pitches you do not hit well. Then in games you must develop the confidence to know a ball from a strike and have the patience to look for your preferred pitch to hit. Only after you have two strikes do you want to swing at any pitch that has the chance to be a strike, so that's a good time to "go with the pitch," as discussed earlier.

Overswinging

You've hit the ball twice reasonably hard but the first one was a high fly ball caught near the fence, and the second one was a hard-hit line drive caught by the left-center fielder. Frustrated, the next time at bat you swing even harder and hit under the ball slightly. A pop-up for an easy out results. Now you're really bummed out! Overswinging is a common problem among power hitters and even among place hitters when they are struggling.

When batters are stressed, because they hit poorly previously, are facing a pressure situation, or both, they often respond by trying extra hard. Extra hard manifests itself in several ways:

- Reaching back farther in the loading phase, which disrupts timing so that the movement forward begins too late. The batter hits the ball before getting full acceleration on the bat.
- Striding out farther than usual, which has the unintended consequence of lowering the body more than expected, resulting in hitting underneath the ball. In addition, the hips are unable to rotate powerfully because of the extended position.
- Tensing the muscles excessively, which makes movement difficult because the muscles pulling the bat in the swing are held back by the tensed counter muscles that must relax to generate the force. Consequently, the batter is in a tug-of-war with his or her own muscles.

- Flailing at the ball in an effort to generate more bat speed (see Offense→Advanced Hitting→Flailing at the Ball on the DVD). Rather than the usual smooth, coordinated swing, the batter appears to be thrashing about, often throwing the hands forward too soon. Batters describe it as being loose in the swing, almost swatting at the ball rather than performing a tight, well-timed swing. When batters flail they also tend to introduce extraneous movements in their swing, which further disrupts their timing mechanism.
- Squinting the eyes and pulling the head off the ball as part of making a greater effort, resulting in poor vision at the critical moment when the batter needs to see the ball clearly.

All these mistakes cascade into a mistimed, mechanically poor swing, resulting in lousy contact with the ball. Frustration abounds, leading to trying even harder, and suddenly you find yourself in a major slump. Just when you want to do better you do worse! Although it sounds counterintuitive, not trying so hard is the obvious answer for breaking out of a slump caused by trying too hard, but that's easy to suggest and much more difficult to do. The section "Psychology of Hitting" on page 251 in chapter 11 offers some useful advice about how to break out of a slump.

Swinging to the Ball

A big mistake in hitting is swinging *to* the ball, not *through* the ball (see Offense→Advanced Hitting→Swinging to the Ball on the DVD). This fault can be caused by poor mechanics but more commonly is caused by hitters wanting to make sure that they contact the ball. Rather than ripping through the ball with a good follow-through swing, the batter never generates much bat speed or begins decelerating the bat just before the point of contact. The batter appears to be pushing the bat at the ball rather than swinging the bat. This cautious swing causes the ball to come off the bat with low velocity. A lazy fly ball is often the result because as the bat decelerates it drops lower in its plane and thus contacts the ball slightly under its center.

The best way to correct this problem is to focus on swinging through the ball, trying to knock a hole in the middle of the ball as you swing. In addition, shortening your backswing may help you focus on accelerating the bat as you contact the ball.

Erratic Timing

A skillful bat swing is a series of timing events as described in this chapter and chapter 1. You must time the start of the swing and each phase of the swing based on your observation of the pitch. You can begin the load phase, stride, or swing too soon or too late.

Precise timing mostly comes about through quality practice. Through repetition you must learn when to initiate the swing, which begins with the forward stride after the load phase, the most critical part of the timing of the entire swing. Then through practice and game experience you want to learn the rhythm of your swing, which is the sequencing of each part of the swing.

Pitchers will try to disrupt your timing by throwing pitches at different heights and locations. You'll not hit as well as you're able if you're an undisciplined hitter and swing at pitches that throw you out of your rhythm.

Stress also disrupts timing. The tension in muscles when stressed will change the speed of the movements, which disrupts your rhythm. Stress also creates interference in the mind. Batters who lack self-confidence may ponder too long whether or not a pitch is one they should swing at and thus start their swing too late. Good timing is a result of continued practice and self-confidence in your ability.

SEEING BETTER

Seeing the ball well is vital to hitting it well. So if you're having difficulty seeing pitches as you bat, the first thing to have checked is your visual acuity. A vision acuity problem can most likely be corrected with glasses or contact lenses, or in some cases with minor surgery.

When you have your eyes tested by reading lines of letters on a chart, you're being tested for static acuity. What's equally important in softball is dynamic acuity—your ability to see clearly when you or the ball is moving. If you think that you have a dynamic vision problem, an optometrist or sports vision specialist can administer a simple test to determine your ability to see a moving object.

Another important component of vision is depth perception—your ability to judge accurately the distance between you and the ball and thus determine the speed and trajectory of the oncoming pitch. Depth perception is achieved by viewing objects with both eyes and integrating the slightly different view from each eye in your brain to give you stereoptic vision. If you're having timing problems with your hitting, you should have your depth perception checked.

Beyond seeing problems, other reasons may cause you not to see the ball well when you're hitting. As we look at each reason, consider whether this is a visual problem or something else.

Control Your Gaze

Top baseball hitters actually don't watch the ball all the way to the bat. They track the ball from the pitcher's hand to a few feet in front of the plate and then fixate on hitting the ball at that point. Because of the speed of a baseball pitch, batters do not have time to adjust the swing when the ball is closer than 24 feet (7 m), so tracking the pitch beyond that point offers no benefit. But slowpitch is different because the ball travels much more slowly and batters can make minute adjustments to the swing much closer to the point of impact. So in slowpitch you should track the ball all the way to the point of contact with the bat.

A common mistake among slowpitch hitters is shifting their gaze (what they watch) to where they want to hit the ball. Often batters are not aware that they do this because it has become habitual and is thus difficult to stop.

Why do batters do this? The flippant answer is that we don't want to miss seeing those beautiful hits we make. A better explanation is that our minds are wired to automate routine activities. We walk without thinking about firing the muscles necessary to make our legs move. We type without thinking about each keystroke, and after playing slowpitch for a while we learn that it is not hard to hit the ball. Thus the brain learns to calculate the trajectory of the pitch, and we begin looking where we're going to hit just before making contact with the ball. Unfortunately, the result is that although we still hit the ball, often we don't hit it dead center.

FIGURE 2.6 Practice controlling your gaze so that you watch the ball until it makes contact with the bat.

How do you correct this problem? The bad news is that your brain is doing this without your permission; that is, it happens automatically. The good news is that you can override this automated behavior by concentrating on watching the ball all the way to the bat (see figure 2.6). Breathing is also an automatic behavior—thank goodness—but if you want to take control of your breathing you can slow it down, speed it up, and take shallower or deeper breaths. Although you want to be able to execute a good mechanical swing automatically, if you are not automatically watching the ball to the bat, then consciously practice controlling your gaze to avoid this mistake. Nothing is more important in hitting.

Keep Your Head Still

When trying to hit the ball extra hard, batters may turn the head away from the ball with the rotation of the shoulders as they swing, making it more difficult to see the ball clearly. The head is turning away from the pitch as it comes toward the strike zone, as shown in figure 2.7. Consequently, at the most critical moment

FIGURE 2.7 *(a)* Batter swinging with his head pulled out. *(b)* As the ball nears the plate, the batter who turns his head sees the ball with less acuity through peripheral vision of only one eye.

to see the pitch, the last few feet before impact, head-turning batters are able to view the ball with only one eye (the back eye when facing the pitcher), and if the head turns far enough, they see the ball only out of the corner of the eye.

Try looking askance with one eye to see how fuzzy your vision is. And, of course, if you see the ball with only one eye, you don't have the depth perception provided by two eyes. When batters swing and completely miss the ball in slowpitch, the reason almost always is that they pulled their head away from the pitch and didn't see the ball clearly or at all. So to hit better and make solid contact with the ball, keep the head still and focus both eyes on the ball as it approaches the plate.

Keep Your Eyes Open

No, we're not going to tell you that some batters close their eyes when they swing, but some do squint, which reduces the sharpness of their vision. When we try extra hard to do things, especially things involving power, some of us have a tendency to squint. As you bat, try to determine whether you squint, or if you can't tell, ask a teammate to watch you to see whether you make this mistake. If you do, simply practice keeping your eyes relaxed and open as you swing.

Keep Your Eyes Quiet

If, as discussed earlier, you look up to where you think you'll hit, or you pull your head away from the ball, or your eyes jump from point to point rather than tracking the pitch smoothly, your eyes won't be quiet and your hitting will suffer. Based on substantial research in many sports, evidence now shows that elite athletes have superior control over what they focus on when playing their sport. This ability has been called the "quiet eye". In slowpitch softball it refers to maintaining a single focus on the ball when hitting, even when all the movements of the swing are going on and potential distractions may exist. You can train your eye to be quiet after you become aware that it is not.

Control Your Attention

We all are familiar with the experience of seeing something that we really didn't see, or hearing something that we really didn't hear. You can have a still head and both eyes wide open and focused on the ball, but if you're not paying attention, you may see the ball technically but not "perceive" it; that is, your brain may fail to register the ball fully.

If you let your mind pay attention to other things in the external environment, such as someone yelling a comment to you, movement by the defense, or the catcher telling you how wonderful a hitter you are (intended to disrupt your concentration), you won't see the ball as well as when your attention is fully focused on the pitch. If you enter the batter's box full of self-doubts and your mind is spewing forth a litany of negative self-talk, you won't see the ball as well either.

So how well you see is immutably linked to how well you think. So when batting you want not only a quiet eye but also a quiet mind.

Improve Your Vision

If you Google for "sports vision" you'll see that a number of training programs are offered to help you improve. Also, listed in appendix A is a book published on sports vision that may be helpful. But most of these programs and the book recommend training that is not sport specific, and they are not supported with extensive research.

For physical vision problems you'll need the help of an optometrist or ophthalmologist. For the other problems, the first step to correct them is recognizing that you're making that mistake. You should be able to do that yourself, but if not, a teammate or coach should be able to help you. Then through thoughtful, focused practice while you're hitting, you can learn to make the adjustments. In our opinion that's better than the non-sport-specific exercises advocated by some of these sports vision training programs.

In conclusion, to hit well you must not only see the ball really well but also perceive it. Your head needs to be still, your eyes must be fully open, and you must watch the ball to the point of contact. Forget about looking at the defense or where the ball will go. Focus your full attention on the ball and hitting it squarely with the bat.

Learning to Hit

If you understand how you learn to hit, your knowledge will influence how you go about practicing to hit. Sport scientists used to think that athletes learned motor skills by developing a mental blueprint through repeated practice, but as they studied athletes' performance of complex skills like hitting, they discovered that these skills consist of many different responses of a similar type. A mental blueprint would be useful only in conditions identical to those under which it was learned. In slowpitch you would need millions of blueprints to match the many variations under which you hit. Even if your brain could learn all those blueprints, you wouldn't be able to recall the correct one fast enough when hitting.

Scientists today believe that instead of learning by developing blueprints, you learn to hit by developing abstract rules. Each time you swing, your brain has the unique ability to take key pieces of information about how you performed to create rules about how to swing in the future. We call this complex set of rules a motor program. This way of learning to hit is far more efficient when so many variables change each time you're at bat. By the way, you learn language the same way. Instead of learning every possible combination of words to understand their meaning (blueprint approach), you learn a set of rules that lets you use language in a far more functional and creative way.

When you practice hitting, your brain seeks to abstract the following information:

- The condition of the environment (e.g., the playing field, weather, position of the defense)
- The demands of the movement being performed (e.g., speed, direction, power)
- The evaluation of your swing as you perceive it
- A comparison of the actual outcome with what you intended

As you practice and use feedback to adjust your technique, your brain continues to synthesize these abstracted pieces of information to shape your motor program.

Under the blueprint approach we believed that after you started to swing you could not make adjustments to your swing, but we now know that you can make minor adjustments. For example, you begin your swing in anticipation that the ball will be in a certain location, but then it begins to curve. If you've developed your motor program to adjust for changes in the trajectory of the ball, as you swing you will be able to make adjustments to hit the ball in its changed location.

Rather than a detailed blueprint the motor program is only a generalized plan to hit the ball. With practice the motor program enables you to make a skillful swing in a wide range of conditions. To hit the ball correctly, however, you must determine the exact trajectory and location of the pitch.

Many factors influence how readily you develop a motor program for hitting. Your motor ability, cognitive ability, concentration, and motivation to practice and play are all important variables that determine whether you become a successful hitter. See pages 48–49 for seven principles to improve your practice.

PRACTICING BETTER

The journey to becoming a better hitter requires an investment of considerable practice time, but many players practice ineffectively and inefficiently. In this section we'll share with you the knowledge acquired by sport scientists about how to practice more effectively. You'll gain more from this section if you have read the sidebar "Learning to Hit" on page 45.

The road to becoming an excellent slowpitch hitter goes through three stages of learning—the mental stage, the practice stage, and the automatic stage—which we describe next.

Mental Stage

When you first learn to hit the emphasis is on *what* to do to swing correctly, which takes a great deal of cognitive activity as you begin to develop a motor program of the correct technique. For that reason this step is called the mental stage. In this stage it's helpful to have a coach demonstrate the technique and provide feedback to help you swing correctly. Without a coach, you can learn to swing by watching other players or DVDs. A knowledgeable coach is much better than no coach, but no coach is better than an uninformed coach.

When in the mental stage of learning to hit, focus on hitting the ball squarely at first. That is, the emphasis should be on accuracy. As you move into the practice stage, you should begin increasing the speed with which you swing, emphasizing both accuracy and power.

Feedback, although valuable in all stages of learning, is especially critical in this mental stage. You want to correct your errors quickly so that you do not learn the wrong technique at the outset. As you know, it's much harder to unlearn a skill and then learn a new one.

Feedback comes in two forms—intrinsic and extrinsic. As you practice, you'll get feedback about your hitting intrinsically by the way that the swing feels to you and how well you hit the ball. Extrinsic feedback, also referred to as augmented feedback, comes from an external source, usually another person observing you or from video of you hitting.

Learning a complex skill like hitting can be frustrating. Multiple errors may occur each time you swing. You or your coach may be tempted to correct several of those errors at once, but don't do that. Correct one error at a time. With the help of a knowledgeable coach, identify which error is more critical to swinging correctly and correct that error first. Then move on to correcting the next most important error.

When you make an error you need to determine what caused the error and how you can correct it. You almost certainly will need help from a knowledgeable coach to do so when you're in the mental stage of learning.

Practice Stage

As you practice in the mental stage you gradually are able to focus less on understanding what to do and work more on executing the swing correctly. As that change occurs you move into the practice stage of learning. Your mechanics are improving, but consistency is elusive. You swing well one time, but on the next swing your timing is off, or you dip your shoulder, or whatever . . . and on and on.

The good news is that errors are minor compared with what happens in the mental stage, and you are better able to detect and correct some of these errors based on intrinsic feedback. But quality feedback from good coaching can shorten your learning process.

Automatic Stage

With further practice, you can execute the mechanics of your swing with little thought about when to start the swing and how to execute it. You've entered the automatic stage. As you begin to achieve greater consistency, you also learn to master hitting a variety of different pitches. Nevertheless, you still occasionally mis-hit the ball and thus want to correct minor errors.

Correcting a minor error in the automatic stage is more difficult because identifying the error and determining how to correct it is harder. After you know what needs to be corrected, you must consciously focus on that part of your swing, taking it out of the automatic stage so that you can repair the motor program. After you've made the correction, you have to integrate that change into your entire swing. You don't want to be trying to do that during competition, so you should work on making the change in practice sessions.

Unautomating a well-learned skill is no easy task but can be done with thoughtful practice and the help of a patient coach. In slowpitch softball, the most common skill to unautomate is hitting. When a player has learned to hit with incorrect mechanics or begins looking to where he or she is going to hit a split second before making contact, the player must consciously recognize the problem, learn the correct skill, and then automate the correct skill in order to execute it in a game.

Principles of Hitting Practice

The following are seven principles for effective and efficient practices. They are based on our observation and experience in the sport and on extensive research over the last 50 years in the sport sciences.

1. *Practice with the intent to improve.* Too many players come to practice sessions to swing mindlessly at balls and socialize with teammates. That's fine if you don't want to improve, but if you want to become a better player you need to be motivated and focused on improving.

2. *Practice the correct technique.* This is another principle that seems to be obvious, but it's often violated. We've heard players boast that they practice hitting 100 balls every day. But it's not just how many balls they hit; what counts is hitting those balls correctly. If you hit 100 balls incorrectly in practice, you're only automating an incorrect motor program. We all have room for improvement, so every practice should be a mindful exercise in further automating what you do correctly and working to improve any imperfections. It is not only the quantity of practice that counts, but the quality of that practice.

3. *Practice as you want to play.* This principle is based on the widely supported specificity-of-learning principle. With regard to hitting it says that the best learning experiences are those that come as close as possible to hitting in the game. Based on this principle, do you think that it is a good idea to use a weighted bat in the on-deck circle before hitting? Many batters do so, but it is counter to the specificity-of-learning principle, although it can help loosen up the muscles.

   Also, in practice you see batters swinging at pitches that would be balls and certainly should not be swung at in games. If you swing at balls in practice, you're more likely to swing at them in games. And from a pitching perspective, batting practice pitchers often try to groove the ball by not throwing it as high as you are likely to see in a game, thinking that they are helping you with your swing. Whether you're hitting in a dedicated practice session or just before you play a game, make the practice come as close as possible to the way that you play the game.

4. *Practice in shorter rather than longer sessions.* This principle is based on the finding that we learn better when practice is distributed over time rather than when it is massed together. When you are in the mental stage of learning, 15- to 20-minute sessions are long enough. When you are in the practice and automatic stages of learning, you can have longer sessions, but you can make those sessions far more effective when you distribute the batting practice. Also, keeping in mind the principle of practicing like you play, rather than having each player hit 20, 30, 40, or more balls at one time, have two batters ready to hit. As a warm-up round have each batter hit 10 and then step out. Then have each batter hit 3 to 5 pitches and step out. Next have each batter hit 1 pitch and rotate out, but do that three to five times. Conducting batting practice in this way gives batters an opportunity to warm up, work on technique, and hit as they do in a game. If batters have the need for additional work on mechanics, then you can organize a special session for them.

5. *Practice in gamelike conditions.* Along with observing the previous principles, it is beneficial to practice hitting with defenders in their positions and to create various offensive situations, although you may or may not actually have runners on the bases. The best

approach is to simulate a game with defensive players in their positions, but if that's not possible you can simulate gamelike conditions with you and your pitcher. Place cones where the defensive players would be standing and then you or the pitcher can call out a game situation (sixth inning, runners on first and second, one out) and practice hitting for that situation.

If you cannot arrange to practice hitting on a regular playing field with a pitcher throwing to you, a batting cage where the ball is pitched by machine is a useful option to practice the mechanics of your swing and your gaze control. These artificial conditions, however, are not nearly as useful as hitting in gamelike conditions.

6. *Be receptive to feedback*. After you've played this game for a while and have experienced success, you may find yourself less receptive to suggestions for improvements from coaches, teammates, or spouses. You'll need to sort out whether the feedback is useful or not, but watch out that you don't close the door to efforts by others to help you improve your hitting.

7. *Observe what better hitters do*. You can learn much from role models who are better than you are by observing closely and asking them questions.

Each time you practice batting, apply the seven principles for effective practice.

PSYCHOLOGY OF HITTING

In practice you hit the ball well, but in games you all too often pop up, hit weak grounders, or loft lazy fly balls to the outfielders. You obviously have learned the swing mechanics to hit the ball well because you do so in practice. So why can't you hit well in games? Working hard to develop your physical skills but then not being able to execute them in the game is frustrating. As you likely know, hitting well is as much a mental skill as it is a physical one. See chapter 11 for a thorough discussion about how to develop the right mind-set for hitting, how to prepare mentally to hit, and how to deal with occasional failures.

SUMMARY

- Hit with more power by increasing your strength and improving the mechanics of your swing.
- Place hitting is more about accuracy than power and about selecting pitches in the right location to hit.
- When you have two strikes, hit the ball into the holes dictated by the location of the pitch, what we call "going with the pitch."
- Step into the batter's box with a plan of what you want to do but adjust the plan based on the ball–strike count.
- Be patient and select good pitches to hit.
- Swing under control. Avoid overswinging, which causes many mechanical errors.
- Swing *through* the ball, not *to* the ball.
- Practice, practice, and practice to get the timing of your swing perfect.
- To hit well, you must not only see the ball but also perceive the ball. Your head needs to be still, your eyes must be fully open, and you need to watch the ball to the point of contact. Don't look to where you want to hit as you swing.
- Practice with the intent to improve, practice the correct technique, and practice your hitting in conditions that are as gamelike as possible.
- Practice in shorter rather than longer sessions, be receptive to feedback, and learn by observing better hitters.
- Hitting is as much a mental skill as it is a physical skill.

CHAPTER 3

Baserunning

Baserunning is a fun part of slowpitch softball, and because there is so much hitting in the game you get to do a lot of it. We've seen many games won and lost because of smart and dumb baserunning, yet amazingly this part of the sport is seldom coached or instructed. Watch only a few games and you'll see runners not hustling to put themselves in a position to take an extra base, missing opportunities to tag on fly balls and advance, and using poor judgments about trying to stretch singles into doubles. In this chapter we'll cover baserunning rules, proper running technique, the four principles of baserunning, sliding technique, the technique to run to each base, and coaching the bases.

SLOWPITCH BASERUNNING RULES

To become a smart base runner, you first need to know the rules that apply to baserunning in slowpitch softball. Then we'll get into the technique and tactics of running the bases.

No Bunting, Leading Off, or Stealing

Unlike in baseball, in slowpitch softball you cannot bunt, lead off a base, or steal a base (with one exception noted shortly). The runner must stay in contact with the base until the ball is batted, touches the ground, or crosses the plate or strike mat. The runner can advance to the next base only when the ball is hit or the batter is walked. The Independent Softball Association and some local leagues, however, play a version of the game in which runners can steal bases after the pitched ball hits the strike mat or ground (the ball is ruled dead if it bounces off home plate).

FIGURE 3.1 When a play is being made at the base, the batter-runner must step on the safety base when running to first.

Safety Base at First

As mentioned in the introduction, many softball organizations have adopted the double base, or safety base as we'll call it, at first base. As shown in figure 3.1, this safety base is connected to the regular first base but lies outside the foul line. When you are running to first and a play at the base is likely, you must step on the safety base to avoid a collision with the first baseperson, and the first baseperson must make contact only with the regular first base to get you out. When batters hit the ball safely they may step on the regular first base as they round the base and consider going to second. If you do not step on the safety base when there is a play at first base, you will be called out. If the first baseperson mistakenly steps on the safety base, you will be called safe. After you've arrived safely on first base you must keep your feet on the regular first base, not the safety base, or you'll be called out.

Avoiding Collisions on the Bases

When running to second or third you cannot interfere with a defensive player who is attempting to field or throw the ball, and defensive players who are not fielding or throwing the ball cannot interfere with you when you're running the bases. In addition, slowpitch softball rules mandate that you avoid collisions when running to a base by either moving out of the way or sliding.

A leading cause of injury in slowpitch is a collision at home between the runner and catcher. To eliminate this potential injury, many softball organizations, and all senior softball organizations, have adopted the scoring plate, similar in concept to the safety base at first base. The scoring plate is located 8 feet (2.4 m) from the regular home plate and outside the foul line, as shown in figure 3.2.

When the scoring plate is in use and a play occurs at home, the catcher stands on the strike mat or home plate (rules vary among organizations). If he or she catches the ball before the runner touches the scoring plate, the runner is out. But, you ask, what if a runner starts to go home and then decides to return to third? To make this modification work, the rule makers created a commitment line located 20 feet (6.1 m) from home plate, as shown in figure 3.2. After runners pass this line, they are committed to running home. A runner who mistakenly runs to home plate or the strike mat will be called out.

Commitment line

FIGURE 3.2 Running to the scoring plate to avoid collisions with the catcher.

Infield Fly Rule

As a runner you will want to be aware of the infield fly rule, which states that a batter is immediately out when he or she hits a fly ball, not a line drive, which can be caught in the infield with runners on first and second or on first, second, and third with less than two outs. The ball remains live. After the ball is caught or touched by the fielder or hits the ground, you can advance at your own risk. The reason for the infield fly rule is to protect the offense from the defensive tactic of intentionally letting the ball drop and then turning a double or even triple play.

Many players misunderstand the infield fly rule. Take note of the conditions that must exist for an infield fly rule to be applied:

- Runners must be on first and second bases or first, second, and third bases.
- There must be less than two outs.
- The ball must be fair.
- The ball can be caught with ordinary effort by an infielder.

Umpires are to call "Infield fly" when the ball reaches its apex in flight and the rule applies, and if the ball is near the foul line, they are to call "Infield fly if fair." Our experience is that umpires occasionally forget to make this call, so you'll need to be aware of when the rule applies.

Running Outside the Baselines

Occasionally you may encounter a play in which the defensive player has the ball and is attempting to tag you out as you run to the next base. The rule says that when running toward any base you cannot run more than 3 feet (90 cm) in either direction from a direct line between the bases to avoid being tagged, as shown in figure 3.3.

FIGURE 3.3 The base runner cannot run more than 3 feet in either direction from a direct line between the bases to avoid being tagged.

STARTS AND RUNNING TECHNIQUE

The fastest runners can travel the 65 feet (19.8 m) from home to first in about 4.0 seconds, and it takes about 3.0 seconds on average to catch a hard-hit ground ball in the infield and throw a runner out at first. So if the ball is hit slowly or to a location difficult for the infielder to reach or the fielder bobbles the ball, with good running technique you can beat out an infield hit. In this section we'll look at

- the start after hitting the ball,
- the start from any base, and
- guidelines for good sprinting technique.

Start at Home

Right-handed batters drop the bat and take the first step with the right, or back, foot (see figure 3.4, *a* and *b*). The first few steps should be short strides with arms pumping hard. Left-handed batters take the first step by crossing the left, or back, foot over the right and then powering toward first base (see figure 3.5, *a* and *b*). See Offense→Baserunning→Start at Home on the DVD for a demonstration.

FIGURE 3.4 Right-handed start. *(a)* Push off with the right foot and *(b)* take a powerful stride toward first.

FIGURE 3.5 Left-handed start. *(a)* Push off with the left foot, which crosses over the right foot, and *(b)* take a powerful stride toward first.

Start at Any Base

The more common method of starting from first, second, or third base is the stationary start shown in figure 3.6. Facing the base that you will run to, place one foot on the base and the other about 2 to 3 feet (60 to 90 cm) in front and in a comfortable sprinter position. As soon as the batter contacts the ball, take a small jab step with the front foot to start the sprint and then push off the base with the back foot to take a full stride.

The less common method of starting is called the rocker start shown in figure 3.7. One foot is placed behind the base, and the other is in contact with the front edge of the base. Most of the body weight is on the front foot. As the pitch is delivered the runner rocks back and then steps forward with the back foot and pushes off with the front foot. You can also see both of these starts on the DVD (Offense→Baserunning→Start at Any Base).

FIGURE 3.6 Stationary start. *(a)* Start with one foot on the base and the other 2 to 3 feet in front, *(b)* take a short jab step with the front foot, and *(c)* push off the base with the back foot to take a full stride.

FIGURE 3.7 Rocker step start. *(a)* Start with one foot behind the base and the other in contact with the front edge of the base, *(b)* then rock back and take the first step forward with the back foot.

The key to the rocker start is timing the pitch so that the foot does not leave the base until the ball is hit. Although less commonly used, the rocker start has the advantage of allowing the runner to gain momentum quicker and thus reach the next base a split-second faster as long as the start is correctly timed. It has the disadvantage that the runner can be thrown out when a line drive is caught in the infield and the runner doesn't have time to reverse his or her momentum toward the base.

Sprinting Technique

You're on your way to first or one of the other bases with a good start, and now you want to run as fast as you can to the next base. You may think that to run fast you have to bear down, stay low, and power out, but running fast actually requires you to stay relaxed and keep your body in a natural upright position (see figure 3.8 and Offense→Baserunning→Good Running Form on the DVD). When trying too hard, runners make the mistake

FIGURE 3.8 Good running form between the bases with the body in a natural upright position.

of overstriding, which significantly reduces speed. In practice try running using different stride lengths to find out which length lets you run the fastest. Good arm action is helpful in improving your speed. The arms should pump up and down from the shoulders but without excess tension. Also lean slightly forward as you sprint but don't exaggerate the lean.

Many people are under the false impression that speed is inherited and can't be improved. But you can become faster through strength and power training and better mechanics. To learn how to improve your speed, see the references in appendix A.

BASERUNNING PRINCIPLES

We see more unnoticed errors in baserunning than in any other aspect of the game. Many players work hard at improving their hitting and fielding but consistently make running errors of which they are unaware that cost their team runs. You can substantially improve your baserunning by applying the four principles discussed next.

Make Smart Decisions

Speed is a huge asset in baserunning, but fast and dumb on the basepaths gets you thrown out or standing on second base when you should have been on third base. So along with improving your speed you want to become a smart base runner. In fact, even if you don't have great speed, you can be an excellent base runner by always running at your best speed and making good decisions about when to run and when not to run. Throughout this chapter we'll provide you with guidelines for making good decisions. Then you'll need to practice those just as you do other skills of the sport.

When a player is easily thrown out trying to stretch a single into a double, the mistake is obvious to everyone, especially the runner who made it. But many of the mistakes in baserunning are failures to take advantage of the opportunity to advance a base, and those mistakes are often unnoticed by the runner, his or her teammates, and the coach. You can only correct a mistake if you first recognize that you made one. We'll discuss specific decisions about baserunning and the mistakes that runners can make when we take our tour around the bases later in this chapter.

To be a smart runner in slowpitch, you need to think differently about the risks that you should take to advance to the next base compared with the risks that you might take in baseball and fastpitch softball. Team batting averages in baseball and fastpitch softball are typically in the .250 to .275 range, or about 1 hit out of 4 times at bat. So as a runner if you see that you have a 50% chance or better of taking an extra base, that is a good calculated risk. But in slowpitch, teams bat .600 to .700, and thus batters are getting on base 6 or 7 times out of 10. Consequently, when running in slowpitch you want to try to advance to the next base only when your chances are considerably higher, say a certainty of 90 to 95%.

So as a general principle, run the bases more conservatively in slowpitch softball. You don't want to take the bat out of the next batter's hands, especially when he or she may be your leading hitter.

Know Where the Ball Is

You may hear what seems to be conflicting advice from a coach or teammate about baserunning:

"You should always know where the ball is when you're running the bases."

"Don't watch the ball; just run."

Confusing advice? Not really!

It's correct that you should always know where the ball is when running the bases. Always! But that doesn't mean that you always watch the ball. At times you should watch the ball, and at other times you should not, but even when you aren't watching it you can know where it is by reasonable estimation and with help from the base coaches. When a ball is hit to right field and you're rounding second, you should not be trying to watch the ball because you'll be running sideways. You want to rely on your third-base coach to tell you whether the ball is being thrown to third and whether you need to slide.

After you've rounded a base and decided not to advance to the next base, you want to watch the ball to see whether it is relayed cleanly and whether a misplay will allow you to advance to another base. You want to watch the ball after rounding a base to make certain that the ball is not thrown behind you to pick you off. Occasionally you'll see a runner round the bag and turn his or her back to the field while walking back to the bag. An alert shortstop or second baseperson may see this and make a quick throw to the player covering the base to catch the runner napping.

We'll discuss the specifics of when to watch the ball and when not to when we do our tour around the bases later in this chapter, but as a general guideline you should watch the ball at all times except when it interferes with your running at top speed.

Watch the Runner in Front of You

You hit the ball well and you're sure that it is a double, but the runner on first is unsure whether it will be caught and waits at first to make sure that it is a hit. The ball does drop in for a hit, and you assume that the runner on first will go to third. You're watching that beautiful hit of yours and running hard to second, but the runner on first decides to stop at second. Oops, now there are two of you at second base. You just violated one of the key principles of running the bases: You must watch the runner in front of you when making the decision about advancing to the next base.

Run Hard to the Next Base

The most common mistake made by base runners is not running hard to the next base. It's not unusual to see this: You hit a ground ball through the infield for a base hit and quickly surmise that it's good for a single and no more. So you go into your half-speed trot to first base. Meanwhile, the ball squirts away from the outfielder. You could have made second base if you had run hard to first base and rounded the bag to be in a position to advance.

Well, not such a big deal, you think. You did get a base hit. But here comes the pain. The next batter hits a ball in the 5-6 hole. The shortstop makes a terrific backhanded stop and throws to second base to force you out, the only play he could have made to get an out. Because you loafed to first, instead of having runners on first and second with no one out, you have a runner on first and

Always run to the next base as fast as you can to put pressure on the defense to stop you.

one out, and you took a hit away from your teammate. And your running mistake could have been even more disastrous. The ball could have been hit directly to the shortstop, who then might have executed a double play!

As a coach or teammate it's hard to accept a player who consistently loafs when running the bases, especially when it costs you a run and maybe the game. We all have greater tolerance for teammates who have less ability, in this case, less speed, but we have a low tolerance for teammates when they don't try hard.

Not running hard to each base hurts your team in the following ways:

- You will be thrown out more often.
- On a hit you will not be in a position to advance to the next base should the opportunity arise.
- You don't remove the force-out situation.
- You slow down the runners behind you.
- You don't put pressure on the defense to hurry their fielding and throwing, which may increase the chances of their making an error.

So as a principle, always run hard. Go as fast as you can until you can go no farther. Force the defense to stop you, running so that you pressure them to "worry and hurry."

SLIDING

Sliding is a helpful skill if you're playing competitive slowpitch softball, yet many players never practice it and thus either don't slide or slide incorrectly. Although sliding is a leading cause of injury in softball, failing to slide can also cause injuries. Learn to slide so that you can run full speed to a base and stop quickly without overrunning the base. Sliding is also useful to avoid collisions, break up double plays, and avoid being tagged out by the fielder.

Because slowpitch is played recreationally as well as competitively and by people of all ages, including seniors in their 70s and 80s, you'll have to decide whether sliding is a skill that you want to learn and use. Also, consider the condition of the playing field. Some fields are extremely hard and consist of finely ground rock (used to improve drainage) that can cause painful abrasions. (We'd like to see those responsible for maintaining softball fields be required to slide on them at least one time per year!)

If you do decide that you want to slide, learn to do it well and with confidence. Sliding is not something that you want to do without full commitment. We'll show you how to slide safely and effectively next, and then we'll offer some suggestions for practicing. We'll demonstrate only the bent-knee slide and the hook slide. We recommend that you *not* slide headfirst because of the risk of serious head and neck injuries.

Bent-Leg Slide

The bent-leg slide is an easy and safe slide to execute. It involves three parts: the takeoff, the slide, and contact with the base as shown in figure 3.9. Read this section and then watch Offense→Baserunning→Sliding→ Bent-Leg Slide on the DVD.

In the takeoff you run straight at the base, not slowing down at all, and then 10 to 15 feet (3 to 4.5 m) from the base you begin the slide by throwing one leg forward, keeping it somewhat straight and pointing it at the base. At the same time you lift up the other leg, bend it at the knee, and tuck it under the straight leg, creating a figure-4 look. Players can select either leg to be the straight leg, but most often the straight leg is the dominant leg. As you throw your feet forward to begin the slide, you lean back slightly from the waist. You don't leap or jump toward the base, or slow up and drop down.

The slide phase begins when your butt contacts the ground. Some players lean straight back, contacting the ground with both cheeks, but most players prefer to slide slightly on the side of their bent leg. You place one hand on the ground as slight support and balance, but you don't want to put your arms out to support or break the fall. That action is a common source of injury in sliding. If you need to break the fall, you're not taking off correctly. An effective slide is a quick but smooth transition of the body from an upright position to the prone position.

In the last phase you're sliding and reaching out with your straight leg to make contact with the base. If you see that the defender may attempt to tag you out, look to place your foot where it is more difficult to make the tag. If you slide with too much momentum, you should be prepared to absorb the momentum by bending the straight leg with contact.

FIGURE 3.9 Bent-leg slide. *(a)* The takeoff, *(b)* the sliding position with the bottom leg bent to form a figure-4, and *(c)* contacting the base with the top leg.

FIGURE 3.10 Hook slide to the left. (a) The takeoff, (b) the sliding position with the left leg reaching out and the right leg trailing in preparation to hook the base, and (c) contacting the base with the trailing right leg.

Hook Slide

You're on first base and the ball is a base hit to the outfield. You round second and head toward third, but 30 feet (9 m) from the base your coach is telling you to slide. You focus on the third baseperson, watching her position herself to field the throw and put the tag on you. She's standing on the outside corner of the bag. She catches the ball and reaches to tag you, but you've made a hook slide to the inside of the base, catching just the corner of the base with your toe, avoiding the tag. With the next batter you score the winning run on a sacrifice fly.

If you're a competitive softball player, the hook slide will give you an edge, perhaps the winning edge. You use it to avoid the tag, so you'll want to learn to hook slide to either side of the base. Study the description that follows (see figure 3.10) and then watch Offense→Baserunning→Sliding→Hook Slide on the DVD.

In the takeoff phase, as you approach the base you determine whether you'll hook slide to the right side or left side of the base. When sliding to the left side, you begin the takeoff about 10 feet (3 m) from the base and aim your body not directly at the base, as in the bent-leg slide, but about 3 feet (1 m) to the left of the base. In the slide phase your left leg goes in that direction and you contact the ground with your left cheek, but not too much on your left side. Your right leg is bent slightly back as you lean back into the slide. You complete the slide by reaching out to hook the corner of the base with the toe of your right foot. Sliding to the right side of the base is done exactly the same way, except, of course, you throw your right leg 3 feet to the right and hook the base with your left toe.

The hook slide definitely requires practice to master it from both sides. You must accurately assess how far from the base you can slide and still be able to hook it. Also, if you slide too late you may not be able to stop your momentum on the base with only your toe contacting it. Now let's see how to practice the bent-leg and hook slides by using a progression to avoid injury.

Practice Progression Sliding

Watch Offense→Baserunning→Sliding→Sliding Practice Progression on the DVD and read this section until you think that you have a good mental image of what to do in the bent-leg slide. If you know someone who knows how to coach sliding, recruit his or her assistance, but if not proceed this way.

1. Lie on the ground in the position shown in figure 3.9*b* to get the sense of what you'll be doing. This is the position that you want to assume when sliding.

2. Do one of the following: Find a long piece of heavy-duty plastic, lay it out on the grass, and water it down. Alternatively find a piece of cardboard at least 4 feet (120 cm) long and 3 feet (90 cm) wide (don't water it). With an old pair of pants and with an old pair of socks or running shoes, run fast to the cardboard or plastic. Just before you step on the plastic launch your takeoff. Don't jump into the takeoff; lean back into it. Slide on your butt or slightly on one side but don't land fully on your side. You have little padding there. Don't try to cushion your fall with your hands; just use them to help balance yourself. Practice this technique until you feel comfortable with it (see figure 3.11*a*).

3. Next put on long pants, a sweatshirt, sliding pads, and kneepads. Now practice sliding on a softball infield that is relatively soft and uses nonabrasive dirt (see figure 3.11*b*). Practice until you have the technique down and feel confident you can execute the bent-leg slide in a game. Follow the same sequence for learning to do the hook slide.

FIGURE 3.11 Practicing the bent-leg slide *(a)* on a sheet of watered-down plastic and *(b)* on a soft infield.

A TOUR AROUND THE BASES

Join us now as we take a running tour of the bases. We'll describe how to run to the next base and what to watch for. Running the bases often involves making split-second decisions about whether to advance or not. We'll guide you through those decisions as you move from base to base under various game situations. And we'll remind you of the running mistakes to guard against.

Running to First

We've discussed how to start your sprint from the batter's box to first on page 54. After you have taken your first two steps you should look up to see where the ball is to determine whether you'll be running through the base at first or rounding the base for a possible run to second. If you know that an infielder is likely to field the ball, turn your focus toward first and running through the base. The route to follow is a straight line from the batter's box, and just to the right of the foul line, to the safety base. Sometimes novices run to the base, slowing down as they approach it. Of course, you know that you'll get to first faster if you run *through* the base, not *to* the base. You should step on the front of the bag with either foot, not trying to adjust your steps to hit the base with one foot or the other. Also, don't leap at the bag; that's a few milliseconds slower than running through the base. When you're two steps past the base, slow down quickly and look and listen for an overthrow at first. Then quickly decide whether you can advance to second base. See Offense→Baserunning→Running to First on the DVD for a demonstration.

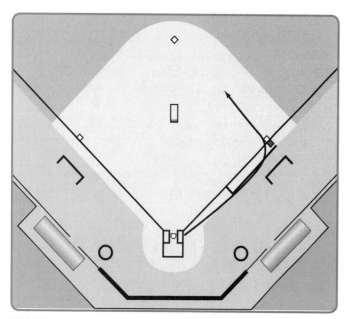

FIGURE 3.12 Running route to first base when the ball is hit into the outfield.

Occasionally you'll see someone sliding headfirst into first base to try to beat the throw, but that's not a smart play. Sliding into the base is definitely slower than running through it, and you put yourself at greater risk of injury. The only time that you may want to slide at first is to avoid being tagged out by a first baseperson who has come off the base to catch the ball. Even then you should slide feet-first.

If the ball is hit through the infield on the ground or is a fly ball to the outfield, you should run to round first base, anticipating that you'll be going to second base unless the defense stops you. The route to take when you're rounding first base is shown in figure 3.12.

As you approach first base step on the inside front corner of the base, lower your left shoulder, and turn as sharply as you can toward second without losing speed. Step on first with either foot rather than adjusting your stride to touch it every time with one foot or the other (see figure 3.13).

FIGURE 3.13 Step on the inside corner of the base and lower the left shoulder to make the sharpest and fastest turn possible.

What to Watch

As mentioned before, the first thing that you'll want to watch is whether the ball is being played in the infield or outfield. You'll then know whether to run straight through first base or round it toward second. When there is no play at first base, as you're approaching the base you want to see where the ball is and then quickly look to first base so that you don't miss the bag. When running through first base, watch the first baseperson to determine whether the ball may be overthrown or whether you can avoid a tag from a throw that pulls the first baseperson off the bag. Next you'll look for an errant ball in foul territory, especially if you don't hear the ball pop in the first baseperson's glove.

Be aware of this little rule: If you run through first base without making any intention to run to second base, you cannot be tagged out as you return to first. But if you see an overthrow to first and begin to break toward second base but then think better of it, you become a live runner and can be tagged out.

Decision Making

As a batter–runner you will have the following decisions to make:

- Whether to run straight through first base or round it.
- If you run straight through, you may have the opportunity to make a decision about going to second if the first baseperson misses the ball.
- When rounding first base the major decision that you're making is whether to run to second. If you decide not to advance, round the bag as far as you safely can without being thrown out. Sometimes you'll find lazy first basepersons who don't go back to the bag to cover first. You can then round the bag as far as the first baseperson is away from the bag and even a little farther. When you round the bag on a hit to left or left-center field and stop, face toward the infield but look directly at the outfielder who is fielding the ball so that you are in a good position to advance to second base if there is a miscue in the field or quickly return to first (see figure 3.14a). When you round the bag on a hit to right or right center and decide to stop, face toward the outfielder with the ball (with your back to the infield) and be in the same ready position to advance or return to the bag (see figure 3.14b).

FIGURE 3.14 After rounding the base, look directly at the outfielder fielding the ball and be in a good position to advance to second base or return to first base. (a) Face the infield on a hit to left or left center; (b) face the outfield on a hit to right or right center.

Mistakes

The most common mistake that batters make is not running at top speed to first when they think that they have hit a single. Avoid this mistake by leaving the batter's box thinking that you're going to second until you see that the defense will stop you.

Another common mistake that batters make is hitting a high fly ball and assuming that it will be caught. Sometimes batters do not even leave the batter's box, but even if they trot to first, if the ball is dropped they are not in a position to advance as far as they could have if they had been running hard from the start. This dumb mistake is easy to make when you're disappointed with a poor hit.

The penalty for not running can be even worse when a runner is on first base with less than two outs. If a pop-up is hit to an infielder who sees that the batter is not running, he or she can let the ball hit the ground untouched, pick it up and throw to second for one out, and then watch a teammate relay it to first for a double play. Ouch, that hurts!

Another mistake is thinking that there are two outs when there aren't. For example, you're up to bat with a runner on first and hit the ball to the second baseperson. Thinking that there are two outs and that the play will be a force-out at second, you think that running to first won't make a difference, so you loaf. But by not running hard the defense gets not only the force-out at second but you at first as well—a double play! One lesson in this example is always to know the number of outs when you're batting. The second lesson, which applies to each of the mistakes described, is always to run at your best speed every time you hit the ball.

Running to Second

Good, you didn't make any of the mistakes described in the previous section and you're safely on first base. You take your starting stance, either the stationary stance or the rocker stance, in preparing to run to second base, making the same decisions that you made when leaving the batter's box. If the hit ball is going to create a play at second, you're running in a straight line to the base as quickly as you can. If you can potentially advance to third base on the hit, you'll round second base, stepping on the inside corner of the base, and be in a position to advance to third base. If the ball is hit to left or left center, you'll round the bag and face the outfielders in a ready position to advance to third base or return to second base. If the ball is hit to right center or right, you'll round the bag and face the infield but look over your shoulder to the outfielders.

What to Watch

From your starting stance at first base you're in an excellent position to see the whole field. You'll want to note the outfielders' positions. Are they playing in close or deep, or are they shifted to the right or left side? When the ball is hit on the ground you'll immediately sprint to second, watching the ball and the defensive player covering second base to help you make the decision about whether to run straight to the base or round it. As you approach the base, watch the defensive player covering second to determine whether you'll need to slide or can stand up. If in doubt, slide. When the ball is hit along the first-base line, you can't watch it and run at top speed. Instead, rely on your first-base coach to tell you whether to run to second base or round it.

When the hit ball is a line drive or a fly ball, you need to quickly decide whether you should stay on the base, tag up, or advance halfway or all the way to second.

When a runner is on second base, you need to watch him or her to determine whether you'll be able to advance to second on a caught fly ball in the outfield. Likewise, you watch the runner ahead of you on a base hit to determine whether you'll be able to go beyond second base to third or home. When you've run to second base and have arrived safely, don't quit watching the ball. If the defensive team throws errantly, you may be able to advance to third.

Another situation to watch for is the first baseperson who plays even with the base rather than back behind you. If the ball is hit on the ground sharply to the first baseperson, because you must avoid making contact with a defensive player making a catch, you may be trapped. The first baseperson can touch you and then step on the bag for an easy double play. The best way to avoid this play is to get the best start possible off the base and for the batter not to hit the ball to the first baseperson.

Decision Making

You've gotten a hit and are proud of yourself as you stand on first base, but do you have your head in the game, thinking about what you need to do next? Let's hope so.

As a heads-up base runner you need to know the game situation, particularly the number of outs, the inning, and the score. You make a mental note of the defensive positioning. You've observed from the bench which outfielders have strong, average, and weak arms. You know who's batting and how he or she tends to hit the ball. Knowing the game situation helps you determine the risk that you're willing to take in trying to advance a base or two.

When the ball is hit you have these decisions to make:

- If the ball is hit on the ground you know that you must run because it is a force-out at second.
- When the batter hits a line drive watch the ball through the infield before you leave the bag; otherwise you are likely to be thrown out if an infielder catches it. This play happens so fast that even if you take only two or three steps off the bag, you may find it impossible to reverse your momentum and get back to the base safely.
- On an infield fly ball with less than two outs when the infield fly rule is *not* in effect, come off the bag no farther than a point from which you can safely return to the base if the ball is caught. If it is dropped, you'll run straight for second. If the infield fly rule is in effect, stay on the base.
- On any fly ball with two outs, run as soon as the ball is hit until the ball is caught or the defense stops you.
- On a short to medium fly ball to the outfield with less than two outs, you need to decide whether it will be a certain hit or whether a fielder has a chance to catch it. If there is a chance that a fielder will catch it, you need to advance as far toward second as you can while still being able to return safely to first if the ball is caught. If you don't advance far enough and the ball is not caught, a fielder may retrieve the ball quickly and be able to force you out at second.

- On a medium to long fly ball with less than two outs, you need to decide whether it will be a certain hit or whether a fielder has a chance to catch it. If there is a chance a fielder will catch it, you need to decide whether you have a high probability of making it safely to second by tagging up at first.
- When a fly ball is hit into foul territory, even if it is close to the infield, always tag up and look for the opportunity to advance if the ball is caught.
- When you're running in a straight line to second base and you anticipate a force-out attempt at second, you'll need to decide whether to slide or stand up.
- When the ball is hit to the outfield you need to decide whether you can safely round second base, giving the appearance that you may go to third, or whether the outfielders are playing so close that you must run straight to the base. If you determine that you can round the base safely, then you must decide whether you can advance to third.

Mistakes

A common mistake is not judging quickly and correctly that a ball will drop safely in the outfield for a hit, thus delaying your sprint to second base or beyond. By observing games and knowing where the outfielders are playing, you can develop the knowledge to discern quickly when the ball is a safe hit and when it has a chance of being caught.

Another mistake that runners make is forgetting to tag up on sufficiently deep fly balls or being indecisive about whether the ball is deep enough and thus wandering off the bag a few feet. If the ball is caught, they do not have enough time to retreat to first and then advance. A lost opportunity!

Another common mistake is failing to slide when running to second to beat the throw on a force-out play at that base. Some players lack the skill to slide, and others just don't like getting dirty, but failing to slide can cost the team a win.

A rare mistake is to stand on the safety base rather than the regular base when in the start stance, or touching the safety base when tagging up.

Running to Third

Running from second to third base is much the same as running from first to second base. When starting from second base you take the same stance as you took at first base, and you will be making the same decisions about running straight to third base or rounding third base for a possible run to home.

When you're coming from first and rounding second to decide whether to run to third, you can watch the ball on the left side of the field but not the right side. After you're halfway to third turn your attention to the third-base coach and the third baseperson. The third baseperson's positioning will give you a clue about whether a play will be made on you at third. You're now in the hands of the third-base coach, who must let you know whether to continue running to home, to round third and stop, to come into third standing up, or to slide to one side of the base or the other.

What to Watch

From your starting stance at second you'll want to watch the hit ball, which sometimes is difficult to do when it is hit up the middle because you're screened out by the pitcher. As you watch you're looking to determine whether it is a hit or a possible out. If you're running directly to third and not rounding the base, after you arrive you want to turn immediately to face the field to see where the ball is and look for any opportunities to run home on a miscue in the field. When rounding third and setting up for a possible run to home, you will, of course, turn to your left to watch the ball.

When a runner is on third but no runner is on first, you're not in a force-out running situation at second base, so you must watch the third-base runner to know whether you can advance to third.

Decision Making

From second base you need to know all the same information as you do when you're on first. Then you have the following decisions to make:

- You must be cognizant of whether a runner is on first, which would put you in a force-out situation at third. If a runner is on first and the ball is hit on the ground, you know that you immediately have to sprint to third.

- If no runner is at first and the ball is hit on the ground, you have to decide whether you can advance safely to third. Here's the rule to follow: If the ball is in front of you, that is, it is hit to the third baseperson or shortstop, don't run, at least not immediately. But if those fielders throw to first and in your judgment you can run safely to third before the first baseperson can throw the ball to third, then do so. If the ball is behind you, that is, it is hit to the second or first baseperson, you definitely want to advance to third.

- When the ball is hit to the outfield you need to make a quick judgment about whether it is a certain hit. If it is, you'll run to third to round the base, looking for the opportunity to run home. The third-base coach, not you, almost always decides whether you should run home. If you don't happen to have a coach, then you'll have to decide.

- When a ball goes to the outfield and has the potential to be caught, you need to decide whether the ball is deep enough to tag the base and run to third or if it is too shallow to tag. Keep in mind that throws from right and right center are now longer than those from left and left center. If the ball is too shallow, you need to come part way off the base so that if the ball is not caught you can make it safely to third. When tagging up at second, if the ball is to the left, left-center, or even right-center fielder, position yourself on the base with your right foot touching it and slightly facing the outfield so that you can see when to push off. If the ball is hit to right field, put your left foot on the base and turn to the infield so that you can see the ball when it is caught.

Mistakes

All but the last mistake listed earlier about running from first to second are applicable when running from second to third. Some other mistakes are the following:

- With two outs the batter hits a fly ball. You assume that it will be caught and run lazily toward third. If the ball is dropped you are unable to score, but you could have scored if you had been running at top speed.

- You fail to listen to the third-base coach when instructed to slide or instructed to run home or not run home.

- You look over your shoulder trying to watch the play while you run, which slows you down a bit.

- When arriving at third you begin visiting with the coach and not watching the ball until it is ruled dead. With some regularity you'll see the relay person not catch the ball, and if you are alert you can sprint home.

- When a ground ball is hit to an infielder and you are not in a force-out situation, you jump off the base in an effort to distract the fielder and get picked off.

- The last mistake we'll mention here is getting trapped between the bases. Of course, it can happen between first and second, between second and third, and between third and home. You decide to advance to the next base but suddenly realize that you've made a bad judgment or that the runner in front of you made a bad judgment and is returning to the base in front of you. Now you're trapped. What do you do? Here are two guidelines.

  - Make the defense chase you to the next base, the one closer to home.

  - Take as much time as possible in the rundown so that other runners can advance.

Running Home

When your start from third base, place your left foot on the outside front corner of the base and your right foot in foul territory. If you get hit with the ball when in fair territory, you're out, unless you're standing on the base. You're not out if you get hit with the ball when you're in foul territory.

From third base, if no scoring plate is being used, you want to run in a direct line to home plate. If a scoring plate is being used, line yourself up to run to that base and remember that after you cross the commitment line . . . well, you are committed, so sprint to the scoring plate as fast as you can.

What to Watch

You don't have any runners in front of you to worry about, so you can focus your attention entirely on where the ball is hit to make your decision about whether to run home. If you're not playing with the scoring plate, watch the catcher to determine whether there will be an attempt to get you out at home. Also, listen to the batter on deck, who should be telling you whether or not to slide. If a scoring plate is being used, the on-deck batter should also let you know whether the defense is going to make a play on you; however, when a scoring plate is used you'll be called out if you slide.

Decision Making

Although good decision making is important at every base, not making a mistake seems more critical at third when you're so close to scoring a run. So here are the decisions that you're facing:

- You must know the number of outs and whether you are in a force-out situation, which would exist when runners are on first and second.

- If it is a force-out situation and the ball is hit on the ground, you must sprint home as fast as possible.

- On a line-drive hit, do not leave the base until you are certain that an infielder has not caught it. When it clears the infield and you know that it is a hit, you have plenty of time to run home.

- If it is not a force-out situation but the ball is hit to an infielder, you need to make a judgment about whether you can run home. If the ball is hit sharply, the infielders are playing close in, and the ball is fielded cleanly, you probably should not run. If it is hit slowly, you may have a chance. And when the ball is thrown to first or second, you must decide whether you are able to score.

- When a runner is on first with less than two outs and the ball is hit to an infielder who has a good chance of turning a double play, you have a decision to make about running home. We recommend that you run home in almost any circumstance. If the infielder throws home, you've prevented a double play, and tactically, with good teams batting .600 to .700, it makes sense to sacrifice a runner on third for a runner on second to save an out. When running home, if you can see the infielder throwing home and judge that you will likely be out, try to stop before you cross the commitment line, if a commitment line is in use. If you get in a rundown you may be able to save the out. If there is no scoring plate and you can see that you're going to be out at home, do the same—get in a rundown. Meanwhile, the runners are safe at first and second. But don't dilly-dally running home. If the infielder goes to second for a force-out and the shortstop or second baseperson covering second base sees you loafing, he or she may throw to home to get you out too.

  The one tricky judgment in this play is determining the chances of a double play. If the ball is hit slowly, if it is hit to the first baseperson who has to turn a 3-6-3 double play, or if you have a fast batter–runner, you have to judge whether it will be a double play. If the ball is hit slowly to the pitcher or in front of the first or third baseperson and the fielder sees you steaming home, the only possible play may be to throw to home. As a rule though, if it looks like a double-play situation, streak home as fast as you can.

- When the ball is hit shallow to the outfield so that you are not able to advance by tagging up, you should go partway toward home but only far enough that you can return to third safely if the ball is caught. When the ball is hit deeper and you judge that you can safely tag up, stay on the base until the ball is caught or drops in for a hit.

Mistakes

The most common mistake we see is not running to home when there is a double-play situation with a runner on first. Next, we see runners coming partway off third, thinking that the ball will be a hit, and then being unable to tag up and make it to home in time when it is caught. There is no reason to leave third base on any ball hit deep enough to the outfield that you know you can score by tagging up. If the ball is caught, you're in good position to run. If the ball is dropped, you'll have plenty of time to score.

Another mistake occurs when runners loaf home, anticipating that the play will be made at another base, and then are surprised by a quick throw home. A related mistake occurs when a runner loafs home when there are two outs and another runner in a non-force-out play is tagged out at another base before the runner crosses the plate. The runner would have scored if he or she had crossed the plate before the tag-out.

Again, good decision making and hustling prevent those mistakes!

COACHING THE BASES

In baseball and fastpitch softball the first- and third-base coaches are typically individuals who are not playing and regularly coach the bases. That situation is uncommon in slowpitch softball. Typically, the coaches are players who are not in the game at that time or at least not due to bat soon. Consequently, within a game and from game to game, a team could have many base coaches, resulting in great variability in the quality of coaching. Thus, having a session with the team about how each person is to coach the bases is helpful.

You can be a better base coach by learning as much as you can about the opposing team's defensive capabilities. Knowing the throwing ability of the outfielders is especially helpful in making the decision about whether to advance to the next base. You should also know your team's position about the level of risk that you want runners to take at various stages of the game.

Good base coaching earns players' confidence in the judgment of the coaches and helps your team win. They must be totally into the game, paying attention to every situation, and then apply good judgment in fractions of a second. When done well, coaching the bases is a gratifying way to assist the team.

Coaching Mistakes

Watch the sport for a while and you'll see the following examples of poor base coaching:

- Failing to tell the runner useful information. For example, on a close play at third the coach doesn't tell the runner to slide. She comes in standing up and as a result is tagged out.
- Not communicating clearly, either by voice or hand signals.

Avoid visiting with the runner when coaching the bases until the play is completed.

- Not knowing the game situation (the count, the number of outs, the inning, the score, the runners on base, the position of the defense).

- Not reminding runners of the situation and the likely decisions that they'll need to make.

- Visiting with the runner when he or she arrives at the base rather than alerting the runner to watch the ball until time is called.

- Visiting with the opposing players or spectators on the sidelines rather than paying attention to their coaching duties.

- Making poor judgments about having runners advance to the next base.

Nearly everyone agrees that coaching third is important, especially in making the decision to send a player home. Coaching first base is typically considered less important, but it shouldn't be. Effective coaching of the bases is another small part of the game that can make the difference between a loss and a win. So whether you're a player who is coaching or a full-time coach, take the duties of coaching the bases seriously.

Coaching First Base

When coaching first base you have the following responsibilities:

- When batter–runners are running straight to the base, as they approach remind them to hit the safety base if one is in use and to run through the base.

- When batter–runners are not hustling to first, encourage them to do so.

- When a throw is being made to first, alert the batter if it looks like a potential overthrow so that he or she can be prepared to make the decision about going to second.

- When runners have gotten a hit and are rounding first, assist them in making the decision about going to second, and as they approach second help them make the decision about sliding into second or going to third by clearly yelling what to do.

- When runners round first base and return to first, remind them to continue watching the ball until time is called and warn them of any throw being made to first.

- When runners are on first base remind them of the game situation, especially the number of outs and the location of other runners on the bases, if any.

- When runners are on first base review with them the likely options for the situation at the time. For example, with less than two outs say: "If it's a ground ball, run immediately. If it's a line drive, don't break until the ball is through the infield. On a shallow fly ball hit to the outfield, go partway. On a deep fly ball, tag up." With two outs you would remind the runner to break toward second as soon as the ball is contacted.

- When runners are on first help them make judgments about whether a ball is a safe hit or has the potential to be caught and whether to tag or to go partway toward second. Also, assist them in deciding whether to go to third base.

- After you've helped the first base runner as much as you can, quickly turn your attention to the batter–runner to assist him or her in reaching the base.
- Provide lavish praise to batters when they get a hit *after* the ball is dead and the runner is standing on the base. Well, maybe lavish praise may be a bit too much, but how about saying, "Nice hit."

Coaching Third Base

When coaching third base you have these responsibilities:

- When a runner is rounding second you assume responsibility for letting the runner know whether to continue to third or stop at second base.
- When runners are on second base or third base or both, you should remind each runner of the game situation, review the likely play situations that may occur, and go over the decisions that will need to be made.
- When runners are coming to third let them know whether to stop at third standing up, to slide and to which side of the base they should slide, to round the bag and hold, or to run home. Use arm and hand signals to indicate clearly what to do as shown in figure 3.15 and in Offense→Baserunning→Coaching Third Base on the DVD.

FIGURE 3.15 Common signals used by the third-base coach. *(a)* Come to the base standing up, *(b)* slide straight into the base, *(c)* slide to the left side of the base, and *(d)* round the base and then stop (note that the coach has left the third-base coaching box and positioned himself 20 to 30 feet [6 to 9 m] toward home plate to have a little more time to decide whether the runner should go home and to be in a position where the runner can see him).

- When you have to make a close decision about sending the runner home or having him or her hold at third, leave the coaching box and position yourself about halfway between third and home to give yourself a little longer to decide whether to send the runner home. Warning: Be sure to stay well in foul territory and stay out of the way of the runner. You cannot touch the runner when the ball is live.

- When runners are on third remind them especially to run home on a double-play situation, with the exceptions noted earlier.

- After you've sent a runner home quickly shift your attention to helping any runners who are following.

On-Deck Player

When you're on deck you have a coaching responsibility as well. When a runner is coming home, you should let him or her know whether there will be a play made at home. If a runner knows that there will be no play, he or she can slow up a bit to save energy. If a play is going to be made you can alert the runner to give all-out effort. Also, if the scoring plate is in use you may want to remind the runner to run to it if he or she is not used to doing so. And if the bat is in the way and you can retrieve it without interfering with the catcher, umpire, or runner, do so.

Coaching From the Bench

In a key situation the runner is coming to third with a possible chance to score. You yell from the bench, "Go home, go home," but the third-base coach is telling the runner to stay. The runner becomes confused, runs home, and is thrown out. Your team loses the game. If you're not coaching one of the bases, do not yell running instructions from the bench or sidelines. Not only may you be wrong, but you undermine the base coach. Just don't do it!

SUMMARY

- Know the rules of slowpitch softball that pertain to running. Especially know whether a safety base is in use at first base and whether a scoring plate with a commitment line is used at home.

- Speed is obviously a valued attribute for good baserunning, but being a smart runner is equally if not more important.

- Learn and practice good technique for leaving the batter's box quickly.

- Use the stationary or rocker start to run from one base to the next.

- You can likely improve your speed through training.

- Know where the ball is at all times, but don't always watch the ball because when it is behind you or sharply off to your side, watching it will slow you down.

- Always key off the runner in front of you to avoid forcing him or her into an out.

- Loafing when running the bases creates many mistakes and missed opportunities.

- Sliding is a valuable skill when running the bases. We recommend learning the bent-leg slide and the hook slide. Avoid the headfirst slide because of the higher risk of injury. Know when to slide.
- When there is a play at first, run straight through, stepping on the front of the base and on the safety base if it is being used.
- When rounding a base to advance to the next base, step on the inside corner of the base with either foot.
- From each base know what the game situation is, especially how many outs there are, whether a runner is in front of you, and if there is a force-out play at the base to which you are running.
- When running from each base know the decisions that you'll need to make when the ball is hit. Then apply good judgment in making those decisions.
- First- and third-base coaches provide valuable assistance to runners, but to do so they need to know the same information that runners should have and be especially good at making split-second judgments.
- When coaching either first or third base, know all your responsibilities and communicate to the runners in a clear voice and with hand signals when appropriate.

CHAPTER 4

Offensive Strategies and Tactics

The inherent goal of any sport contest is to win. Winning in slowpitch softball is often achieved not only by superior physical play but also by advanced mental play, or what is called strategy and tactics. The plan of action that your team takes to win the game is called strategy, and the calculated actions that take advantage of opportunities in the game are called tactics. In this chapter we focus on offensive strategies and tactics, including hitting with different ball–strike counts and hitting in various game situations.

STRATEGIC OPTIONS

Many teams, perhaps most, approach each game without any thought of a strategy other than hit the ball and score more runs than the opposing team does, a no-brainer strategy. Although slowpitch softball has fewer offensive strategies than baseball and fastpitch softball because base stealing (in most leagues) and bunting are not allowed, the sport is not devoid of offensive strategies.

Although the coach is customarily responsible for determining team offensive strategies, all players should know what factors are important in determining the team's strategies and then how tactical decisions when batting fit into those strategies. Those factors include

- the speed of each player,
- the hitting power of each player,
- the ability of each player to place hit,
- the strengths and weaknesses of the defense,
- tournament or league rules,
- the playing field, and
- the environment.

Considering these factors, your team may employ several potential strategies:

- You have excellent speed on your team, and the opposing team's outfielders do not have strong throwing arms and are playing deep. The infield surface has good footing and the grass in the outfield is a bit long, slowing down ground balls. Part of your team strategy will be to run the bases more aggressively than usual.

- You're playing on a small field that has fences at 275 feet (84 m). Although your team is not particularly a power-hitting team, at these distances you decide to swing for the fences more often.

- You're playing in a tournament that has a limit of five home runs per team; any home run thereafter is an out. You have six power hitters who are instructed to try to hit home runs only when at least two runners are on base to make the home runs more productive.

- The defensive outfielders are excellent, fast with strong throwing arms, but the infielders are relatively weak, especially on the right side. As a team, your strategy is to exploit this weakness by hitting ground balls and line drives to the right side. Your coach inserts into the lineup two left-handed batters who normally would not start, and you have several excellent place hitters who are instructed to hit to the right side. (Note: A major offensive strategic decision is how the lineup is made. See pages 288–290 in chapter 14 for further discussion about creating the lineup.)

- The wind is at gale force blowing in from left field. You have five right-handed power hitters, but with this wind the chances of their hitting home runs are markedly reduced. As a team strategy you decide not to swing for home runs.

- The opposing pitcher has a history of control problems. As a team you decide to look at more pitches in an effort to draw walks. This strategy can be particularly important for the men on coed teams, because most coed leagues and tournaments have rules in place to prevent pitchers from walking the men in the hopes that the women will be less powerful hitters and more likely to make an out. The typical rule is that if a man walks, he gets to take two bases and go directly to second. Some leagues also include a rule, usually based on the number of outs, about whether the woman following the man who walks is required to bat or can take a walk herself.

Knowing the team strategy instructs you on the tactics that you'll employ when batting and running the bases. In other words, you must know what your role is in the offensive lineup. Are you expected to be a power hitter or a place hitter? Does the team look to you for the big hit, or do they expect you to be on base 7 out of 10 times and let the batters behind you bring you home? Are you expected to run aggressively or be cautious on the basepaths?

In chapters 1 and 2 we focused on hitting technique. In the remainder of this chapter we look at the tactics that you employ when you're batting. In the next section we look at hitting with various ball–strike counts, and in the final section we review the tactical decisions that you will want to consider for various game situations.

HITTING WITH VARIOUS BALL–STRIKE COUNTS

In making any tactical decision you need to know the situation. When playing slowpitch softball the first thing you'll want to know is how many balls and strikes determine walks and strikeouts. Really?

Yes, because some leagues and tournaments play slowpitch with a standard count of four balls and three strikes, what we'll call a long count, whereas others play by starting with a one ball and one strike count, what we'll call a short count. (We'll use the term *full count* to refer to a count of three balls and two strikes.) In addition, leagues and tournaments differ on third-strike-foul rules. Usually a third-strike foul is an out, but sometimes when starting with a 1 ball, 1 strike count, the first third-strike foul is not an out unless it is caught, but the second third-strike foul is an out. When a tournament has had weather delays the tournament officials may attempt to complete the tournament by shortening each game. They do so by going to one-pitch play. If the pitch is a strike the batter is out. If the pitch is a ball, the batter walks. Seven-inning games take about 30 to 40 minutes to play under this rule.

Looking for Your Pitch

In the batter–pitcher duel, the pitcher is trying to get you to swing at pitches that you don't want to swing at. On the other hand, you're looking to swing at a pitch that is in your hitting zone, and if you're a power hitter, in your power zone. If you're playing with a long count, you should swing at the first pitch only when it is perfectly located in your hitting or power zone. Otherwise, a good tactic is to take the pitch and look for a better one to hit.

If you're playing with either a short count or a long count when you have one strike, you may be less picky about getting a perfect pitch in your hitting zone. Some players do not like batting with two strikes because they fear getting a pitch that will be difficult for them to hit. If you're confident about your hitting, however, you'll likely hit better if you avoid hitting a pitch outside your hitting zone, even if it results in strike two.

Batting With Two Strikes

When you have two strikes your hitting tactics should change to a more defensive approach. If the count is two balls or less, the pitcher will likely try to throw a pitch that is on the edge of the strike zone, perhaps a low outside or deep inside pitch that may just catch the corner of the strike zone. If you're certain that the pitch is a ball, you will not want to swing, of course, but if the pitch looks close to being a strike, you'll want to swing—and swing with a more defensive swing.

What is a defensive swing? It's a swing for accuracy and not as much power (remember the speed–accuracy tradeoff that we discussed in chapter 2, page 35). You want to be sure that you hit the ball fair and in the best location you can given the location of the pitch. If you're a place hitter and your plan is to hit to the opposite field, you may need to abandon your plan when you have

When batting with a long count, be patient selecting a pitch in your hitting zone.

two strikes. If the ball is pitched low and inside and likely to be a strike, hitting to the opposite field is nearly impossible. So you will be wise just to hit the pitch the best you can.

Taking a Pitch

Obviously, you want to take a pitch when you judge that it will be a called ball and, as just discussed, when you have no strikes and are looking for a pitch in your hitting or power zone. When playing with a long count batters often take the first pitch as part of a tactic to look for a walk. You'll especially want to consider doing this after the pitcher has walked a batter or when you see that the pitcher is having control problems. A common tactic is to continue to take pitches until the pitcher throws at least one strike. If the count is three balls and one strike, batters often take the next pitch, looking for a walk.

Almost all batters take a pitch when they have a 3-0 count. A batter who does not is likely viewed as not being a team player, someone unwilling to give up a time at bat for a likely walk. Now there may be an exception to that conclusion if the batter is a high-average power hitter and the batter to follow is a low-average hitter. See "Probability of Walking" on the next page to understand your odds of getting on base by a free pass from the pitcher.

SITUATIONAL HITTING

As you formulate your hitting plan when preparing to bat, you'll want to know the following:

- the number of outs,
- the location of base runners,
- the inning and score,
- the defensive alignment and the strengths and weaknesses of the defense, and
- the players batting behind you.

Probability of Walking

We all play slowpitch softball to hit, but the safest way to get on base in slowpitch is to walk. So if walks are part of your team strategy you should know the odds of getting a walk. Let's consider the variables involved and make some assumptions to come up with some probabilities.

The most significant factor will be the pitcher's ability to throw strikes consistently. You can't simply count the number of balls and strikes thrown to determine a pitcher's control because pitchers often throw balls intentionally, depending on the count. Some pitchers almost always throw a ball on the first pitch, hoping that the batter will swing at a not-so-good pitch, and they will do the same when they are ahead in the count. Another factor is wind. In a strong wind, especially a crosswind, pitchers have more difficulty throwing strikes when they want to. By watching the pitcher in the early part of the game, you should have a good idea of whether he or she has good control that day.

Another variable to consider in estimating the probability of walking is the count on the batter. Obviously, as the number of strikes increases, the chance of walking decreases, and vice versa.

In our analysis, we'll assume two things: that the pitcher throws strikes 50% of the time and that the batter does not swing. Based on these assumptions, here are the odds of getting a walk when you have various counts.

Count (ball–strike)	Probability of walking
0-0	43%
1-0	50%
0-1	33%
2-0	60%
1-1	40%
0-2	20%
3-0	75%
2-1	50%
1-2	25%
3-1	66%
2-2	33%
3-2	50%

What does all this mean? If you want to get on base without the risk of making an out in the field, here's a tactic that you may want to adopt when playing with a long count. You take the first pitch. If it's a ball, you continue taking pitches until the pitcher throws a strike. After you have a strike, you swing at a pitch if it is in your hitting zone. Otherwise you take it for a ball or strike. When you have two strikes obviously you need to swing at any pitch that has a chance to be a strike.

You not only want to know these things but also to understand what they mean in terms of the tactics that you employ when hitting. We now consider those tactics for various situations.

Leading Off the Inning

Typically, the leadoff batter at the start of the game is a high-percentage hitter who has excellent speed. Thereafter, anyone in the lineup can be a leadoff batter in later innings. What's the best thing you can do as a leadoff batter? The best thing is to hit a home run over the fence (assuming that there are no home-run limits, in which case a home run is wasted without runners on base), but it is not the safest thing to do because if the ball does not go over the fence, it may be caught for an out. The safest thing to do is to walk.

When a walk is not forthcoming, where's the best place to hit? Because no one is on base, the field is yours. Although you may need to hit wherever the pitch permits you to hit, keep in mind your team's assessment of the defensive strengths and weaknesses and any environmental or field conditions that might work to your advantage.

Hitting a Sacrifice Fly

A sacrifice fly is a fly ball hit with fewer than two outs that is caught by an outfielder and permits a runner to score. You always want to hit a sacrifice fly in two game situations:

- When you have a runner on third, the score is tied, and you're batting in the bottom half of the last inning and there are less than two outs
- When playing under rules that limit the number of runs per inning (frequently five runs), you have a runner on third, less than two outs, and you've scored one run fewer than the maximum number allowed

Do you want to hit a sacrifice fly in the second inning when a runner is on third and the score is tied or close to being tied? Probably not. You more likely would try for a base hit to go for a higher-scoring inning. Would you want to hit a sacrifice fly in the bottom of the sixth inning when the score is tied or you're down one run? Would you want to hit a sacrifice fly in the top of the seventh inning when the score is tied? The decision is not as straightforward as it was in the second inning. You want to weigh your confidence in getting a hit, the batters to follow you, and the scoring potential of the opposing team. More often than not, good teams will score more than one run in an inning, so playing to tie the game or gain a one-run lead in late innings is a risky tactic.

When hitting a sacrifice fly you should consider which outfielder to hit the ball to, especially if you have the place-hitting skills to do so. Although all outfield positions are equidistant to home, the obvious choice would be to hit to the outfielder with the weakest throwing arm, and second, the one with the weakest catching skills.

Scoring the Runner From Third Base

One of the keys to winning is not leaving runners stranded on third base. If you have less than two outs and you aren't in one of the two sacrifice-fly situations described in the previous section, your tactic should be to hit the ball to the outfield, with either a line drive or a fly ball. You're not trying to hit a sacrifice fly—you're aiming for a hit in the outfield—but if a fly ball happens to be caught the unintended sacrifice fly scores the run. If you're a skilled place hitter, a good place to hit is the 3-4 hole, seeking to get enough height on the ball that it can't be caught by an infielder but not hit so high or far that it will be caught by the right or right-center fielder. Even if you miss the 3-4 hole but force the first or second baseperson to field the ball on the run, the runner from third may be able to score. But if you hit the ball sharply and directly at either of those infielders, you'll fail to bring the runner on third home.

Where should you avoid hitting the ball? Don't hit in the third-base zone or to the shortstop. The runner has almost no opportunity to advance when the ball is hit to those fielders. In addition, a ball hit up the middle obviously has the risk of being caught by the pitcher, in which case the runner will not score.

Hitting the 3-4 Hole

An important offensive tactic in baseball and fastpitch softball is hitting behind the runners. What that means is that the batter hits the ball to the right side of the field behind the first-base runner, who is breaking for second base. In slowpitch the runner cannot leave first base until the ball is hit, so only if you hit the ball very near the foul line would you be hitting behind a runner on first. Instead, the tactic in slowpitch is to hit the 3-4 hole, the zone between first and second base.

If you're a power hitter who hits home runs frequently or you hit the long ball and have a high on-base average, then you shouldn't bother thinking about hitting behind the runners. Just blast away! But if you're not a frequent home-run threat and have developed your place-hitting skills, then you should know when it may be appropriate to hit into the 3-4 hole. Hitting this hole offers certain advantages except when no runners are on base.

With a runner on first base and less than two outs, hitting to the 3-4 hole is a good tactic because if the ball is caught by the first baseperson or second baseperson, it is more difficult to execute a double play than if the ball is hit to the pitcher, third baseperson, shortstop, or the second baseperson moving into

Hitting the 3-4 hole has several advantages when runners are on base.

the 1-4 hole. To turn a double play when the first baseperson catches the ball, he or she must throw to second and then retreat to first or the pitcher must come over to cover. The shortstop must throw the ball accurately to the covering fielder, who is on the run, and all that must be done in less than 4 to 5 seconds.

If the second baseperson catches the ball moving toward the 3-4 hole, he or she must stop, turn, and throw to the shortstop covering second, who must relay the ball to first. That play is less difficult than the ball hit to the first baseperson, but it is still a challenging double play. And remember, hitting to the right side of the infield increases the chances of scoring a runner from third.

The other benefit of hitting to the 3-4 hole, assuming that the ball goes into the outfield, is that the base runners may more readily advance two bases. With a runner on first base, a hit to right field has a greater probability of advancing the runner to third because the throw from right field to third base is longer than the throw from center or left field. In addition, you have a greater chance of scoring runners from second because they can get a better running start than they can on a ball hit into the 5-6 hole. One other possible advantage of hitting the 3-4 hole is that first basepersons are often less mobile than other players and right fielders may be weaker in fielding and throwing than the other outfielders.

Avoiding Double Plays

Hitting into a double play is a backbreaker for the offense in slowpitch, but with smart hitting you can reduce the odds of doing so. Hitting a home run is a wonderful way to avoid a double play! And hitting a ball over the head of an infielder and in front of or between the outfielders is an excellent way to avoid a double play and advance the runners.

We just identified one other way: hit toward the 3-4 hole. But with a runner on first, if you miss the 3-4 hole and hit the ball to a first baseperson who is playing close to the baseline from first to second, he or she may catch the ball, tag the runner on first, and step on the base for an easy double play.

With a runner on first or runners on first and second, hitting just to one side or the other of the pitcher (the 1-4 and 1-6 holes) is often a good place to hit because after the ball is past the pitcher the holes are usually wide open to the outfield. But if you hit to the pitcher, it's one of the easier double plays to execute.

When the bases are loaded, don't hit the ball to the third baseperson. He or she can step on third base and then throw to the catcher to tag out or force out (if the scoring plate is in use) the runner going home, a disastrous double play that removes the two leading runners from the bases.

Where you choose to hit when a double-play situation exists depends mostly on your confidence about where you hit best and where the pitch is located, but if you're not able to hit to the 3-4 hole you can increase your odds of avoiding a double play by hitting the ball to the outfield.

Hitting When You're Ahead and Behind

When your team gets a big lead in a game you feel less pressure to get a hit, and as you've learned, hitting when relaxed usually produces good results. When your team has a good lead you can take the risk of swinging for extra-base hits and take more chances in advancing on the basepaths. Sometimes teams become too relaxed, however, and begin to make mistakes or try to hit home runs that fall short. This tendency opens the door for the opposing team to make a comeback by having a good offensive rally that changes the momentum of the game.

When your team is losing by a substantial margin, players may think that they must swing for home runs even though they are only occasional home-run hitters, and that they should take extra chances on the basepaths. Usually this tactic backfires. A better tactic is to continue playing your game, staying within yourself by not trying to do more than what you can and employing the offensive tactics that we've discussed earlier.

SUMMARY

- With no strikes on you, look for a pitch in your hitting or power zone. If you're a confident hitter, continue looking for a pitch in your hitting or power zone when you have one strike on you.
- When you have two strikes on you, adopt a defensive tactic by hitting any pitch that has any probability of being a strike. Unless the pitch is in your power zone, swing more for accuracy and location than for power.
- Know the odds of getting a walk and don't swing until the odds turn against you or you receive a pitch in your hitting zone.
- To know the right offensive tactic to employ, you need to know the game situation, the positioning of the defensive players and their fielding strengths and weaknesses, your strengths and weaknesses, and the strengths and weaknesses of the batters following you.
- When you're leading off an inning the best thing that you can do is hit a home run (assuming that there are no home run limits), but the safest thing to do is get a walk.
- Hit a sacrifice fly when it will win your team the game or score the last run in an inning when playing under inning-run-rule limits.
- Hit to the outfield or the 3-4 hole to score the runner from third base with less than two outs.
- With a runner on first base or runners on first and second base, a smart tactic is to hit the ball in the 3-4 hole.
- Know where to hit to reduce the odds of hitting into double plays.
- When your team has a big lead don't become complacent, which can open the door for the opposing team to rally and defeat you. When you're losing big, don't try to do more than you can. Continue to play within yourself.

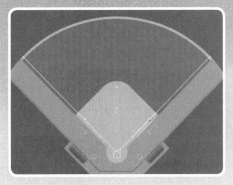

PART II
DEFENSE

Slowpitch softball is known as an offensive game, but a lot of offense creates the opportunity to play a lot of defense. Even when elite teams with full lineups of home-run hitters play, a key to winning is making the outs when the opportunities to do so present themselves. Arguing that offense is more important than defense or vice versa is fruitless; both are important. In some games your offense may lift you to victory, and on other days it may be the defense.

In part II we begin with chapter 5, "Pitching." We explain and demonstrate the various pitching techniques and provide a thorough analysis of pitching tactics. We close chapter 5 with an examination of defense in the pitching position. We'll cover setting up to catch balls hit up the middle, the pitcher's responsibilities in covering various bases in different defensive plays, the pitcher's role in double plays, and backing up the bases.

Chapter 6 is devoted to infielder skills. We'll cover fielding skills, throwing skills, and tagging runners at the bases. Then we look at how to play each infield position and how to make some special plays. Chapter 7 does the same for outfielders, covering fielding and throwing skills,

and learning some other responsibilities. In these two chapters we provide brief summaries of the basic skills and demonstrate them in the DVD, but we don't dwell on them because many other books and videos are available that cover these fundamentals. Instead we focus on those aspects of defensive play that are especially relevant to playing slowpitch softball.

Defensive strategies and tactics are the focus of chapter 8. We first consider some defensive team strategies based on the offensive team's abilities, your team's defensive abilities, the playing field, and the environment. You'll learn the tactics of positioning yourself and the team for various defensive situations. We provide a thorough description of how to execute relays and cutoffs for most defensive play situations. Next we look at the tactics involved for numerous double-play situations and some other special plays. Finally, we discuss the role of communication in defensive play.

By studying these chapters and reviewing the video segments that show these skills and tactics in action, you'll be ready to practice these tactics for your upcoming competition.

CHAPTER 5

Pitching

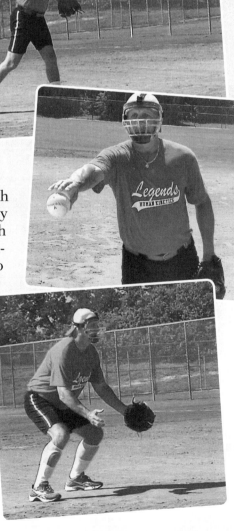

Foremost, slowpitch pitchers need to be able to throw strikes when and where they want. If pitchers become tight armed in pressure situations, they'll walk batters, and as soon as batters see pitchers struggling to throw strikes, they'll look for walks. But as a pitcher you can do much more than just throw strikes. You can make it easy for the batter to hit the ball or much more difficult.

In baseball and fastpitch softball, pitchers commonly dominate the game, and their importance in determining the defensive outcome of the game is estimated to be from 60% to 90%. Pitching in slowpitch softball is obviously not that influential; pitchers rarely strike out batters. Yet pitching is far more important than many players and coaches recognize.

Pitchers who can locate the ball precisely where they want with varied pitches make it much more difficult for batters to hit safely and with power. Although pitchers do not dominate the slowpitch game, which, by the way, is one reason that the sport is so popular, they can cause batters to hit pitches that they'd prefer not to hit and thus increase the chance of their making an out. In addition, pitchers can disrupt a batter's timing. We estimate that good pitching combined with good defensive play by the pitcher determines about 25% of the defensive outcome of the game.

Amazingly, slowpitch pitching has received little critical analysis. So let's put slowpitch pitching under the microscope to see how master pitchers execute this unappreciated skill. We begin by examining the objectives and goals of pitching and then move on to the various pitching techniques. Next we'll provide you with an in-depth analysis of the tactics of pitching. In the last section, you'll learn how to play defense in the pitching position.

PITCHING OBJECTIVES AND GOALS

Obviously, the big objective is to get the batter out, and if you aren't able to do so, the objective is to minimize the damage that the batter does. Within those larger objectives, successful slowpitch pitchers have two goals that they consistently try to achieve:

1. get batters to swing at pitches they don't want to swing at, and

2. disrupt batters' timing in swinging at pitches.

Before we dig into those two goals let's first look at the rules that apply to slowpitch pitching to understand what pitchers must do. Traditionally, pitchers were required to have one foot on the pitching rubber, which is located 50 feet (15 m) from home plate. More recently, though, many slowpitch softball associations have switched to a pitching box, which extends 6 feet (1.8 m) from the pitching rubber toward second base and is the width of the pitching rubber, 2 feet (61 cm). Pitchers may pitch from anywhere inside this box. The box gives pitchers the opportunity to be farther from the batter, giving them a little more time to react to hit pitches.

Pitchers must deliver the ball with an underhand motion with a trajectory that has a minimum height of 4 (1.2 m) to 6 feet (1.8 m) from the ground and a maximum height of 10 (3 m) to 12 feet (3.7 m), as shown in figure 5.1. A strike is called when a ball is pitched within those limits and passes through the strike zone or hits the strike mat. (See chapter 1, pages 12–13, for more information about the strike zone.) Pitches that fail to meet these height limits are to be called illegal by the umpire, although sometimes they forget to make that call. Illegal pitches are balls, but batters may legally swing at illegal pitches if they wish to do so.

Although the strike zone is a small target for a pitcher to hit standing 50 feet (15 m) away, it's a little bigger than what it might seem. A 12-inch (30 cm) softball (12 inches refers to its circumference) is nearly 4 inches (10 cm) in diameter. If any part of the ball passes through the strike zone or touches the mat, it's a strike, and thus with 4 inches added to each side of the strike zone, it is nearly 25 inches (64 cm) wide. Women typically play with an 11-inch (28 cm) softball, which has a diameter of 3.5 inches (9 cm), resulting in a 1-inch (2.5 cm) smaller strike zone.

FIGURE 5.1 Minimum and maximum arc limits.

In table 5.1 on page 114 you can review the major pitching rules for the leading slowpitch softball associations to see the similarities and differences. Most of the many local, state, and regional slowpitch associations adopt the rules of one of the national associations, often those of the Amateur Softball Association, but they also make minor changes. So always check what the pitching rules are when you're first playing in a league or tournament.

Now you know what requirements the pitch must meet to be called a strike, but remember that your goal is not just to pitch a strike but to get the batter to swing at what he or she doesn't want to swing at or to disrupt his or her timing. So let's analyze these two goals further.

Your goal is to pitch the ball to a location outside the batter's hitting and power zones but where it will still be called a strike (if the batter doesn't swing at it) or be so close to being a strike that the batter will swing at it. Of course, you'll not always be able to keep your pitches outside the batter's power zone or even outside his or her hitting zone and be able to throw strikes. So the second goal is to disrupt the batter's timing in executing the swing. Successful pitchers achieve that goal by varying the location of the pitch—its speed, trajectory, and movement (e.g., straight, curve, or knuckle).

Some players, especially those lacking good control, simply throw the same pitch over and over to batters, who are then able to learn to time the pitch. Those players are throwers, not pitchers. Pitchers confront each batter with pitches that keep the ball away from the batter's hitting zone or disrupt his or her timing.

Do you recognize the challenge and see why pitchers are the most important defensive players? Excellent slowpitch pitchers continually strive to do the following:

- Throw strikes to avoid walking batters
- Locate the ball in or near the strike zone, trying to avoid the batter's hitting zone and especially staying away from the batter's power zone if he or she has one
- Vary their pitches in an effort to disrupt a batter's timing
- Master the mechanics of pitching, our next topic, after which we'll dig into the tactics of the pitcher–batter duel
- Make numerous defensive plays, which we'll examine in the last section of this chapter

PITCHING MECHANICS

The mechanical principles of pitching slowpitch are not nearly as difficult as those in fastpitch softball or baseball. Thus the key to success is complete mastery of those principles so that you can pitch the ball with the trajectory that you want and to the location that you think is optimal for that hitter in that situation. If you pitch in coed slowpitch, pitching is even more challenging because you throw the 12-inch (30 cm) ball to the men and the 11-inch (28 cm) ball to the women. Learning to pitch two balls of differing in size and weight with pinpoint accuracy is no easy feat.

In this section we'll describe two styles of delivery and five types of pitches, illustrating the basics of each.

Delivery Methods

You'll see many unique deliveries by pitchers as they add their own personal styles, but most deliveries consist of taking one step as the pitch is thrown or not taking a step forward as the pitch is released. Let's consider the advantages and disadvantages of each type of delivery.

One-Step Delivery

The one-step pitching delivery is widely used because it's the way that we all learn to throw, whether overhand or underhand. The disadvantage of the one-step delivery is that pitchers are reducing the distance between themselves and the batter, which further reduces the time that they have to catch a ball hit to them. Some pitchers are able to take a slight step forward and then immediately take several steps back to get set up defensively, but not all are able to make this adjustment. The steps in executing this delivery are shown and explained in the series of photos in figure 5.2 and in Defense→Pitching→Delivery Methods on the DVD.

FIGURE 5.2 One-step delivery. *(a)* Beginning in back of the rubber, which is permitted by some rules, place the right foot in front and the left foot slightly behind. *(b)* After bringing the ball up to your chest, begin the down motion of the backswing, and at the same time begin the stride with the left leg. The backswing ends when the hand is back about waist high. *(c)* When the left foot contacts the ground, begin the forward swing of the right arm and release the ball at about waist height, with the ball rolling off the fingertips. *(d)* The pitching arm follows through so the hand ends up well over your head.

No-Step Delivery

In the no-step delivery pitchers place one foot on the rubber or in the pitcher's box and the other foot comfortably to the side and slightly behind them (see figure 5.3 and Defense→Pitching→Delivery Methods on the DVD). Some pitchers use the foot opposite the throwing arm that they throw with as the lead foot and others use the same foot. The key here is being comfortable and well balanced in this stance so that the arm swing when delivering the pitch is well controlled. Another factor to consider is whether it is easier for you to back up starting with your right or left leg.

If you can achieve the same level of control with the no-step delivery that you can with the one-step delivery, it's the preferred method because you are able to retreat and set up faster, increasing your chances of fielding balls hit up the middle and reducing your chances of getting injured.

FIGURE 5.3 No-step delivery. *(a)* Place the right foot on one side of the rubber and the left foot to the side and slightly back. *(b)* After bringing the ball up to the chest, begin the down motion of the backswing and at the same time crouch down. The backswing ends when the hand is back about waist high. *(c)* In a rhythmic motion swing the arm forward and at the same time come out of the crouch, letting the ball roll off the fingertips when the hand is about waist high. *(d)* The pitching arm follows through so the hand ends up well over your head.

Types of Pitches

We'll look at the technique for throwing five types of pitches:

- Vertical topspin
- Vertical backspin
- Left curve

- Right curve
- Knuckleball

You don't need to master all these pitches to be successful, but you'll definitely need to master one and preferably two or three of them. These pitches are demonstrated in figures 5.8 through 5.12 and in the Defense→Pitching→Types of Pitches section of the DVD.

Before you read about pitching curveballs, read "Softball Aerodynamics." Then you'll appreciate the physics involved in throwing this pitch.

Softball Aerodynamics

Why do baseballs and softballs curve? Why do knuckleballs knuckle? Why do balls hit with topspin dive down and those hit with backspin lift up? Understanding softball aerodynamics may help you as a pitcher and, if nothing else, may satisfy your curiosity about why softballs do not always travel in a straight trajectory.

Sport biomechanics (people who study the physics of human motion) tell us that Daniel Bernoulli and Gustav Magnus, who lived in the 1700s, developed the principles that we can use to explain how baseballs and softballs can curve.

Bernoulli's discovery, called the Bernoulli principle, states that faster-moving fluids (air is considered a fluid) exert less pressure laterally than do slower-moving fluids. This principle explains how air passing over the wings of birds and airplanes gives them lift so that they can fly. With a correctly shaped wing, the air molecules passing under and over the wing reach the back of the wing at the same time, which means that the air passing over the wing must travel a greater distance, as can be seen in figure 5.4. Bernoulli's principle says that the faster-moving air flowing over the wing exerts less downward pressure than the air flowing under the wing, which is applying upward pressure. The imbalance of pressures creates an upward lift.

You can experience this lift force by placing your hand outside the window of your car when it's moving at a reasonable speed. With the palm down and fingers pointing forward, shape your hand like a wing and feel the upward lift. Then try a fist and see how that works.

You now understand how birds and airplanes fly, but you're probably asking what that has to do with softballs. Enter Gustav Magnus, who discovered that Bernoulli's

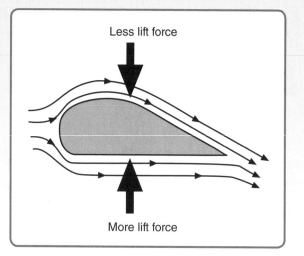

FIGURE 5.4 Bernoulli's principle.

Adapted, by permission, from P.M. McGinnis, 2005, *Biomechanics of sport and exercise*, 2nd ed. (Champaign, IL: Human Kinetics), 206.

principle applies to spinning balls. Figure 5.5 will help you understand.

Let's use an example to explain. A fly ball is hit to your left-center fielder, who catches it. The runner on second tags and tries to advance to third. The left-center fielder has a rocket arm and throws the ball to the third baseperson with such velocity that the ball seems to lift up as it arrives in time for the player to tag the runner out. Is it possible that the ball actually lifted up, or are we seeing an optical illusion?

The first point is that the upper surface of a ball thrown overhand has a backward spin relative to the center of the ball and the lower surface has a forward spin, as shown in figure 5.5. The air molecules around the ball all have a backward velocity relative to the center of the ball as it travels forward. Now here's where it gets interesting. When the air molecules strike the lower surface of the ball, they slow down more because they are moving against the surface of the ball. The air molecules striking the top surface are moving in the same direction as the spin of the ball and are slowed down less. In short, the air molecules on top of the ball are moving faster than those underneath the ball.

Now applying Bernoulli's principle, the faster-moving air above the ball exerts less downward pressure than the slower-moving air underneath the ball, creating upward pressure, or lift on the ball. Consequently, the ball indeed rises. This lift force, when applied to spinning balls, is called the Magnus force in honor of the discoverer of this phenomenon.

One caveat here: You don't always see overhand balls rise because they must be thrown with enough velocity to create enough upward lift to counteract another substantial force—gravity.

The Magnus force works in the opposite direction with a ball that has a lot of topspin (see figure 5.6), which is commonly seen when a batter hits a fly ball slightly above the center of the ball. Now the air molecules striking the top surface of the ball are moving in the opposite

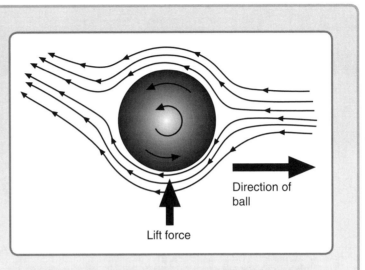

FIGURE 5.5 Gustav Magnus applied Bernoulli's principle to spinning balls, called the Magnus force, to explain why balls curve. A ball with backspin, as shown here, will lift up.

Adapted, by permission, from P.M. McGinnis, 2005, *Biomechanics of sport and exercise*, 2nd ed. (Champaign, IL: Human Kinetics), 207.

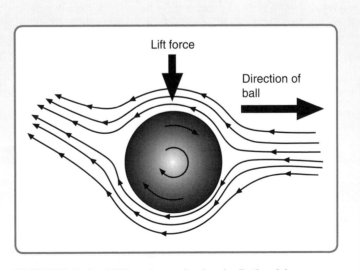

FIGURE 5.6 With a topspinning ball, the Magnus force applies downward pressure on the ball.

Adapted, by permission, from P.M. McGinnis, 2005, *Biomechanics of sport and exercise*, 2nd ed. (Champaign, IL: Human Kinetics), 207.

(continued)

direction as the spin of the ball and are slowed down more, whereas the air molecules striking the lower surface of the ball are moving in the same direction as the spin of the ball and thus are moving across the surface of the ball more quickly. Consequently, the Magnus force in this case is greater in a downward direction, causing the ball to dive downward.

So now you know that you weren't just seeing things. So let's see if you understand softball aerodynamics by answering these questions:

1. If you want to get more upward lift on a ball thrown overhand, would you grip it *with* the seams or *across* the seams? **Answer**: Gripping it across the seams would cause more resistance to the air molecules passing over the top of the ball, thus creating more lift.

2. If a tennis ball and a softball are moving at the same speed and spinning with the same velocity, which would create the greatest Magnus force? **Answer**: The tennis ball would create greater Magnus force because it has a rougher surface than a softball. That's also why Wiffle balls curve so readily.

3. Applying Bernoulli's principle and the Magnus effect, why are pitchers able to throw curveballs? **Answer**: Curveballs, whether they break away from or into the batter, are simply balls with spin applied with a rotation other than vertical. If a right-handed pitcher is throwing to a right-handed batter, the pitcher must apply a counterclockwise spin on the ball with the spin or rotation shifting from the vertical axis to as close to horizontal as possible to have it break away from the batter (see figure 5.7). With this pitch, the right side of the ball spins against the flight of the ball, creating more resistance, and the left side spins with the flight of the ball, thus moving across the surface of the ball more quickly and producing less force than the right side does. Thus the Magnus force pushes the ball toward the left. To have a pitch break into a right-handed batter, the pitcher wants to apply a clockwise spin as close to the horizontal axis as possible.

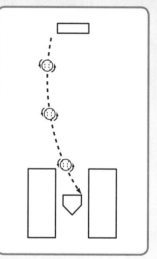

FIGURE 5.7 To throw a curve to a right-handed batter, a right-handed pitcher applies a counterclockwise spin to the ball.

4. Why do knuckleballs move erratically? **Answer**: Knuckleballs move erratically because without spin the air molecules pass over the ball without direction, randomly causing the ball to flutter. The term *knuckleball* comes from the way that some pitchers throw the pitch using their knuckles and thumb to release the ball without rotation.

5. Does humidity influence the Magnus effect? **Answer**: Air would seem to be heavier when moist, but as you learned in "Atmospheric Conditions and Ball Flight" in chapter 1, the opposite is true. The density of air decreases with increasing humidity. Consequently, humidity creates less drag or friction, which decreases the Magnus force, causing the ball to curve less. Unfortunately from a pitcher's perspective, more home runs are likely to be hit.

6. Does temperature and barometric pressure influence the flight of the ball? **Answer**: As air warms it becomes less dense, so it offers less resistance to the flight of the ball. Likewise, as the barometric pressure decreases, the air becomes less dense. Thus, rising temperatures and decreasing barometric pressure cause curveballs to curve less and batted balls to go farther.

FIGURE 5.8

VERTICAL TOPSPIN

Start position.

Backswing.

Release.

The most common pitch, the vertical topspin pitch is thrown with the palm up, fingers underneath the ball, and the thumb on the side or top. As the arm swings forward the ball rolls off the fingertips. The fingers are usually placed across the wide part of the seams, but the ball can be thrown holding it with the seams. The ball leaves the hand rotating clockwise on a horizontal axis, with what is commonly called topspin. The trajectory is usually very straight (unless it's windy), so this is an excellent pitch when you want to throw to an exact location, which you most often want to do.

Grip—palm up, fingers underneath the ball, and the thumb on the side for balance, with the fingers placed across the wide part of the seams.

Release—as the arm swings forward the ball rolls off the fingertips at about waist height.

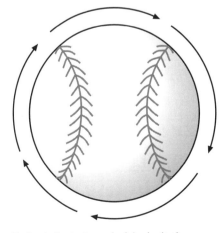

Ball rotation—topspin (clockwise).

VERTICAL BACKSPIN

FIGURE 5.9

Start position.

Backswing.

Release.

This pitch is somewhat more difficult to control, but we've seen a few pitchers master it. This pitch is thrown with the palm facing *down,* fingers on top of the ball, and thumb on the side for control. The ball is released by rolling it off the fingertips. As the arm swings forward the wrist is cocked downward, and at the moment of release it is snapped upward to produce the backspin. This pitch, like the vertical topspin, travels in a straight line.

With the ball spinning counterclockwise, some think that the vertical backspin pitch is more difficult to hit, but there is no physical reason that this would be true. Theoretically (see "Softball Aerodynamics"), the vertical backspin pitch should have a slight upward lift, resulting in its reaching the apex of its trajectory slightly later and then dropping down more steeply than the vertical topspin pitch does. But this difference is slight and probably unnoticeable to the batter.

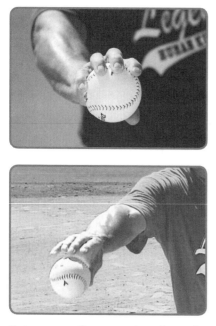

Grip—palm facing down, fingers on top of the ball, and the thumb on the side for control.

Release—as the arm swings forward, the ball rolls off the fingertips at about waist height.

Ball rotation—backspin (counterclockwise).

FIGURE 5.10

LEFT CURVE

Start position.　　　　　Backswing.　　　　　Release.

A left curve is simply a pitch that breaks to the left when the pitcher is facing the batter. It is thrown by a combination of grip and wrist action that produces a near-horizontal spin on the ball; let's call it an oblique spin. To throw this pitch, place the index finger along seam A in such a way that the finger can apply pressure to the stitching to put spin on the ball. Then place the thumb on seam B. Here's how to throw a left curve if you're a right-handed pitcher. Starting with a vertical topspin delivery (palm up), as you are releasing the ball, rotate your wrist sharply in a counterclockwise direction and at the same time flick the index finger and thumb in a counter-clockwise direction to create the spin. The ball then rotates in a counterclockwise direction at an oblique angle so that it curves to the left.

If you're a left-handed pitcher you use the same grip, but you need to flip-flop these instructions and use the instructions for the right curve. The description makes it sound more difficult to do than it is. This pitch, of course, takes good timing and lots of practice to do correctly, but with patience and some help from the enclosed DVD you can learn to throw it.

Grip—palm facing up, with the index finger along seam A (the wide seam) and the thumb next to seam B.

Release—as the arm swings forward, rotate the wrist sharply in a counterclock-wise direction to the left and at the same time flick the index finger and thumb in a counterclockwise direction to create the spin by applying strong pressure to the left as the ball rolls off the fingers at waist height.

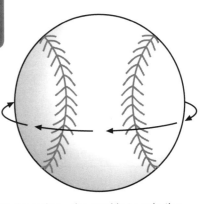

Ball rotation—the goal is to spin the ball counterclockwise to the vertical axis.

RIGHT CURVE

FIGURE 5.11

Start position.

Backswing.

Release.

Yes, this is a curve pitch that breaks to the right when the pitcher is facing home plate. This pitch is thrown with essentially the same grip as the left curve, but some pitchers prefer to put the index finger on the other side of the stitch to obtain a little more grip when releasing the ball. For right-handed pitchers this pitch begins with a vertical topspin delivery, but unlike the left curve, the palm is facing to the left, not up. Here's why: As the arm swings forward, just at the point of release the pitcher must sharply rotate the wrist clockwise. Try putting your palm up and then rotating it clockwise. As you can see, there's little room for further rotation in a clockwise direction, but you can apply clockwise spin to the ball if you begin with the palm facing to the left. And then remember to push with the index finger and thumb to increase the clockwise spin.

If you're a left-handed pitcher, flip-flop these instructions or follow those for a left curve when you want to throw a right curve. Mechanically, it's easier for right-handed pitchers to throw a left curve than a right curve, and the opposite is true for left-handed pitchers.

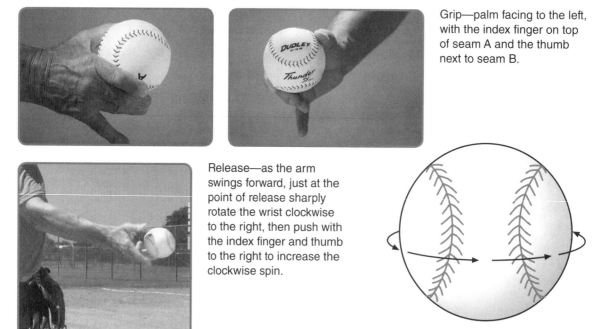

Grip—palm facing to the left, with the index finger on top of seam A and the thumb next to seam B.

Release—as the arm swings forward, just at the point of release sharply rotate the wrist clockwise to the right, then push with the index finger and thumb to the right to increase the clockwise spin.

Ball rotation—the goal is to spin the ball clockwise to the vertical axis.

FIGURE 5.12

KNUCKLEBALL

This pitch is delivered with a grip that results in no or little spin on the ball. If the wind is blowing straight out from the batter to the pitcher, the uneven airflow over the nonspinning ball may cause it to move erratically. In our opinion, this pitch is more difficult to control, but with mastery it is valuable as a change of pace that can keep the batter unsettled.

The most common grip used to throw the knuckleball in softball is digging the fingernails of two, three, or four fingers into the ball. The thumb is on the other side to balance the ball in the hand. Less common is gripping the ball with the first knuckles (which is easier to do with a baseball than a softball). The pitch is typically delivered with the palm up as the arm comes forward, and often with a stiff wrist.

The key to this pitch is in the release. To obtain no rotation on the ball, you need to release the pressure on the ball applied by the fingers or knuckles on one side of the ball and the thumb on the other side of the ball at exactly the same moment. You don't want the ball gaining any spin from the fingers or thumb.

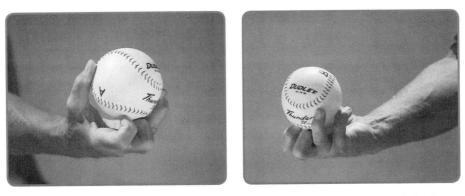

Grip—although there are many ways to grip a knuckleball, the most common is to dig the fingernails of two or three of the fingers into the ball with the thumb on the other side for balance. Here you see the pitcher using only two fingers.

Release—execute the backswing with the same motion as the vertical topspin delivery. As the arm comes forward from the backswing keep a stiff wrist, and at the point of release the ball leaves the hand with equal resistance from the fingernails and the thumb so that the ball does not spin.

Ball rotation—none.

Learning to Pitch

If you're new to pitching in slowpitch we recommend that you begin with the no-step delivery, which keeps you farther from the batter and gives you more time to field your position. Focus on gaining superb control with one pitch, probably the vertical topspin pitch. You can vary the trajectory from the minimum 6 feet (1.8 m) to the maximum 12 feet (3.7 m). After you master that pitch see whether you can master the right and left curve pitches to give you a little more firepower to keep the batters off balance.

You've probably seen many other variants of the pitches that we've described here. Some pitchers like to dance around and throw with many different motions in hopes of distracting the batters. Because batters have so much time to watch the ball when batting, we believe that whatever might be gained in distracting the batter is likely less helpful than what the pitcher loses by having less control or not being set to field the ball. If you can locate your pitches on the perimeter of the strike zone or just outside of it with consistency and variability in height, you'll be an effective pitcher.

PITCHING TACTICS

Remember that your objective is to get the batter out or to minimize the damage that a batter does. Your goal is to get batters to swing at pitches that they don't want to swing at or to disrupt their timing. You're not going to achieve those goals all the time, but as you acquire greater control and apply the tactics that we discuss next, you'll achieve them more often than not. Your three weapons as a tactical pitcher are (a) location, (b) variation, and (c) knowledge of the batters. Let's understand these weapons and how to put them to use.

Location

Just as in real estate, the key to success in slowpitch pitching is location, location, location. It's your most powerful weapon to encourage batters to swing at pitches that they don't want to swing at. You want to pitch the ball to a location that is outside batters' hitting zones but appealing enough that they swing at the pitch or it catches a corner of the strike zone for a called strike. Obviously, achieving that goal requires superb control of your pitches.

In baseball and fastpitch, pitchers control location primarily in two dimensions—height and width. Within the strike zone, pitches can be up or down, and to the right or left side of the plate. Technically, there is a third dimension of depth, which is the distance from the front to the back of the plate, so that a curveball may be a strike over the front outside corner of the plate but be out of the strike zone by the time it reaches the back of the plate.

When using the strike zone without the mat in slowpitch, pitchers can control the same three dimensions of height, width, and depth as shown in figure 5.13. But because the ball is thrown with an arc between 4 (1.2 m) to 6 feet (1.8 m) and 10 (3 m) to 12 feet (3.7 m), the depth dimension becomes much more prominent than it is in baseball or fastpitch softball. Furthermore, varying the height of the arc changes the time taken for the ball to arrive at the plate and the angle at which it goes through the strike zone, thus influencing the batter's timing.

When using the strike mat something interesting occurs—we lose a dimension. Now that can't really be, can it? Look at figure 5.13 and visualize that strike zone being placed on the ground as shown in figure 5.14. Poof, the depth dimension collapses into the ground, leaving only the two-dimensional strike zone of height and width, but the height dimension of the strike zone becomes the depth dimension, and consequently we've lost the height dimension in the strike zone.

So that we're consistent and clear in describing the tactics in pitching to various locations, we'll use the following terms for the three dimensions of the strike zone and for the height of pitches.

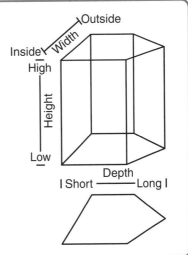

FIGURE 5.13 The three dimensions of the strike zone when the strike mat is not in use.

- Height of pitches: Pitches are low (low arc) to high (high arc).
- Height in strike zone: Pitches are low as they pass through the strike zone or high.
- Depth in strike zone: Pitches are short (front of the strike zone) to long (back of the strike zone).
- Width in strike zone: Pitches are inside (close to the batter) to outside (away from the batter).

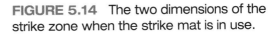

FIGURE 5.14 The two dimensions of the strike zone when the strike mat is in use.

When describing the location of pitches we'll describe them in the order of height, depth, and width in the strike zone and will make separate reference to the height of the arc. For example, with an 0-0 count, we may suggest that you pitch high-long-outside, or with a 2-2 count, we may recommend that you pitch low-short-inside. In reference to location of pitches, it does not make any difference whether the batter is batting from the right or left side of the plate with these descriptions.

Variation

So location is the big gun for pitchers, but variation is the next best weapon, especially to disrupt timing. Variation is achieved in the following ways:

- Varying the location of the pitch relative to the batter's position at the plate.
- Varying the speed of the pitch. You have less ability to vary speed in slow-pitch, but you can change it some by throwing with a low arc compared with a high arc.
- Varying the trajectory or path of the ball with straight pitches, right and left curves, and maybe even a knuckleball.
- Varying the time taken to deliver the ball. You can pitch quickly after the batter steps in the batter's box, perhaps catching him or her not fully ready to hit, or you can hold the ball for a longer time, trying to heighten the batter's anxiety.

- Varying the motion used to deliver the pitch. As mentioned earlier this is a useful way to achieve variation, but don't sacrifice location to get this type of variation.

Obviously, being able to vary all these elements takes great skill, which you can achieve only through dedicated practice. If you have less control of some of these pitches, avoid using them in important game situations so that you don't lessen the probability of pitching to the location that you've decided on. Instead, practice these variations when the game is well in hand so that you can build up your arsenal of pitching weapons.

Knowledge of the Batters

What do you want to know about batters to help you determine your pitching tactics? You want to seek answers to four questions:

- Is the batter a power hitter or a place hitter?
- Does the batter usually hit the ball to the same area, or does he or she hit to all fields?
- What are the batter's hitting and power zones?
- Is the batter patient at the plate and willing to walk, or is he or she impatient, often hitting the first pitch?

So how do you get reasonably good answers to these questions? Here are the obvious possibilities:

- You've competed with the player before and know his or her tendencies.
- You observe the player, maybe even formalizing your observation into a scouting report.
- You ask others who know the player.
- You review your scorekeeper's score sheet and notes.

And finally, if you don't have answers from those sources, you can get some clues to answer your questions when the batter comes to the plate. What are these clues?

- **Hitting style.** Power hitters are more likely to bat third, fourth, fifth, or sixth in the lineup and are usually bigger and more muscular. Power hitters more often do not play defensively but are designated hitters or are catchers and first basepersons. They are more likely to use the power grip rather than a traditional grip (see chapter 2). Place hitters are likely to be those who don't fit into the power category, although you'll likely find an exception or two in the lineup. Of course, none of these are absolutes; they're only clues or possibilities. But in the absence of better information, it's worth developing your tactical approach based on these clues.
- **Hitting location.** Knowing whether a batter hits consistently to one field or sprays the ball around is even more difficult to know without direct observation. The batter's position at the plate is a small clue. Batters who are close to the plate tend to pull the ball more than batters who stand away from the plate. Those who stand away are more likely to step into the pitch and hit to the opposite field.

- **Hitting and power zones**. You must observe a batter many times to know his or her hitting and power zones or learn them from someone who knows the batter well. If that information is not available to you, remember that most hitting zones are between the armpits and midthighs and the width of the strike zone. And the power zone is usually from the shoulders to the waist and the inside half of the strike zone.

- **Judging patience**. Determining batters' patience also comes from seeing them bat numerous times. One clue, however, is the batter's mannerism as he or she takes a position in the batter's box. You may surmise that the batter is impatient if you see a lot of fidgetiness as he or she prepares to bat. Likewise, a batter who swings at the first pitch, especially if it's outside the strike zone, is probably impatient.

Of course, you understand that these are just clues, hints of what a batter likes to do. Obviously, you'll have more reliable information if you can observe batters before you pitch against them. As the game proceeds and batters come up for the second, third, and fourth time, you'll have more information to consider, but you must be able to recall how they hit the previous times at bat. That's not easy to do in the fast-moving slowpitch game.

So if you have trouble recalling tendencies, get help from your team score-keeper or a player not playing defense. Have them record the results of your opponents' previous at-bats and let you know whether the batter hit with power (you'll likely remember whether he or she hit a home run) or was a place hitter, where the ball was hit, and whether he or she swung at the first pitch.

But another person may be able to help you—the catcher. Generally, in slowpitch softball the pitcher makes all the decisions about how to pitch to a batter, but just as in baseball and fastpitch softball, the catcher can assist you in deciding what pitch to throw to each batter. Your catcher can flash you signals about where he or she recommends that you pitch. These can be subtle touches to the catcher's body (see figure 5.15). For example, the catcher can use the glove hand to signal a low pitch and the throwing hand to signal a high pitch. Touching the knees signals a short pitch, and touching the shoulders signals a long pitch. So if you have a right-handed batter, when the catcher touches the left knee with the glove hand, he or she is calling for a low-short-inside pitch. Touching the right shoulder with the throwing hand is the signal for a high-long-outside pitch.

You may not always agree with the catcher's opinion, but you should consider it. Between innings and before and after games you'll want to discuss tactics with your catcher so that you understand what each other is thinking.

FIGURE 5.15 The catcher calls for a low-short-inside pitch by subtly touching his glove hand to his left knee with a right-handed batter.

TACTICAL PRINCIPLES

OK, now let's put everything together as you prepare to pitch your next game. Your goal is to get batters to swing at pitches that they don't want to swing at or to disrupt their timing. You'll achieve those goals through location and variation. You've mastered one pitch, of which you have superb control, and you're making progress with a couple of other pitches that you'll use occasionally. You prepare to pitch by observing the opposing team as they take batting practice. As each batter comes to the plate for the first time, you look for clues about the type of batter that he or she is and his or her patience. You input that information into the computer sitting on top of your shoulders, and the output is your tactical plan for each batter.

Next we'll discuss a set of tactical principles based on five important factors:

- Batter position in relation to the strike zone
- Hitting style
- Ball–strike count
- Batter patience
- Game situation

You should consider these tactical principles as guidelines based on the mechanics of hitting and the judgments of expert pitchers. These tactical principles are not absolutes, but probabilities that you'll achieve your pitching goals more often with the recommended pitch than with another pitch. Remember, though, that even when you locate the pitch perfectly, skillful batters will still get hits sometimes, and on occasion when you throw that "oh no" pitch into a batter's power zone, he or she may pop it up. Nevertheless, you want to play the probabilities.

When a tactical location is recommended, unless noted otherwise, the pitch is to be thrown for a strike. Later we'll discuss throwing to a location when you want the pitch to be a ball.

Batter Position

An important factor in determining your pitching tactics is the batter's position at the plate or strike mat because batters position themselves to increase the chances of getting a pitch in their hitting zones and preferably in their power zones. Without the strike mat batters typically stand farther back in the box, but with the strike mat most batters stand even with or in front of the strike mat because a ball thrown with a 6- to 12-foot (1.8 to 3.7 m) arc will likely reach the batter at waist to shoulder height—the typical hitting zone—and because they want to protect against the low-short pitch that just catches the front of the strike mat for a strike. You also want to consider whether the batter is standing close to or away from the plate or strike mat.

Principle 1. Pitch low-short to batters who stand back in the box, causing them to reach to hit the ball, and high-long to batters who stand in the front of the box, forcing them to swing above their power zone.

> **Principle 2**. Pitch inside to batters who stand near the plate or mat, reducing their chances of extending their arms and thus jamming their swing, and pitch outside to those standing away from the plate or mat, causing them to reach.

For batters who take a center position to the plate or strike mat, and many do, you can use any of the four pitches described, but vary them. Just make sure to avoid the power zone.

Most batters are squatters (they stay set in the box when the pitch is thrown), but occasionally you'll encounter nomads who move when the pitch is thrown to try to put themselves in the optimal position to hit the pitch. Most nomads tend to start far back in the box and then move into the pitch. The high-deep-outside pitch and the low-short-inside or low-short-outside pitch are usually more effective against these batters.

Hitting Style

Remember that power hitters try to hit the ball as hard as they can without much concern about where they hit it as long as it is fair and that place hitters try to hit the ball to a specific location. You'll see two types of place hitters—those who hit to the same location consistently and those who spray the ball to all fields. Some power hitters are versatile and hit with power when they get a pitch in their power zone and place hit when they do not.

Power Hitters

Right-handed power hitters usually pull the ball to left field, and left-handed hitters usually pull the ball to right field. Although that's not always true, it's more probable than not. To pull the ball, power hitters like the ball on the inside half of the strike zone or mat between their waists and armpits. It's their power zone. You don't ever want to throw a pitch in this zone!

So where do you pitch power hitters? What's the toughest pitch for them to hit? From a biomechanics perspective, generating power is more difficult when hitting a low-arc pitch that is low-short-outside. The next most difficult pitch for batters to power out of the ballpark is the high-long-outside pitch, especially if the batter is standing toward the front of the strike zone. A low-short-inside pitch is also effective as a variation pitch, but if the batter is right-handed, warn your third baseperson that he or she is likely to get a hard-hit ground ball. If you have two strikes and less than three balls on the batter, a high-long-inside pitch that's 6 to 12 inches (15 to 30 cm) out of the strike zone is a good pitch to try to get the batter to pull the ball and foul out.

> **Principle 3**. Pitch power hitters low-short-outside when they are standing even or back of the plate or mat and pitch them high-long-outside when they are standing in front of the plate or mat.

Same-Location Place Hitters

The tactical principle here seems to be straightforward. Pitch the ball where it is more difficult for the batter to hit to his or her preferred location. For example, if a right-handed batter is a 5-6 hole hitter, pitch the ball low-short-outside. If a left-handed batter is a 5-6 hole hitter, pitch the ball low-short-inside.

> **Principle 4.** With same-location place hitters, pitch the ball where it is more difficult for the batter to place the hit.

Spray Place Hitters

When the third baseman is playing off the line, spray place hitters hit down the third-base line. The next time at bat they see a big gap in right-center field and pop the ball into that hole for a double. So how do you pitch to these versatile batters? The most difficult pitch to place hit is the low-short-inside pitch. Without any other information, this is a good probability pitch.

Also, recognize the game situation and what the batter would likely prefer to do. Then pitch the ball to make that type of hit more difficult, as you would with a same-location place hitter. For example, you have runners on first and second with nobody out. A smart place hitter will likely try to hit the 3-4 hole or go to right field. If you throw a high-short or deep-outside pitch to a right-handed batter, you're making it easier for him or her to hit the ball to the right side of the field. If you throw a low-short-inside pitch, however, the batter is more likely to hit the ball to the third baseperson, shortstop, or you, giving you the opportunity to turn a double play.

> **Principle 5.** With spray place hitters, recognize the game situation and determine where the hitter would prefer to hit in that situation. Then pitch the ball to make that type of hit more difficult.

If a spray place batter seems to go with the pitch (pulls the ball when the pitch is inside and punches the ball to the opposite field when the pitch is outside), and the game situation doesn't dictate a place that the batter would prefer to hit, apply this principle.

> **Principle 6.** As another tactic for spray place hitters, pitch the ball to a location where the batter is more likely to hit to your strongest defensive players or where you have the best chance of getting a force-out or double play.

Ball–Strike Count

Let's look at how to pitch with different ball–strike counts, taking into account the factors discussed earlier. We'll assume that you're playing with a full count of four balls and three strikes. Many leagues and tournaments start with a 1-1 count, and if so, apply the tactics described here beginning with that count. Remember that the first number is the number of balls.

A batter can have 12 different combinations of balls and strikes before he or she walks or is called out on strikes (0-1, 2-2, 3-2, and so on). What pitch do you want to throw for each of these counts? To answer that question more easily, we've identified three tactical pitches, one of which is recommended for each of the 12 ball–strike counts. We've named them the option pitch, unequivocal strike, and teaser pitch, so named to help you remember them with the acronym OUT.

- **Option pitch**. Throw the option pitch when the count is 0-0, 1-0, 1-1, or 2-2. You want to get a strike on the corner of the plate, but if you miss a bit off the plate it's OK because you're not behind the batter in the count. If you throw the option pitch with the 2-2 count, you must be confident that you can throw the unequivocal strike next if you miss the strike zone. But remember that when the batter has two strikes she or he is more likely to swing at balls that are slightly outside the strike zone.

- **Unequivocal strike**. Throw the unequivocal strike when the count is 2-0, 3-0, 2-1, 3-1, or 3-2. You're behind in the count and you need a strike for certain. Even so, you want to keep it out of the batter's hitting zone if possible.

- **Teaser pitch**. Throw a teaser pitch when the count is 0-1, 0-2, or 1-2. You don't want to throw a strike, especially a strike in the hitting zone. Instead, you want to tease the batter with a pitch that he or she may be willing to chase because you're ahead in the count. Many pitchers believe that the first pitch is the pivotal pitch. When playing with a full count (four balls and three strikes) many batters take a first pitch. If you can get an option pitch in for a called strike, you then can use the teaser pitch to get the batter to chase a ball outside the strike zone. But don't throw waste pitches. For example, you have an 0-2 count on the batter, so you throw a pitch with a 16-foot (4.8 m) arc that is 2 feet (0.6 m) from the plate or strike mat as a teaser pitch, but it isn't a teaser pitch at all. It's a complete waste. It's obvious that it's a ball to the hitter and the umpire, who calls it too high. You've missed an opportunity to develop your pitching tactics. Don't waste pitches, whether they are too high, too low, or too far outside the strike zone. Instead, keep the pitch away from the batter's hitting zone but close enough that an impatient, less disciplined batter is tempted to swing at a less than desirable pitch.

Principle 7. Throw the option pitch when the count is 0-0, 1-0, 1-1, or 2-2.

Principle 8. Throw the unequivocal strike when the count is 2-0, 3-0, 2-1, 3-1, or 3-2.

Principle 9. Throw a teaser pitch when the count is 0-1, 0-2, or 1-2.

Principle 10. Don't waste pitches when you're ahead in the count; instead, throw a teaser pitch.

Batter Patience

If you've played the game for a few years, you most likely have seen Jumping Jack at bat. He's yet to see a pitch he doesn't like. He jumps on the first pitch if it's anywhere close to the strike zone. His hitting philosophy is this: "It's a hitter's game, and I'm swinging away." On the other hand, you also are likely to have seen Patti Patient. She's only going to swing at a ball in her hitting zone, which she widens only when she has two strikes. She's happy to take a walk if the pitcher doesn't throw strikes.

You can usually identify Jumping Jack and Patti Patient reasonably quickly in a game. If you have the opportunity to scout the opposing batters before you play them, make a note of the hitters who are patient and impatient. The obvious tactical principle with impatient hitters is to start them out with a teaser pitch that may be even a little more outside the strike zone than usual, but not too much.

> **Principle 11**. Throw the first pitch to impatient batters outside the strike zone and to patient batters in the strike zone, locating the pitch based on the other tactical principles.

Walks

The tactical principles reviewed earlier apply to most game situations, but it's inevitable that you'll face game situations in which you'll want to weigh the merit of intentionally walking a batter. An intentional walk may be useful in several situations:

- To avoid letting a particular batter hit
- To create a force-out situation for the defense
- To get an out on a substitute runner who is due to bat (in leagues that allow players already in the lineup to serve as substitute runners)

We analyze the decision to walk a batter intentionally more fully in chapter 14, page 295.

To be a master pitcher, you must have superb control; otherwise, you can't employ the tactics discussed in this chapter. As you nibble at the corners of the mat, you still must be able to get strikes. Walks are the bane of pitchers and a team. The defense has no chance to get the batter out, and when pitchers throw lots of balls the defensive players find it hard to maintain their concentration.

Consider an unintentional walk as an unofficial error on the pitcher. Giving up three, four, or more walks in a game gives the other team a big advantage. So work on your pitching using the delivery with which you have the best control so that you can throw unequivocal strikes when you must.

> **Principle 12**. Walk batters intentionally when you conclude that the probability of their doing harm is higher than the damage from a free pass to first.
>
> **Principle 13**. Avoid giving batters unintentional walks.

PITCHER DEFENSE

No defensive position is more vital to a strong defense than the pitching position. Pitchers who can catch rocket line drives, scoop up ground balls to their right and left, initiate double plays, cover first, second, and third base, and back up bases on overthrows can help their teams win. In this section we'll help you become a better defensive pitcher.

Before we cover the various defensive plays that you will make as a pitcher, a cautionary word about this position is in order. With the high-tech bats used today and the power and skill of many batters, balls can be hit at you at speeds exceeding 100 miles per hour (160 kph), giving you a reaction time of less than 0.40 seconds to catch the ball. Knuckleballs are especially dangerous because they come at you erratically, making it even more difficult to catch the ball or protect yourself. Balls hit hard on the ground can hit a divot or the pitching rubber and take a bad hop to hit you.

So please consider the risks involved in pitching and recognize your own ability to react to the ball. We highly recommend protective gear for pitchers, the extent of which depends on your fielding ability. For males a protective cup is a wise investment, as is a chest protector for women. Shin guards and a facemask are also worth considering, especially for senior softball pitchers. (See chapter 9 for information about various protective equipment.)

Setting Up

As stated earlier we recommend using the no-step delivery because of the advantage it gives you in fielding the ball. Whether you use the one-step or no-step delivery, you will be a much better fielding pitcher if you can take from two to four steps back as the pitch is in the air and then set up to catch the ball (see figure 5.16).

FIGURE 5.16 Pitcher setup position from the no-step delivery. *(a)* After the pitch is released, *(b)* take a large step back with the left foot, *(c)* a large step back with the right foot, *(d)* then bring the left foot back even with the right and crouch into the ready position. Note that our model has a protective mask and shin guards on.

The setup is the most critical part of a pitcher's defensive play. If you are still backing up, you'll not be able to bend down or move laterally quickly enough to field hard-hit ground balls. Even if you don't take any steps back, you definitely want to be set up when batters start their swing, foremost for your own safety and secondarily to be in a good fielding position.

The setup position is shown in figure 5.16 and demonstrated on the DVD (see Defense→Pitching→Defensive Setup). After taking as many steps back as you have time and energy for, you want to stop, square up both feet to the batter, and be well balanced on the balls of your feet, ready to move in any direction.

Backing up and setting up on every pitch is not easy. You're concentrating on throwing pitches to a particular location, and to backpedal constantly and then set up to catch the ball is a great deal of work, especially if you pitch several games in a day. Most pitchers hedge a bit by determining whether the batter is likely to swing at the pitch that they've just released. If they don't think that the batter will swing they don't back up, but if the pitch looks hittable they do. Even if you decide not to back up on a pitch, you definitely want to set up so that you are in a ready position if the ball is hit to you.

Covering the Bases

Pitchers are responsible for covering various bases in different defensive situations, which we'll review now. A pitcher who recognizes that his or her responsibilities extend beyond just pitching the ball and then covers each of the bases in appropriate situations can make a tremendous difference. That's another reason why the pitching position is the most important defensive position. See Defense→Pitching→Covering the Bases for demonstrations of the skills discussed in this section.

Covering First Base

On a ground ball hit to the right side of the infield, you should break immediately toward first base. If you see that the second baseperson is going to catch the ball and that the first baseperson will be at first base, then you can stop. If the ball is hit to the first baseperson, then you want to continue toward first. If the first baseperson indicates that he or she will run to the bag without your help, you can stop. Otherwise, you need to continue to first to receive the throw to get the batter out.

When you are covering first you want to run to the foul line about 5 feet (150 cm) to the home-plate side of first and then turn to run parallel with the foul line to avoid collision with the base runner (see figure 5.17). Ideally, the first baseperson will be able to toss you the ball before you get to the bag so that you can catch it and then look to step on the base. Sometimes, however, time doesn't permit that to occur, so you're catching the ball as you're stepping on the base.

The most frequent mistake that the pitcher makes in this play is forgetting to cover first or getting a late start and not being able to get to first in time. You can avoid this error by making it a habit to break toward first each time the ball is hit to the right side of the infield.

FIGURE 5.17 Pitcher covering first base when the ball is hit to the right side.

Covering Second Base

When a pop fly is hit that both the shortstop and second baseperson go after, the pitcher is responsible for covering second base. In addition, when you have a runner on first and two outs, as a pitcher you can cover second base for the force-out. By doing so, the shortstop and second baseperson can play back farther because they don't have to be in position to cover second.

This play is executed when the ball is hit on the ground to the third baseperson, shortstop, or second baseperson. You immediately run to second, face the fielder throwing the ball, and position yourself on the side of the base closer to the fielder throwing you the ball for the force-out (see figure 5.18).

FIGURE 5.18 With two outs and a runner on first base, the infielders can play deeper when the pitcher covers second base on an infield ground ball.

Covering Third Base

When a pop-up is hit that the third baseperson goes after and a runner is likely to advance to third or is tagging up from third, the pitcher must cover third base. Also, when an overthrow occurs at third base and the third baseperson chases down the ball, the pitcher is likely to be in the best position to cover third.

Covering Home

When a runner is attempting to score on an overthrow at home that the catcher must chase, the pitcher is responsible for covering home plate or the strike mat. If the catcher retrieves the ball in time, he or she can flip the ball to the pitcher to get the runner out.

Pitcher-Initiated Double Plays

Pitchers often have the opportunity to initiate double plays. We look at how to execute the two most common double plays in this section and in Defense→Pitching→Pitcher-Initiated Double Plays on the DVD.

Second to First

Your most likely double plays as a pitcher occur when a runner is on first base and the ball is hit to you. You turn quickly and throw the ball to the shortstop or second baseperson covering second base, and that person relays it to first. Before you pitch the ball, you, the shortstop, and the second baseperson should agree on who will be covering second base. The customary rule is that with a right-handed batter the second baseperson will cover and with a left-handed batter the shortstop will cover. If a batter is known to hit more frequently to the right or left side of the field, however, you can adjust the coverage accordingly. (Note the exception to the coverage of second base on a double-play ball hit to either side of the pitcher. See chapter 6, page 144.)

When you catch the ball you quickly turn to look for the fielder covering the base and throw it immediately, leading the fielder to the base. Don't wait until the fielder reaches second to throw the ball. When throwing, try to place the ball about chest high to the fielder. If you're within 10 to 12 feet (3 to 3.7 m) of the fielder, throwing the ball underhand is faster and better. If you're farther away, a dart throw (nonwindup overhand throw; see chapter 6, page 132) is better (see figure 5.19).

FIGURE 5.19 *(a)* The pitcher catching a ground ball with a runner on first base, *(b)* then quickly turning and throwing to the shortstop covering second base to start a double play.

Home to . . .

When the bases are loaded with less than two outs and the ball is hit to you when pitching, you'll need to decide which way to attempt a double play. If the ball is hit slowly and you have a fast batter–runner, you're best play is to throw home and then have the catcher throw to first or third for a possible second out. If the ball is hit sharply and you field it cleanly, your best play may be to throw to second base for a faster double play, but that decision will also depend on your confidence in the ability of your shortstop and second baseperson to execute the double play, the score of the game, the level of risk that you want to take, and the speed of the batter.

Backing Up Plays and Throws

The pitcher can prevent runners from advancing extra bases by backing up the throws coming from the outfield to one of the bases. You need to do two things to back up the bases effectively:

1. You want to anticipate to which base the ball will be thrown. Usually you will be backing up the base ahead of where the lead runner is advancing.
2. You want to leave at least 30 feet (9 m) between you and the base that you're backing up, or as far back as the field permits up to 30 feet, so that if the ball is missed you have time to react to the errant ball. Sometimes pitchers are so close to the fielder that they cannot react to a missed ball.

Forgetting to back up the throw from the outfield is a common occurrence. Along with all the other work that the pitcher needs to do to field the position effectively, it's easy to become a spectator and forget to back up the base. But preventing a runner from advancing just once in a game could be the difference between winning and losing.

The pitcher is also involved in relays and cutoffs from the outfield. We'll cover the pitcher's role in these plays in chapter 8, "Defensive Strategies and Tactics."

SUMMARY

- As a pitcher your objective is to make it easier for your defensive team to get batters out. You do that by trying to get batters to swing at pitches that they don't want to swing at and to disrupt batters' timing in swinging at pitches.
- Master the mechanics of at least one pitch so that you can locate it precisely where you want in and near the strike zone.
- Learn as much as you can about the batters' hitting behavior so that you can apply the appropriate tactical principles.
- Practice, practice, practice so that you can master control of the location of your pitches.
- Disrupt the timing of batters by varying the pitches—low to high, short to long, inside and outside.
- Apply the 13 tactical pitching principles summarized on pages 104–108.
- Pitchers are a vital part of the defense, often executing more plays than fielders at any other position.
- Recognize the hazards of pitching and wear appropriate protective gear based on your ability to field the position.
- Whether you use the one-step method of pitching or the no-step method, back up several steps as the pitch is in the air, and most importantly, set up as the batter begins the swing so that you're in a good defensive position to field the ball.
- Know what bases to cover for various defensive plays and make a habit of always doing so.
- Recognize double-play situations and know to whom you will throw the ball if it is hit to you.
- Back up the base that the outfielder or relay person will likely throw to and keep sufficient distance from the base so that you have time to react to a missed ball.

TABLE 5.1　Major Pitching Rules for the Leading Slowpitch Softball Associations

	Amateur Softball Association (ASA)	Huntsman World Senior Games (HWSG)	Independent Softball Association (ISA)	International Senior Softball Association (ISSA)	International Softball Federation (ISF)	National Softball Association (NSA)	
Strike zone or strike mat	Zone—area over home plate between batter's front knee and back shoulder when in natural batting stance, except for seniors, who use 17 × 24 in. (43 × 61 cm) mat (or 17 × 32.5 in. [43 × 83 cm] mat when including the plate).	Zone—area over home plate that is lower than the top of the batter's back shoulder and higher than the bottom of the front knee.	Zone—area over home plate between batter's front knee and highest shoulder when in natural batting stance.	Mat—17 × 34 in. (43 × 86 cm).	Zone—area over home plate between batter's front knee and back shoulder when in natural batting stance, except for seniors, who use 17 × 34 in. (43 × 86 cm) mat.	Zone—area over home plate between batter's front knee and highest shoulder when in natural batting stance, except for seniors, who use 17 × 32.5 in. (43 × 83 cm) mat.	
Arc	6–10 ft (1.8–3 m); 6–12 ft (1.8–3.7 m) for seniors.	5–12 ft (1.5–3.7 m).	4–10 ft (1.2–3 m).	6–12 ft (1.8–3.7 m).	6–12 ft (1.8–3.7 m).	6–10 ft (1.8–3 m).	
Pitch count	Begin with 1 ball, 1 strike (except masters and seniors, who use 4 balls, 3 strikes).	4 balls, 3 strikes.	3 balls, 2 strikes with courtesy foul on second strike.	4 balls, 3 strikes.	4 balls, 3 strikes.	Begin with 1 ball, 1 strike.	
Pitching box	No pitcher's box, except for seniors. Box is the area from the front edge of the pitcher's plate (50 ft [15 m] from home plate) extending back 6 ft (1.8 m) and 24 in. (61 cm) wide.	Pitchers path from the front of the pitching plate (50 ft [15 m] from home plate) and extending 6 ft [1.8 m] perpendicular to the pitcher's plate is used.	Box is the area from the front of the pitcher's plate (50 ft [15 m] from home plate) extending back 6 ft (1.8 m) and 24 in. (61 cm) wide.	Box is the area from the pitcher's plate (50 ft [15 m] from home plate) extending back 6 ft (1.8 m) and 24 in. (61 cm) wide.	No pitcher's box, except for masters and seniors. Box is the area from the pitcher's plate (50 ft [15 m] from home plate) extending back 6 ft (1.8 m) and 24 in. (61 cm) wide.	No pitcher's box, except for seniors. Box is the area from the front of the pitching plate (53 ft [16 m] from home plate) extending back 3 ft (1 m).	

*This table provides general comparisons between organizations and is not meant to serve as a rulebook. Only rules that vary are presented, and then not in their entirety. Rules are subject to change during a yearly review process by each organization. For specific, current pitching rules see the rulebook of each organization.

North American Senior Circuit Softball (NASCS); also referred to as Senior Softball World Series	Senior Softball World Championships (SSUSA)	Softball Players Association (SPA)	United States Specialty Sports Association (USSSA)	Slo-Pitch National Softball (Canada)	Softball Canada
Mat—17 × 32.5 in. (43 × 83 cm).	Mat—19 × 34.5 in. (48 × 88 cm).	Mat—21 × 35 in. (53 × 89 cm).	Zone—area over home plate between bottom of batter's front knee and highest shoulder when in natural batting stance.	Zone—space directly above home plate that is neither higher than the batter's highest shoulder nor lower than the bottom of the batter's front knee, when the batter assumes the natural batting stance.	Zone—area over home plate between bottom of batter's front knee and highest shoulder when in natural batting stance.
6–12 ft (1.8–3.7 m).	6–12 ft (1.8–3.7 m).	6–12 ft (1.8–3.7 m).	3–10 ft (1–3 m).	6–12 ft (1.8–3.7 m).	6–12 ft (1.8–3.7 m).
4 balls, 3 strikes.	4 balls, 3 strikes.	4 balls, 3 strikes. If weather is bad, tournament director can decide to use 1-1 count or 1-pitch if necessary.		4 balls, 3 strikes.	4 balls, 3 strikes.
Box is the area from the front of the pitcher's plate (50 ft [15 m] from home plate) extending back 6 ft (1.8 m) and 24 in. (61 cm) wide.	Box is the area from the front of the pitcher's plate (50 ft [15 m] from home plate) extending back 6 ft (1.8 m) and 24 in. (61 cm) wide.	Box is the area from the front of the pitcher's plate (50 ft [15 m] from home plate) extending back 8 ft (2.4 m) and 24 in. (61 cm) wide.	Box is the area from the front of the pitcher's plate (50 ft [15 m] from home plate) extending back 6 ft (1.8 m) and 24 in. (61 cm) wide.	Zone (box) is the area from the front of the pitcher's area 50 ft (15 m) from the back point of home plate extending back 15 ft (4.6 m) and 24 in. (61 cm) wide.	No pitcher's box. Pitching plate is 24 in. (61 cm) wide and 6 in. (15 cm) deep. It is 50 ft (15 m) from the front of the pitching plate to the outside corner of home plate.

(continued)

TABLE 5.1 *(continued)*

	Amateur Softball Association (ASA)	Huntsman World Senior Games (HWSG)	Independent Softball Association (ISA)	International Senior Softball Association (ISSA)	International Softball Federation (ISF)	National Softball Association (NSA)	
Foreign substances	Pitcher can have tape on the fingers of the pitching arm or a sweatband on wrist or forearm. Batting glove cannot be used on pitching hand.	Pitcher cannot use any foreign substance on the ball, pitching hand, or fingers. Under the control of the umpire, powder resin may be used to dry the hands. Wristbands or batting gloves may not be used on the pitching hand or wrist. A non-distracting colored bandage may be worn on the pitching hand/wrist in case of injury.	Pitcher cannot use tape on the fingers of the pitching arm. Anything on the pitching hand, wrist, or arm that might be distracting to the batter is not allowed.	Pitcher can have tape on the fingers of the pitching arm or a sweatband on wrist or forearm. Batting glove cannot be used on pitching hand.	Pitcher can have tape on the fingers of the pitching arm or a sweatband on wrist or forearm. Batting glove cannot be used on pitching hand.	Pitcher cannot use tape on the fingers or hand of the pitching arm.	
Pitching preliminaries	Pitcher must come to a complete stop with ball in front of body for a minimum of 1 second before delivering the ball. From the time the pitcher receives the ball, it must be delivered within 10 seconds.	One foot must be in line with the pitcher's plate and within pitching path when the pitcher releases the ball. The free foot may take a step in any direction when the pitch is made. Pitcher must come to a complete stop before pitching.	Pitcher must make a required stop before delivering ball. Ball must be delivered within 5 seconds of start of windup or when umpire calls, "Play ball."	Pitcher must come to a complete stop with ball in front of body for a minimum of 1 second before delivering the ball. From the time the pitcher receives the ball, it must be delivered within 10 seconds.	Pitcher must come to a complete stop with ball in front of body for a minimum of 1 second before delivering the ball. From the time the pitcher receives the ball, it must be delivered within 10 seconds.	Pitcher must come to a complete stop with ball in front of body for a minimum of 1 second and a maximum of 5 seconds before delivering the ball.	

North American Senior Circuit Softball (NASCS); also referred to as Senior Softball World Series	Senior Softball World Championships (SSUSA)	Softball Players Association (SPA)	United States Specialty Sports Association (USSSA)	Slo-Pitch National Softball (Canada)	Softball Canada
Pitcher can have tape on the fingers of the pitching arm or a sweatband on wrist or forearm. Batting glove cannot be used on pitching hand.	Pitcher can have tape on the fingers of the pitching arm or a sweatband on wrist or forearm. Batting glove cannot be used on pitching hand.	Pitcher cannot use tape on the fingers of the pitching arm but can use sweatband on the pitching arm forearm or above.	Pitcher cannot use tape or any other substance, including a glove, on the pitching hand or fingers.	A pitcher cannot use any substance other than tape or a bandage on the pitching hand or fingers. No foreign substance is to be applied to the ball, provided that under supervision and control of the umpire, a bag containing powdered resin may be used to dry the hands. A pitcher can have a sweatband on the wrist or forearm of the pitching arm as well. A batting glove cannot be used on the pitching hand.	No foreign substance except resin. Resin must be on the ground, not in the pant pocket. Taping fingers is legal. Batting glove on the pitching hand is illegal.
Pitcher must come to a complete stop with ball in front of body for a minimum of 1 second before delivering the ball. From the time the pitcher receives the ball, it must be delivered within 10 seconds.	Pitcher must come to a complete stop with ball in front of body for a minimum of 1 second before delivering the ball. From the time the pitcher receives the ball or umpire calls, "Play ball," the pitch must be delivered within 10 seconds.	Pitcher must come to a complete stop with ball in front of body for a minimum of 1 second and a maximum of 10 seconds before delivering the ball. Ball must be delivered within 10 seconds of receiving ball from catcher.	Pitcher must come to a complete stop with ball in front of body for a minimum of 1 second before delivering the ball. Ball must be delivered within 5 seconds of the time the pitcher receives the ball.	Pitcher shall take a position with the pivot foot firmly on the ground within the confines of the pitching zone. The pivot foot must remain in constant contact within the pitching zone until the release of the ball. After assuming the pitching position, the pitcher must hold the ball in front of the body (and be motionless for at least 1 second) in either one or both hands, before starting the delivery motion. The ball must be delivered within 5 seconds after the pause. The pitcher must face home plate when starting delivery of the pitch.	Pitcher must come to a complete stop with ball in front of body for a minimum of 1 second before delivering the ball. From the time the pitcher receives the ball, it must be delivered within 10 seconds.

(continued)

TABLE 5.1 *(continued)*

	Amateur Softball Association (ASA)	Huntsman World Senior Games (HWSG)	Independent Softball Association (ISA)	International Senior Softball Association (ISSA)	International Softball Federation (ISF)	National Softball Association (NSA)	
Legal delivery	After the stop, pitcher can't make any pitching motion without delivering the ball. Must be a continuous motion without a stop or reversal of pitching motion. Must be delivered on first forward swing of pitching arm past the hip and can't be behind the back or through the legs.	Pitcher must be facing home plate when delivering the pitch. Any type of windup may be used but ball must be delivered from below the hip at a moderate speed. Ball must be released within 5 seconds of start of windup or when the umpire calls "Play ball."	Any type of windup may be used, but the ball must be delivered from below the hip.	After the stop, pitcher can't make any pitching motion without delivering the ball. Must be a continuous motion without a stop or reversal of pitching motion. Must be delivered on first forward swing of pitching arm past the hip and can't be behind the back or through the legs.	After the stop, pitcher can't make any pitching motion without delivering the ball. Must be a continuous motion without a stop or reversal of pitching motion. Must be delivered on first forward swing of pitching arm past the hip and can't be behind the back or through the legs.	Any windup can be used before the required pause. After the stop, pitcher can't make any pitching motion without delivering the ball. Must be a continuous motion without a stop or reversal of pitching motion. Must be delivered on first forward swing of pitching arm past the hip and can't be behind the back or through the legs.	
Charged defensive conferences	Three charged conferences per seven-inning game between the manager (or other team representative from the dugout) and pitcher; one extra conference per inning after that. Additional conference means removal of pitcher from that position for the game.	Two charged conferences per seven-inning game. Additional conference means removal of pitcher from that position for the game.	Two charged conferences per seven-inning game. Additional conference means removal of pitcher from that position for the game.	Three charged conferences per seven-inning game between the manager and pitcher; one extra conference per inning after that. Additional conference means removal of pitcher from that position for the game.	Three charged conferences per seven-inning game between the manager and pitcher; one extra conference per inning after that. Additional conference means removal of pitcher from that position for the game.	One charged conference per inning; second means removal of the pitcher from that position for the game. If the second conference in an inning is to remove the pitcher, the pitcher can return in that position.	

North American Senior Circuit Softball (NASCS); also referred to as Senior Softball World Series	Senior Softball World Championships (SSUSA)	Softball Players Association (SPA)	United States Specialty Sports Association (USSSA)	Slo-Pitch National Softball (Canada)	Softball Canada
After the stop, pitcher can't make any pitching motion without delivering the ball. Must be a continuous motion without a stop or reversal of pitching motion. Must be delivered on first forward swing of pitching arm past the hip and can't be behind the back or through the legs. Pitcher cannot deliver a pitch from the glove. Any windup that does not conflict with the preceding can be used.	After the stop, pitcher can't make any pitching motion without delivering the ball. Must be a continuous motion without a stop or reversal of pitching motion. Must be delivered on first forward swing of pitching arm past the hip and can't be behind the back or through the legs. Pitching motion cannot continue after release of the ball.	Any windup can be used as long as the pitcher doesn't make any pitching motion without delivering the ball and uses a continuous motion without a stop or reversal of pitching motion. Must be delivered on first forward swing of pitching arm past the hip. Hand must be below the hip and can't use any fakes.	The pitcher can release the ball in any manner using any type of delivery after presenting the ball for at least 1 second. Any windup or arm motions may be used including stops and starts as long as it is within 5 seconds of receiving the ball.	After the pitcher has come to a complete stop, he or she has 5 seconds in which to use any windup or arm motion desired, either in front of the body, above the head, or behind the back including stops and pauses, before he or she must release the ball. Only a definite underhand motion is permitted in the delivery of the pitch. The pitcher may release the pitched ball with the hand above the hip in order to obtain the necessary arc.	Cannot make any motion without immediately delivering the ball. Windup must be continuous motion. Cannot use a windup with a stop or reversal of the forward motion. Must deliver the ball on the first forward motion past the hip with an underhand motion. Pivot foot must remain in contact with the plate until the release of the ball from the pitcher's hand. Cannot pitch behind the back, through the legs, or from the glove. Must be thrown at moderate speed.
Three charged conferences per seven-inning game between the manager and pitcher; one extra conference per inning after that. Additional conference means removal of pitcher from that position for the game.	One charged conference per inning; second means removal of the pitcher from that position for the game.	One charged conference per inning; second means removal of the pitcher from that position for the game. If the second conference in an inning is to remove the pitcher, the pitcher can return in that position.	One charged conference per inning; second means removal of the pitcher from that position for the game.	One charged conference per inning. The second charged conference will result in the removal of the pitcher from the pitching position for the remainder of the game, but he or she can play any other position.	One charged conference per inning; second means removal of the pitcher from that position for the game. If the second conference in an inning is to remove the pitcher, the pitcher can return in that position.

(continued)

TABLE 5.1 *(continued)*

	Amateur Softball Association (ASA)	Huntsman World Senior Games (HWSG)	Independent Softball Association (ISA)	International Senior Softball Association (ISSA)	International Softball Federation (ISF)	National Softball Association (NSA)	
Wind or sun affecting both pitchers	No rule	No rule	No rule	No rule	No rule	No rule	

	North American Senior Circuit Softball (NASCS); also referred to as Senior Softball World Series	Senior Softball World Championships (SSUSA)	Softball Players Association (SPA)	United States Specialty Sports Association (USSSA)	Slo-Pitch National Softball (Canada)	Softball Canada
	No rule	If the umpire thinks that the wind or rain is having a notice-able effect on the accuracy of both pitchers, the umpire may indicate that only strikes count. The umpire may decide to lower the height of the pitch in the case of sun interference.	No rule	No rule	No rule	No rule

CHAPTER 6

Infielder Skills

Playing the infield in slowpitch softball is great fun. As an infielder you will be challenged to field hard-hit ground balls to your right or left, catch knuckleball line drives, and run down bloopers hit over your head. You'll be expected to throw accurately across the diamond, make soft tosses to a nearby teammate covering a base, and relay the ball from the outfield to make a long throw to home. And you'll have the opportunity to execute double plays with split-second timing, tag sliding runners, and chase down runners trapped between bases. This chapter and the accompanying DVD cover fielding, throwing, tagging runners, playing each infield position, and making special plays.

FIELDING

We start this section with a quick review of the basics of catching hits and throws. We consider some reasons why catchable balls are missed and then move into the specifics of fielding ground balls, line drives, and pop-ups. We end the section with a discussion of difficult fielding plays.

Catching Fundamentals

When a ball is hit or thrown to you below the waist, you turn your glove so that the fingers are pointed downward. When the ball is above the waist but not above your head, you turn your glove sideways, and when it is above your head the fingers are extended upward. These positions are shown in figure 6.1.

Sometimes a ball sinks or rises, so you have to adjust quickly to get the glove in the right position. Line drives that are hit with topspin may approach you above your waist but then suddenly drop below your waist. If you don't change positions quickly the glove will be in awkward position to catch the ball.

FIGURE 6.1 *(a)* Point the glove down to catch balls below the waist; *(b)* turn the glove sideways to catch balls between the waist and head; *(c)* point the glove up to catch balls above the head.

Fielding Ground Balls

In figure 6.2 and Defense→Infielder Skills→Fielding Ground Balls on the DVD you see the appropriate ready position for infielders as they set up to field a ground ball. The position is well balanced, and the glove is ready to move in any direction in pursuit of the ball.

From the ready position you move to field the ball. The traditional fielding position that is widely accepted in slowpitch, fastpitch, and baseball is to position yourself so that you catch the ball directly between your legs with your face looking directly at it as shown in figure 6.3.

Because of the wide variability in the quality of infield surfaces in which slowpitch is played, an alternative is to position yourself to field the ball in front of the leg on the glove-hand side as shown in figure 6.4. If the ball takes a bad hop, it is less likely to hit you in the face and your foot may stop it.

FIGURE 6.2 Ready position for fielding ground balls.

FIGURE 6.3 The traditional position for fielding ground balls is to place the glove directly between your legs.

FIGURE 6.4 An alternative position for fielding ground balls is to play the ball off your glove-side foot.

Consider three other important points for fielding ground balls:

1. When you're fielding from the ready position remind yourself to watch the *last* bounce to avoid some of the catching mistakes mentioned on page 127.

2. You can bring your glove up from the ground faster than you can push the glove down to the ground from your knees, according to sport scientists. So get the glove down on ground balls and as you see that last hop adjust it upward as needed.

3. Don't quit on the play if you make an error. If you knocked the ball down it may be within quick reach, so you still may be able to get an out. Or perhaps you slowed up the ball, and it is now rolling to a stop just on the edge of the grass. You're the closest person to the ball and need to retrieve it. Even if the ball goes through your legs all the way to the outfielder, don't stand there grumbling about your error; you have a base to cover or a relay play to make from the outfield. You can feel remorse over your error later.

Fielding on the Move

Wouldn't it be nice if batters always hit the ball directly to you? But, of course, they don't! You have to field many balls on the run. Read about making these plays and then watch Defense→Infielder Skills→Fielding on the Move on the DVD.

On a slowly hit ground ball you will need to charge in to field it on the run. If time permits approach the ball on your glove-hand side (see figure 6.5*a*) and then come up throwing quickly. On occasion time does not permit that approach, so you'll need to pick up the ball barehanded (see figure 6.5*b*) and make the throw.

For balls hit to your right or left, if you have time you can shuffle laterally and get in the fielding position to stop the ball as shown in figures 6.3 and 6.4. But when you don't have that time you'll be running and reaching to make a forehand catch or a backhand one as shown in figures 6.6 and 6.7. For both forehand (glove-side) and backhand (throwing-arm-side) catches, stay low, keep your eye on the ball, and adjust your running so that you catch the ball just in front of your forward foot.

FIGURE 6.5 Fielding a slow roller with *(a)* the glove and *(b)* barehanded.

FIGURE 6.6 Forehand catch. *(a)* Take a quick crossover step in the direction of the ball and *(b)* keep the glove down as you approach the ball. Then move quickly into a position to throw.

FIGURE 6.7 Backhand catch. *(a)* Turn your body toward where you anticipate catching the ball and take a powerful step with the foot away from the ball (left foot here). *(b)* As you approach the ball plant the back (right) foot and reach for the ball with the glove in the backhand position, and then *(c)* set the back (right) foot and come up throwing.

Catching Mistakes

Here are some common mistakes made when catching balls and the corrections to make.

Mistake: You fail to track the ball all the way into the glove. After thousands of catches your brain has excellent ability to estimate the trajectory of the ball, so you may shift your attention to the runner or the infielder to whom you plan to throw the ball. But sometimes the trajectory of the ball can change because of wind, ball flutter, or a bad hop, resulting in your missing a catch that you would easily make otherwise.

Correction: Focus your attention on watching the ball into your glove.

Mistake: You're covering second base on a potential double play. You hear the footsteps of the runner coming fast to second base just as the ball is thrown to you. At the same time you need to find the base so that you can step on it, and you want to avoid the impending collision with the runner. Your eyes dart from the ball to the base to the runner, and, oops, you've missed the throw.

Correction: Focus on the ball, learn to spot the base before you reach it, feel for the base with your feet, and push the runner out of your mind.

Mistake: On a hard-hit line drive directly at your head, you throw your glove up to make the catch, but your glove blocks your vision. When you can't see the ball going into the glove, you don't know exactly when to squeeze it shut, so the ball pops out.

Correction: Quickly move your head to one side.

Mistake: You try to catch the ball with your glove against your body, which greatly reduces your ability to adjust your glove quickly to the location of the ball.

Correction: Move your glove hand away from your body.

Mistake: On a hard-hit ground ball your entire body tightens up, fearing that you may miss the ball or that it will hit you. Those tight muscles greatly reduce your reaction time to catch the ball.

Correction: Catch the ball off to the side until you overcome your fear through practice.

Mistake: You try to catch with hands of steel. The ball hits in the glove, but you don't absorb the impact, so the ball jumps out.

Correction: Develop "soft hands" that cuddle the ball and squeeze the glove shut at the right moment.

Mistake: When running to catch a ball the impact resulting from your movement causes your eyes to bounce and thus not see the ball clearly.

Correction: You can avoid this problem by running on the balls of your feet rather than with the usual heel–toe strike.

Mistake: In an attempt to catch and throw the ball quickly, you stick your throwing hand into the glove before the ball arrives. You not only drop the ball but also put your fingers at risk of being broken.

Correction: Don't do it.

Diving

When running won't get you to the ball perhaps a dive will. Diving for balls is useful when you can recover from the dive in time to throw a runner out at a base or prevent a runner from advancing to another base. Diving for balls that leave you without an opportunity to get an out or prevent the advancement of a runner doesn't make any sense and risks injury. In figure 6.8 and Defense→Infielder Skills→Diving, Bloopers, and Pop-Ups on the DVD you'll see how to make a diving catch, but we had our model do so on the grass to decrease the chance of getting abrasions.

FIGURE 6.8   Diving for a ball. *(a)* Turn toward where you anticipate the ball will be caught, *(b)* push hard with your feet at exactly the right time for a full-extension reach, *(c)* use the throwing arm to help absorb the fall, and *(d)* after the landing, with the ball secure in the glove push up with both arms to a kneeling position to throw.

Catching Line Drives

What may seem like a relatively easy ball to catch can be deceptively difficult depending on how the line drive is hit. The line drive that is hit just slightly above the center of the ball will come at the infielder with topspin. Expect this ball to dip downward, sometimes sharply and right in front of you, making it a difficult one-hop ball to catch. The line drive that is hit just slightly below the center of the ball will look as if it is coming to you, and then because of the backspin it will lift up and go over your head. But by far the most difficult line drive to catch is the ball that is hit dead center and comes toward you without rotation—the fluttering knuckleball.

You'll do better catching these balls when you learn to recognize each of these three types of line drives, anticipate a change in trajectory, and track the ball all the way into your glove. With the sinking line drive that looks as if it may hit the ground just in front of you, if you have time, charge it to catch it on the fly. With the rising line drive, be prepared to jump as it lifts up over your head. With the knuckleball line drive, be prepared to make small adjustments with your glove as the ball approaches you.

Catching Bloopers and Pop-Ups

Fielding looping fly balls just behind the infield and chasing down higher pop flies requires good athletic ability. You need to be able to read quickly where the ball will likely come down, run rapidly to that spot while making adjustments as you continue to watch the ball, and then as you reach the ball see it into your glove. Sometimes you'll be catching the ball as it comes over your head, and at other times you'll be reaching to your right or left to make the grab.

When catching pop-ups don't make the mistake of slowing down with a heel–toe foot strike when you reach the location where the ball is descending. Stay up on the balls of your feet. When you let your heels strike the ground your eyeballs will do an incredible dance that will have you seeing double, more than likely causing you to miss the ball.

Watch Defense→Infielder Skills→Diving, Bloopers, and Pop-Ups on the DVD now to see how to snare pop-ups.

Making Difficult Fielding Plays

The more difficult fielding plays for infielders include

- fielding balls that are in the sun,
- fielding windblown balls,
- fielding fly balls near the sideline fence,
- avoiding collisions with teammates and runners, and
- fielding on poorly maintained infield surfaces.

Let's look at each of these playing situations now.

Balls in the Sun

If you play the game for a while you'll surely run into conditions in which the sun makes it nearly impossible to see the ball. Besides wearing safety sunglasses, you can use your glove or throwing hand to shade the sun and then try to find the ball so that you can catch it (see figure 6.9). Another option is to have the adjacent fielder come over to catch high fly balls from an angle that is not in the sun. When the sun is low in the sky and is directly behind the batter, line drives hit straight at you become dangerous missiles. Wearing good sunglasses and using your throwing hand to attempt to block the sun is all you can do.

FIGURE 6.9 Shield your eyes by blocking the sun with your hand or glove.

FIGURE 6.10 Field fly balls close to the fence by running to it and feeling for the fence with your hand.

Windblown Balls

A strong wind can change the flight of the ball, so you must adjust. A pop-up that looks as if it is coming to the shortstop may be blown over to the second baseperson. With a wind coming in from the outfield a line drive that has topspin will dive downward even more than usual, and a ball with backspin will lift more than usual. When you're getting ready to play, make a mental note of the wind and the adjustments that you may need to make.

Fly Balls Near the Fence

All infielders at times have the opportunity to catch a pop-up near the fence, but in doing so they risk injury. The proper way to play the fence is to run to it while watching the ball, locate the fence with your throwing hand to avoid a collision with it, and then make the catch, as shown in figure 6.10. Another approach is to do a bent-leg slide just as you're approaching the fence to keep you from crashing into it and make the catch as you're in the slide. But we recommend staying on your feet and using good judgment to avoid injuring yourself by crashing into the fence.

Collisions

Another hazard in infield play is the potential for collisions with other fielders chasing high fly balls and with base runners. Collisions with teammates can be avoided by good communication. Players should call out clearly who will catch the ball. Collisions with base runners can usually be avoided by positioning yourself correctly and by base runners' adherence to the rules to avoid collisions.

Infield Surfaces

You'll likely play on some wonderful infields and on some terrible ones. Some fields will be brick hard, and the ball will skip through the infield in a flash. Others will be so soft that moving across them will be like running on the beach. Firm but smooth infields give truer bounces consistently, although the ball gets to you or through the infield in a hurry. Soft infields are great for sliding but not for running or fielding. Although soft fields will slow down ground balls, giving you a greater chance to reach them, the runners on the basepaths and the movements of the infielders will create ugly divots that cause frequent bad bounces. That's why we advise fielding ground balls slightly to the glove side, as mentioned earlier.

THROWING

Infielders need to be able to throw in a variety of ways, depending on the play. The emphasis is always on accuracy. In this section we'll look at five types of throws and offer some ideas about how to throw accurately.

Types of Throws

The five types of throws that you'll need on the infield are the

- overhand throw,
- sidearm throw,
- dart throw,
- underhand toss, and
- backhand flip.

Read about these throws next and then watch the DVD to see these throws being made in action.

Overhand Throw

This throw is a staple for infielders and outfielders alike. With practice this is the most powerful and accurate way to throw longer distances, but it takes more time to set up and execute this throw than the other throws that you'll use in the infield. The grip on the ball should be across the seams as shown in figure 6.11 and Defense→Infielder Skills→Types of Throws→Overhand Throw on the DVD. If you grip the ball in other ways it has a greater chance of not traveling in a straight line. The throw is made with a windup, a strong step forward, and a hard push with the back foot. The arm comes straight over the top with a hard snap of the wrist and a complete follow-through.

If you throw 50 to 100 balls a day, you'll increase not only the distance you can throw but also your accuracy. If you lack arm and shoulder strength, see the strength-training references in appendix A.

FIGURE 6.11 Overhand throw. *(a)* Grip the ball across the wide seams, *(b)* wind up and take a powerful stride forward, and *(c)* throw the ball with the arm coming over the top of the shoulder in a strong forward action.

Sidearm Throw

Accurately named, this throw is made with the arm moving parallel to the ground. The elbow is below the shoulder and the arm action is perpendicular to the ground as shown in figure 6.12 and Defense→Infielder Skills→Types of Throws→Sidearm Throw on the DVD. Some players use the sidearm throw in place of the overhand throw, but generally you use the sidearm throw when you need to make a quicker throw than the overhand throw allows. On a slowly hit ball you may need to throw sidearm from low in the fielding position to eliminate the time required to stand up, wind up, and throw overhand. Although not quite as powerful as the overhand throw, the sidearm throw is a useful way to make a quick throw of 20 to 75 feet (6 to 25 m).

FIGURE 6.12 Sidearm throw. *(a)* Reach back with the elbow below the shoulder, and *(b)* initiate the throwing action by keeping the arm parallel to the ground.

Dart Throw

This throw is a short snap throw in which you bring the ball up close to the ear and throw mostly with the forearm and wrist, as shown in figure 6.13 and Defense→Infielder Skills→Types of Throws→Dart Throw on the DVD. The dart throw is a quick throw for distances in the range of 10 to 30 feet (3 to 10 m), and it is especially useful in turning double plays started by the pitcher, shortstop, or second baseperson, and when executing a rundown play in which you have a runner trapped between the bases.

FIGURE 6.13 Dart throw. *(a)* Begin the throw by bringing the ball up close to the ear, and *(b)* initiate the throw with a short snap of the forearm and wrist.

Underhand Toss

When you catch the ball low and are close to the fielder to whom you are going to throw the ball, the underhand toss is a quick and accurate way to throw, as shown in figure 6.14 and Defense→Infielder Skills→Types of Throws→Underhand Toss on the DVD. Middle infielders and the pitcher use this throw when executing double plays. Use the underhand toss when you are within 20 feet (6 m) of the fielder. Toss the ball with as much speed as you can to get the ball to the fielder quickly but not so fast that the fielder cannot react to the ball.

FIGURE 6.14   Underhand toss. *(a)* Begin the throw with a backswing to about waist high, and *(b)* step forward and swing the arm underhand in the direction you're throwing.

Backhand Flip

This throw is best for short distances when the throwing shoulder is pointing in the direction you want to throw. It is made with the arm swinging away from the body to push the ball out to the fielder, as shown in figure 6.15 and Defense→Infielder Skills→Types of Throws→Backhand Flip on the DVD. This throw is difficult to make accurately, and therefore it is used only in special circumstances. When the pitcher has backed up halfway to second and caught a ground ball, the backhand flip is a quick way to throw the ball to the infielder covering second for a force-out and possible double play. Likewise, the first baseperson may use it to flip the ball to the pitcher covering first, although if time permits an underhand toss is preferable. A right-handed shortstop who runs behind second base to catch a ball may use the backhand flip to get the ball to the infielder covering second base for a force-out; a right-handed second baseperson may also use it to flip the ball to second when fielding a ball close to the base.

FIGURE 6.15   Backhand flip. *(a)* With the elbow pointed out, bring the ball in front of the body, and then *(b)* push the ball out with a backhand action.

Accuracy

Regardless of the type of throw you make, you want it to be accurate. A common mistake that infielders make is hurrying a throw to the point that the intended receiver of the throw cannot catch the ball or can catch it but be unable to make a relay throw or tag a runner.

Do you remember the speed–accuracy tradeoff principle that we reviewed in chapter 2 in our discussion of hitting? The idea applies to throwing as well, and generally it is better to trade speed for accuracy. On a possible double play it's better to get one out for sure with an accurate throw rather than try for two outs by making a hurried, errant throw. And it's much better to take a little more time to throw accurately and not get the out at a base than it is to overthrow the base and allow the runners to advance farther.

Accuracy comes through practice. Players commonly warm up with the overhand throw, but they may seldom practice the other throws. So devote time in practice sessions to making all the throws that you will likely use in a game. It's easy to do so by throwing with a teammate or throwing at targets on a fence.

Difficult Throws

We'll now look at a few throws that are especially challenging to make. After reading about each one watch the DVD to see each throw in action.

Throwing on the Run

The batter hits a slow bouncing ball toward you, and you charge the ball, fielding it on the run. You don't have time to stop and set up to make a good throw to first, so as you are running you throw the ball to the base (see figure 6.16 and Defense→Infielder Skills→Difficult Throws→Throwing on the Run on the DVD). This skill is difficult to execute, but with practice you can master it.

FIGURE 6.16 Throwing on the run. *(a)* Change a slow-rolling ground ball hit in front of you; *(b)* catch the ground ball on the run, positioning yourself to catch the ball on the glove-hand side; and *(c)* lacking time to set up to throw, orient yourself toward first base and throw on the run.

Throwing to a Running Fielder

Occasionally infielders must throw to a teammate who is running to cover a base by leading them—by throwing the ball where the fielder will be, not where he or she is. This throw requires timing the running fielder and throwing accurately to his or her anticipated location (see Defense→Infielder Skills→Difficult Throws→Throwing to a Running Fielder on the DVD). Lots of practice will help you make this play. When leading a teammate throw the ball as quickly as possible, preferably before the fielder reaches the base, so that he or she can first attend to catching the ball and then find the base or tag the runner.

Making the Backhand Catch and Throw

You're a right-handed shortstop, and the bases are empty. The batter hits a ground ball in the 5-6 hole, and you sprint to catch it, making a nice backhand grab. Now you must stop quickly and make the long throw to first base, a difficult play because you don't have time to set up fully and make the usual overhand throw. Instead, you plant your right foot immediately after making the catch, take a short step with your left leg, and throw overhand to first (see figure 6.17). You make the throw mostly with the arm and upper body, with a push from the back leg. The second baseperson has the same play when backhanding a ball hit up the middle, although the throw is slightly shorter.

FIGURE 6.17 Backhand catch and throw. Here the shortstop *(a)* makes a backhand stop in the 5-6 hole and then *(b)* sets up to throw to first.

Relaying Throws From the Outfield

Either the shortstop or second baseperson will almost always make the relay throws from the outfield. Here's a description of how to make these throws.

1. First, you must hustle to a position that is in a direct line between the fielder and the base to which the ball will be thrown, and go out far enough so that the fielder can reach you with a throw in the air.

2. The outfielder should try to throw the ball so that you can catch it chest high and make a quick relay throw.

3. As the ball is coming to you, position yourself to catch the ball with the throwing arm and shoulder turned toward the outfielder and the glove hand toward the infield, as shown in figure 6.18 and Defense→Infielder Skills→Difficult Throws→Relaying Throws From the Outfield on the DVD. From this position you can make the relay throw quickly without having to pivot to throw.

4. Watch the ball come into your glove and then quickly make the overhand relay throw to the base to which your infield teammate has told you to throw. When relaying the ball to a base for a force-out play, try to throw the ball chest high to the fielder covering the base. For a tag play, throw the ball low to make it easier for your teammate to tag the incoming runner.

FIGURE 6.18 Relaying the ball from the outfield. *(a)* The infielder runs into shallow outfield, getting in a direct line between the outfielder and the base to which the ball will be thrown. *(b)* The outfielder throws the ball chest-high to the infielder, who positions himself so that the ball is caught with the throwing arm and shoulder turned toward the outfielder and the glove-hand toward the infield. *(c)* The relaying infielder makes a short throw to the infielder covering the base.

Players make three common mistakes in executing the relay from the outfield:

- The outfielder's throw is not chest high to you, so you need more time to catch the ball and set up for the overhand throw. If the ball is way off target and you can't catch it, a base runner has the opportunity to advance to another base.
- With your back to the infield waiting for the throw, you receive no communication about whether to throw to a base or which base to throw to. Or several of your teammates yell conflicting instructions about whether you should throw or where. Consequently, you must turn around, determine where all the runners are, and decide whether to throw or where, losing valuable time.
- In your rush to make the throw to a base, you begin the throwing action before you catch the ball and therefore drop it.

When Not to Throw

A difficult thing to learn is when to hold the ball. For example, you bobble a ball hit to you. After you get your hands on the elusive ball, in a rush you throw wildly to the base. The runner was only a step away, however, and you had no chance to get an out. The ball ends up in right field or under the opponent's bench. All runners are not only safe but also advance one or two additional bases. In the desperate attempt to make up for a small error, you created a much bigger error. Another common mistake is throwing the ball in an often-futile attempt to get the leading runner out, thus permitting the trailing runner to advance a base. For example, you take a relay from the outfield and make a desperate throw home, but you really have no chance for the out. The batter–runner on first sees you make the throw home and trots down to second.

You need judgment tempered with experience to know when not to make a throw. Also, your fellow infielders can let you know to hold the ball, especially when your focus is on fielding it and they can see the location of the base runners.

Checking the Runner and Then Throwing

When runners are not in a situation when they are forced to run—for example, when runners are on second or third base, or both, but not on first with less than two out—you can look at the runners to "freeze" them as you field the ball, preventing them from advancing to the next base, and then throw to first base to get the force-out. With runners on first and third, you can freeze the runner on third when you know that you can't get a double play and the runner on third does not immediately break for home.

TAGGING RUNNERS

When there is not a force-out play at a base, you can secure an out by tagging the runner, that is, by touching him or her with the ball in your hand or glove when the runner is not on a base. Tag plays usually occur at a base but also can occur in a rundown when a runner is trapped between bases. Read this section and then watch Defense→Infielder Skills→Tagging Runners on the DVD.

When making a tag at a base, you want to get to the base quickly and get in the correct position to catch the ball. The correct position is one in which the fielder can throw you the ball without hitting the runner and you can catch it where you can make the tag without colliding with the runner. If the base runner is directly in line with the fielder throwing the ball, step out to your glove side and hold up your glove as a target for the thrower.

When receiving throws from infielders to make a tag at a base, stand over the base, straddling it at an angle facing toward the thrower as long as you have a clear line of sight with the thrower. By doing so, you give the runner a chance to reach the bag without running into you. (We don't recommend trying to block the base and risking injury.) For example, when making a tag at second base on a throw from right and right-center field, straddle the base facing toward right field, and when receiving a throw from left and left-center field, stand on the right-field side of the base facing toward left field, as shown in figure 6.19.

One mistake to avoid is positioning yourself several feet from the base to avoid contact with the runner. The throwing fielder assumes that you're on the base and throws to you, but now you're out of position to make the tag on close plays.

OK, you avoid making that mistake, and you're in a good position to catch the ball to make the tag. Now the priority is to catch the ball. One of the more common errors in making a tag play is taking your eye off the ball just as you are about to catch it or beginning to move the glove to make the tag before you catch the ball. So remember, catch the ball and then make the tag. If the throw is offline, move to catch the ball first and then come back to the base to make the tag if possible.

FIGURE 6.19 Preparing to tag a runner at second base. *(a)* When making a tag at second base on a throw from right or right-center field, straddle the base and face toward the thrower. *(b)* On a throw from left or left-center field, stand on the right-field side of the base turned toward the thrower.

The one-handed tag, sometimes called the sweep tag, is the most common way of tagging out runners. You catch the ball in the glove, squeeze it shut, and place the tag on the runner (see figure 6.20*a*). The less commonly used two-handed tag is preferred because the runner is less likely to knock the ball out of your glove. When you have sufficient time, you catch the ball, place your other hand over the glove that's squeezed shut on the ball, and then apply the tag (see figure 6.20*b*).

FIGURE 6.20 Tagging runners. *(a)* For a one-handed tag, with the ball in the glove, place the tag on the runner sliding into a base. *(b)* For the more secure two-handed tag, place your hand over the squeezed glove and tag the runner.

If the runner is sliding into the base, place the glove in front of the base and let the runner slide into the glove. When the runner makes contact with the glove, don't keep your arms or wrists rigid. Let them absorb the impact to avoid having the ball jarred loose or injuring yourself. If the runner is coming into a base and not sliding, if you have time take one step toward the runner and to the side so that he or she cannot sneak a foot onto the bag before you tag him or her. Make that step slightly to one side so that you avoid a collision with the runner. Then tag the runner anywhere between the waist and chest, and again let your arms and wrist absorb the impact. Don't tag the runner on the legs or arms because you're more likely to have the ball knocked out of your glove. One last point is to keep the tag on runners for a moment because they may over-slide the base or overrun it.

POSITION PLAY

With practice and feedback you've developed the basic defensive skills of fielding, throwing, and tagging runners. Now let's apply those skills as we look at how to play each infield position. We'll review the typical and sometimes atypical plays that you'll see at each position, describe how to make them, and identify mistakes to avoid. We'll also remind you of your responsibilities in backing up plays at various bases.

Playing First Base

Typically, first basepersons are left-handed, which makes it easier to catch balls in the 3-4 hole. Often, first basepersons are taller and less mobile than players in other positions. Ideally, they are sure handed in fielding both good and poor throws and have quick reactions to field hard-hit balls by left-handed batters.

Receiving Throws at First

The most common play for a first baseperson is catching a throw from one of the other infielders for a force-out at first base. We'll describe how to make this play (we'll assume that you're a left-handed first baseperson), and then you can see it done in Defense→Infielder Skills→Receiving Throws at First on the DVD.

1. Position your feet as shown in figure 6.21 as the throw is being made.

2. Read the throw to determine whether it is on or off target.

3. Adjust your feet based on the anticipated location of the throw.

– If the throw is on target the left foot reaches back to touch the base as the right hand catches the ball. If the play will be close, a stretch out toward the throw will allow you to make the catch a few milliseconds faster and perhaps favorably influence the umpire's decision to call the batter–runner out (see figure 6.22).

– If the throw is low, especially if it is in the dirt, assume a good fielding position that is a well balanced and has a low center of gravity with the glove near the ground (see figure 6.23).

– If the throw is wide toward the home side of first, shift your feet so that your left foot is on the front inside corner of the bag and take as big a crossover step with your right foot as needed to reach and catch the ball backhanded, as shown in figure 6.24. Alternatively, if the throw is so far wide that you must leave the base, then catch the ball and attempt to tag the batter–runner as he or she passes by.

– If the throw is wide to the right-field side of the base, slide your feet toward right field, place your left foot on the back inside corner of the base, and step with your right foot toward right field as far as needed to reach the ball, as shown in figure 6.25.

– If the throw is high but you can reach it without jumping, step on top of the bag with your left foot and as you reach up push up onto your toes without leaving the base (see figure 6.26). If the throw is higher, be prepared to jump and hope to return to the base before the runner touches the base.

One mistake you want to avoid is stretching out for a throw too soon. When you do so you lose your ability to adjust to a throw. For example, the second baseperson is relaying the ball for a double play and you're eager to stretch to save a little time. You lunge out toward second, but the ball is thrown 5 feet (1.50 m) to the right-field side of first. You won't be able to catch that ball, but if you had waited to see that the throw was going to be wide, you could easily have stepped toward right field to catch it.

FIGURE 6.21 The left-handed first baseperson sets up at the base by placing the left foot on the base and the right foot parallel with the left in a well-balanced stance ready to move right or left.

FIGURE 6.22 On-target throw. Stretch out by keeping the left foot on the base and stepping directly toward the thrown ball.

FIGURE 6.23 Low throw. Make a long stretch to prevent the ball from hitting the ground while keeping the left foot on the base.

FIGURE 6.24 Wide throw to the home plate (left) side. Shift the left foot to the front corner of the base and step across with the right leg to reach out and catch the ball.

FIGURE 6.25 Wide throw to the outfield (right) side. Slide the left foot to the inside back corner of the base and step out and reach as far as needed to catch the ball.

FIGURE 6.26 High throw. Step on the base to gain a little advantage in reaching for the ball and go up on your toes as you stretch upward.

A critical decision to make when receiving throws at first base is when to leave the base to make the catch. Of course, it is preferable to catch the ball even when it has pulled you off the bag than to let it get past you, allowing runners to advance another base or two. Knowing when to leave the bag and when you can stretch and reach it comes through practice and game experience.

Fielding Plays at First

Next is a series of play situations for the first base position. Read the description and think through how you would make these plays. You can also watch Defense→Infielder Skills→Fielding Plays at First for a demonstration of the second and third plays.

Batter Hits a Single When a batter hits a ball that is clearly a single, you have the responsibility of moving to first base for a possible throw from the relaying infielder. For some unknown reason we see many first basepersons who become spectators and don't cover the base. When smart base runners see this mistake they know that they can round first farther and be in a better position to advance to second base if a fielder bobbles the ball. Always go back to first whenever you expect a runner will be at first. Always! And if it looks as if a throw may come to you as the runner retreats to first, take a position on the base that gives you a good visual line with the infielder or outfielder throwing the ball to you.

Ground Ball to First, No One on Base After you field the ball you must immediately decide whether you can run to the base before the batter–runner arrives or whether you must toss the ball to the pitcher, who should be coming to cover the base. That decision depends on your location when you catch the ball and the speed of the runner. Of course, the safest thing to do is to run to first if you are certain that you'll win the race with the batter–runner. If you do have to throw the ball to the pitcher, it's best to use the dart throw or the underhand toss (see figure 6.27). Remember to get the ball to the pitcher as quickly as you can to give him or her time to catch the ball and then find the base.

FIGURE 6.27 Ground ball to first, no one on base. After fielding a ground ball, make an underhand toss to the pitcher who is covering first base.

Ground Ball to First, Runner on First or Runners on First and Second
With a runner on first when you're playing well behind the runner, after you field the ball you want to throw to the shortstop covering second base for the

force-out. With less than two outs you may have a chance for a double play, although this double play is difficult to execute in slowpitch because of the shorter bases. As soon as you throw to second you should determine whether you or the pitcher has the best chance to get to first base, and you should let the pitcher know your decision. If there are two outs, you may have a choice of throwing to second for a force-out, running to first base, or tossing the ball to the pitcher covering first base.

With runners on first and second base and less than two outs, you would almost never throw to third base to get a force-out. The only time that you might consider doing so is when the game is on the line and you want to keep the runner off third to prevent the winning run scoring from an outfield sacrifice fly.

Ground Ball to First, Runners on Second or Third   When a ground ball is hit to first with a runner on second, a runner on third, or runners on both second and third but not on first (not a force-out situation), you'll have a decision to make. If a runner breaks for home from third, for example, do you throw home or get the sure out at first? After you field the ball, can you "check" the runner by looking at him or her and appearing ready to throw him or her out and then still get the out at first? Your decision depends on many factors—the game situation, the speed of the runner, and your ability to throw to home.

Ground Ball to First, Bases Loaded   When the bases are loaded with less than two outs, after you catch the ground ball the customary play is to throw home. Then the catcher looks to throw back to first or to third for a double play. On the other hand, depending on the game situation and the location of the hit when you catch it, you may decide to turn a double play by throwing to second and then taking the throw back to first (or having the pitcher take the throw). Or, if you field the ball within a few steps of first, you may be able to step on first and throw home for a double play (either a tag or force play, depending on whether a scoring plate is in use).

Trapping the Base Runner   When you have a runner on first base you'll want to decide whether to play back behind the runner or even with the runner. When you're playing even with the runner and the ball is hit sharply, after you catch it you may be able to tag the runner if he or she doesn't get away from first quickly. You can then step on first for a snappy double play. Even if the runner does get past you, you may get a double play by stepping on first and then throwing to the shortstop covering second, who will then need to tag the runner. (By stepping on first base you remove the force-out at second.)

Backing up the Bases   When you know for certain that you will have no play on runners at first, you should look to back up a base. You're in a good position to back up second base when throws are made from the left side of the field. You also should back up the catcher on throws to home.

Playing Second Base

Second basepersons need to be quick in moving right and left, have soft hands to field the ball, and have a strong arm to relay throws from the outfield. Second basepersons are the relay person on many double plays, so sure hands and a quick release are helpful in making this complex play successful. Read about the following plays and envision yourself executing them.

Ground Ball to Second, No One on Base   With no one on base, after you catch the ball you will, of course, throw to first base. Your target is the chest of the first baseperson. When the ball is hit sharply to you, you may have to give the first baseperson a little time to get to first base before you throw.

Ground Ball to Second, Runner on First   With less than two outs, after you catch the ball you will want to throw as quickly as possible to the shortstop covering second base for a possible double play. Throw to hit the shortstop chest high as he or she is approaching second base (see figure 6.28).

FIGURE 6.28   Ground ball to second, runner on first. After fielding a ground ball, throw the ball to the shortstop chest-high.

If the ball is hit slowly, making it unlikely that you can get a double play, you still want to throw to second if you think that you can force out the runner from first. But if you see that you won't have a play at second base, possibly because you've gone deep into the 3-4 hole to catch the ball, your only play may be a throw to first.

When you have two outs, after fielding the ball, throw the ball to the nearest base—first or second—for the force-out. Some second basepersons in this situation like to take a position in short right-center field. Then when they make the catch they throw out the runner at second base, which the pitcher covers if the shortstop is also playing deep. Playing deep has pluses and minuses. The pluses are that you may have more time to reach a ground ball and you will be able to catch some pop-ups that otherwise would fall in for a hit. The minuses are that (1) you may have to run farther to get to a ground ball than you would if you were playing in closer, (2) if the ball is not hit sharply or you bobble it slightly, you will not be able to throw out the runner going from first to second, and (3) fielding on the grass is generally tougher than fielding on a well-maintained infield.

Ground Ball to Second, Runners on Second or Third   When runners are on second, third, or both bases without a runner on first base (a non-force-out situation), the second baseperson has the same decisions to make as the first baseperson does in this situation. Can you check the runners? If the runners attempt to advance do you attempt to throw them out or get the easier out at first base?

Ground Ball to Second, Bases Loaded   When the bases are loaded, after you field the ball you need to decide whether to throw home or try to turn a double play. That decision will depend on how hard the ball is hit and what the game situation is. If it's the seventh inning, no one is out, and the run on third is the winning run, you have no choice but to throw home. If there is one out, you must decide whether to throw home or attempt a double play. When the game is not on the line and you have a hard-hit ground ball hit directly at you, turning the double play is the preferred option. When there are two outs, after you catch the ball you can throw to first or second, whichever base is easier to throw to.

We review the procedures for executing double plays by the second baseperson and shortstop in the section "Special Plays" in this chapter, beginning on page 150. We also examine the tactics of double plays on pages 197–199 in chapter 8, "Defensive Strategies and Tactics."

Making and Receiving Relay Throws From the Outfield   The second baseperson is responsible for relaying the ball from the right and right-center fielders for a throw to one of the bases. When the ball is hit up the middle the shortstop and second baseperson should agree to let the fielder with the stronger and more accurate throwing arm take the relay. The other person then covers second base. Relays are covered in more detail in chapter 8, page 180.

Whether the ball is thrown directly by the outfielder to second base or by the shortstop relaying it, how you position yourself at second base to receive the relay throw depends on whether the play is a force-out or a tag play. If the play is a force-out, play the base like a first baseperson does, putting one foot on the outfield side of the base and facing the throwing fielder. For a tag play, position yourself as described on pages 137–139, "Tagging Runners," and shown in Defense→Infielder Skills→Tagging Runners on the DVD.

Playing Third Base

Coaches often select players to play third base who have quick reactions, a strong arm to throw across the diamond to first but may not be as mobile as the shortstop or second baseperson. Because most batters are right-handed hitters and right-handed power hitters pull the ball, third base has become known as the hot corner. Read next about the plays made by third basepersons and then practice these plays.

Ground Ball to Third, No One on Base   After you make the catch on a moderate- to hard-hit ball, you'll make an overhand throw to first for the force-out. If the batter tops the ball and hits a slow roller to third, you'll need to charge the ball and will likely throw the ball sidearm or on the run.

For most right-handed third basepersons, one of the toughest plays to make is a ball hit down the third-base line. The play requires a strong lunge with a crossover step with the left foot and a long reach with the glove. Then you must recover quickly from that position to straighten up, plant the right foot, and make a long overhand throw to first.

If you are a mobile third baseperson, you will need some experience to learn how far you can move into the 5-6 hole to field the ball without interfering with routine plays by the shortstop. The general rule is that the third baseperson tries to catch any ball that he or she can reach because the third baseperson is moving toward second base and has an easier throw to second or first compared with the shortstop, who is moving away from those bases when going after a ball in the 5-6 hole.

Ground Ball to Third, Runner on First   With less than two outs you have a double-play situation. You can play moderately deep because you do not need to cover third immediately. When you field the ground ball you'll want to throw the ball to hit the second baseperson in the chest to start the double play. Usually the throw is an overhand throw, but if you've fielded a slowly hit ball in the 5-6 hole you may use a quick sidearm throw from the set fielding position. With two outs you'll have to decide whether to throw to second or to first for the force-out, making that decision based on where you field the ball. Usually second base is the preferred place to throw because it's closer.

Ground Ball to Third, Runners on First and Second   This play situation is interesting with less than two outs. One option is to play deep and, after fielding the ball, to throw to second for an attempted double play. The other option is to play much closer to the baseline between second and third and relatively close to the base. If the ball is hit to you within a few feet of third base, you step on the base and throw to second for the double play. If the ball is hit more than a few feet from third base, however, you won't have time to run to third base and then get the force-out at second. So you would throw the ball to second immediately and try to get the double play from second to first. If the ball is hit slowly and you're certain that you can't execute a double play, then the smart play is to step on third to get the lead out.

Also remember that if the shortstop goes deep into the 5-6 hole to catch the ground ball, making it highly unlikely that a double play can be made, the best throw and perhaps the only throw available to the shortstop is the throw to third base. If you're playing moderately deep, you must immediately decide that the shortstop has a better chance to catch the ball than you do and that you need to sprint to third to be ready to catch the ball from him or her.

When you catch a ground ball with two outs, the location where you catch it will determine whether you run to third for the force-out, throw to second, or throw to first.

Ground Ball to Third, Runners on Second or Third or Both   When runners are on second, third, or second and third (no force-out situation), they are less likely to attempt to advance immediately after the ball is hit. You'll want to check the runners with a quick look and perhaps a fake throw and then throw to first. As you throw to first, however, runners may attempt to advance.

Ground Ball to Third, Bases Loaded   This play is fun when there are less than two outs. If you're not playing too deep and you field the ball without having to move much into the 5-6 hole, the preferred option is to step on third base for the force-out and throw home when you're certain that the runner is going home for a nifty double play that retires the two leading runners (see figure 6.29). If you do have to go into the 5-6 hole to field the ball, you'll do better to throw to second to start the double play.

With two outs you have the option to get a force-out at any base, including home. The safest play is to run to third for the force-out, but if you field the ball too far from the base, you will want to throw to the nearest base for the force-out.

Covering Third Base When runners are on first and second or the bases are loaded and the ball is hit to any other infielder, you must quickly position yourself at third base for a possible throw to third for a force-out. If the throw is from the shortstop or second baseperson who is on the out-field side of the second-to-third baseline, position yourself on the outfield side of the base so that the throw can be made without hitting the runner (see figure 6.30*a*). If the throw is made by the pitcher, catcher, or any other infielder who is located on the infield side of the second-to-third baseline, position yourself on the infield side of third base to offer a clear line of sight and to prevent the throw from hitting the runner (see figure 6.30*b*). Because this play is a force-out, position yourself to make the catch in the same way you would if you were playing first base.

FIGURE 6.29 Ground ball to third, bases loaded. Step on third base and throw home for a double play. If the scoring plate is in use, throw to the catcher standing on the strike mat. If no safety base is used, throw to the catcher, who must tag the runner coming home.

FIGURE 6.30 Positioning of the third baseperson when receiving throws from various positions in the infield and outfield. *(a)* Stand on the outfield side of third base when receiving throws from infielders and outfielders on the left side of the line between second and third base. *(b)* Stand on the home-base side of third base when receiving a throw from right field and infielders who are on the right side of the infield.

On occasion you also may have a force-out at third on a throw from the out-field. Again, you would position yourself to have a good line of sight between you and the outfielder or the relaying infielder.

The most exciting play at third base is a tag play on a runner coming into third. Your position in preparation for the throw is to stand on the home side of third or the left-field side of third depending on the location where the ball will be thrown. You want to give the fielder throwing you the ball a target unobstructed by the runner. If the ball is on target, when you catch it you make the tag as described on page 137, "Tagging Runners," and shown on the DVD.

If the throw is off target, you need to move along the third-base line to get sight of the ball, which is often shielded from your vision by the runner, to make the catch and tag. This play is not easy, and it requires extra concentration to keep your focus on the ball, not the runner. By positioning yourself to one side or the other of the base, you give the runner access to the base and can avoid a collision.

Playing Shortstop

The attributes for playing shortstop are similar to those for playing second base. Shortstops get many balls hit in their direction, so mobility and the ability to catch the ball on the run are useful skills to master. Read through the plays that follow and then practice these skills.

Ground Ball to Short, No One on Base   With no one on base, after you catch the ball you will, of course, throw to first base. When the ball is hit sharply you will have time to make an overhand throw. When the ball is hit up the middle and you make a running catch that puts you on the outfield side of second base, the tough part of the play is stopping your momentum and throwing to first.

Ground Ball to Short, Runner on First   With less than two outs, after you catch the ball you'll quickly throw to the second baseperson to start a double play. The throw should be chest high and to the glove side, if possible. If you field the ball close to second base, you may decide to run to second and then throw to first if in your judgment that will be faster than throwing to the second baseperson.

If the ball is hit slowly, making it unlikely that you can get a double play, you still want to throw to second if you think that you can force out the runner from first. But if you see that you will not have a play at second, your only play will be to throw to first.

When you have two outs, after fielding the ball you'll usually throw to second base because the throw is easier. In this situation some shortstops like to take a position in short left-center field. Then, when they make the catch, they throw the runner out at second base, which is covered by the pitcher if the second baseperson is also playing deep. See the comments on pages 143–145 in "Playing Second Base" for the pluses and minuses of playing deep when you have a runner on first and two outs.

Ground Ball to Short, Runners on First and Second   With less than two outs and runners on first and second base, where you decide to throw depends on how hard the ball is hit and where you make the catch. If you get the ball quickly, you'll want to start a double play from second to first. If the ball is hit slowly or you catch it deep in the 5-6 hole, your better play is to throw the ball to third base to force out the leading runner. If the ball is hit up the middle and you're able to catch it, even if you're sure you won't have time for a double play, you should pitch the ball to the second baseperson covering second base because you probably won't be able stop and throw back to third in time for a force-out.

Ground Ball to Short, Runners on Second or Third   When you have runners on second, third, or both bases in a non-force-out situation, you'll want to make the play in the same way we described for the third baseperson. Check the runners and then throw to first base.

Ground Ball to Short, Bases Loaded   You have the same decisions to make that the second baseperson does when the bases are all occupied. You'll definitely throw home with no outs and the winning run on third. When the runner on third is not the winning run with no outs or one out, you must decide whether to throw home or attempt a double play. If you're confident that you can execute the double play, it's the preferred action.

Making and Receiving Relay Throws From the Outfield   The shortstop is responsible for relaying the ball from the left and left-center fielders for a throw to one of the bases. And when balls are hit up the middle the shortstop and second baseperson must decide who will take the relay and who will cover second base. The shortstop receives the relay throw from the outfield in exactly the same way that the second baseperson does. So review that section on page 145.

Playing Catcher

Without a doubt, catching is the easiest defensive position to play, so often the catcher is a power hitter who is less mobile or doesn't have good fielding skills. Although the position is easier to play than the others, the catcher must make a few plays that can be critical to the success of the team. Read about these plays then see them executed on the DVD (Defense→Infielder Skills→Plays at Catcher).

Pop-Ups   In slowpitch it makes no sense for catchers to squat behind the plate or strike mat as they do in fastpitch or baseball. Stand up and back as far as the umpire will let you so that you are in a better position to catch any pop-ups. Know where the umpire is standing so that he or she does not obstruct you when going after the ball. Keep in mind that you'll often be fielding a pop-up near the backstop or sideline fences. So practice going to the fence, finding it with your throwing hand, and then catching the ball (see figure 6.31). Stay on your toes when catching the ball so that your eyes don't bounce.

FIGURE 6.31   To catch a foul ball near the fence, use the throwing arm to feel for the fence while keeping your eyes on the ball.

Dribblers   When a batter hits a ball that dribbles 10 to 20 feet (3 to 6 m) out in front of home plate, pounce on it like a cat and throw the ball to the base where you have the best chance to make an out. If no one is on base, of course, you must throw to first. If runners are on base, you may have an opportunity to force out the leading runner, depending on how quickly you are able to field the ball.

Force-Outs and Tag Plays at Home If you're playing with the separate scoring plate and the commitment line, when you have a force-out play at home you'll want to stand on the plate or the strike mat. (Currently, some rules require that you stand on home plate and not on the strike mat placed behind the plate. Other rules, especially those that use a strike mat that covers home plate, permit the catcher to stand anywhere on the strike mat for a force-out. So know your rules.) In this position, you'll make the play at home just as the first baseperson does at first. Of course, you hope that the throw will be on target to you. If it isn't, you'll shift and stretch as the first baseperson does.

You also face the decision about stretching for the ball or leaving home plate to catch the ball and prevent runners from advancing another base or two. That decision will depend mostly on what the game situation is and whether other runners are on the bases in position to advance should you not be able to catch the ball.

If you're catching without the separate scoring plate you'll have to tag the runner out at home unless the bases are loaded and the play is a force-out. When tagging a runner at home you'll do so in the way described in "Tagging Runners," pages 137–139, and shown on the DVD. But watch out for runners who are seeking to force a collision with you in order to knock the ball loose when you make the tag.

Double Plays With less than two outs and the bases loaded, if the ball is hit hard to the first baseperson, third baseperson, or pitcher, one option for them is to throw home. You then relay it to third or first, whichever base offers the best chance of getting a force-out. To make this play, stand on the front of the plate or strike mat and make a quick relay throw just as the shortstop or second baseperson would when turning a double play at second base.

SPECIAL PLAYS

In this section we examine the conventional second-to-first double play and the rundown of a trapped base runner.

Second-to-First Double Plays

When a runner is on first with less than two outs, you have the potential for a double play, which is a backbreaker to the offense when successfully executed. In this section we describe the technique for executing the conventional second-to-first double plays, and in chapter 8 we consider the tactics associated with these and other less routine double plays. Read this section and then watch Defense→Infielder Skills→Second-to-First Double Plays on the DVD.

We'll call the person who takes the throw at second the relay person. The general rule for determining who takes the throw at second is that if the batter is right-handed the second baseperson covers, and if the batter is left-handed the shortstop covers (the thinking being that right-handed batters are more likely to hit to the shortstop and left-handed batters to hit to the second baseperson).

If the infield captain knows that a batter tends to hit to the opposite field, he or she may reverse the general rule, making sure that all infielders and the pitcher know who is covering second base.

Also note another exception to the general rule when pitchers field balls hit to their right or left. Let's say that the second baseperson, shortstop, and pitcher agree that the second baseperson will cover second base. A ground ball is hit in the 1-4 hole (between the pitcher and the second baseperson), and the pitcher makes an excellent lunging catch. He turns to throw to the second baseperson, but he's not on second base because he too was moving to field the ball. So in this case the shortstop needs to recognize that the second baseperson won't be able to cover second base and take the throw from the pitcher. The same adjustment needs to be made when the shortstop is to cover second base and the ball is hit in the 1-6 hole. The shortstop may not be in a position to cover second base, and thus the second baseperson needs to cover.

Milliseconds make the difference in executing the double play, so many little actions need to be performed quickly and correctly to produce a successful double play. As a hedge the second baseperson and shortstop should play closer to second so that one of them can reach second base quickly to take the relay throw from the infielder throwing the ball. Ideally, the relay person should reach second base before catching the ball, but often the player must catch the ball while sprinting to the base. The throw from the fielder to the relay person should be chest high and should not force the relay person to lunge for the ball and possibly collide with the oncoming runner.

Figure 6.32 shows the footwork at second base when the second baseperson is the relay fielder. For the shortstop the footwork and throw for turning the double play is shown in figure 6.33.

Here are some keys tips for turning double plays successfully:

- If you are the relay infielder it's much easier to relay the ball if you can get to the base before you have to catch the ball, or if you can catch the ball

FIGURE 6.32 Footwork of the second baseperson turning a 6-4-3 double play. *(a)* As you approach the base, step on second base with the right foot, with the left foot on the first-base side of second. *(b)* After catching the ball, push off with the right foot and stride toward first to make the throw.

FIGURE 6.33 Footwork of shortstop turning a 4-6-3 double play. *(a)* Place the right foot on the back side of second base and the left foot to the right-field side. *(b)* As you catch the ball drag the right foot across the base, moving toward the outfield side of second, and then *(c)* bring the right foot up to the left foot and step with the left toward first base as you make the throw.

well before getting to the base. When you have to catch the ball and step on the base at the same time, and especially if the base runner is sliding into the base, it's easy to lose concentration on the thrown ball.

- You must be quick to turn a double play (you typically have between 3 and 4 seconds to execute the play), but don't rush so much that you err in fielding or throwing the ball, resulting in getting no outs and allowing runners to advance a base or two. Remember the speed-accuracy tradeoff; take a little speed off to be sure to get at least one out.

- When fielding the ball for a double play, don't look up to see where the runner is. Watch the ball come into your glove.

- Errant throws are a common cause of unsuccessful double plays. Even if the relay person can catch the ball, if the throw is low, high, or wide, it will take too much time to catch the ball and make the relay throw to complete the play successfully.

- If the fielder is relatively close to the relay person, don't throw the ball so fast that the fielder can't react to the throw.

- The relay person should be careful not to reach into the glove to throw before the ball is in the glove. That is a frequent cause of misses and broken fingers.

Rundowns

When you have a runner caught between the bases you want to run him or her down with the minimum throws possible to keep other runners from advancing. Read the description of how to do so and then watch Defense→Infielder Skills→Rundowns on the DVD.

The infielder with the ball should run at the trapped runner in such a way to encourage him or her to run back to the base that the runner just passed. The ideal play is that the infielder with the ball tags the runner without having to throw, but if the infielder has to throw, he or she should run hard at the runner and then use the dart throw (figure 6.13) to throw the ball to the fielder covering the base. The throw should arrive in time for the receiver to make the tag but not so soon that the runner can stop and change directions. The fielder catching the ball should be two to three steps in front of the base and should begin running at the runner as he or she catches the ball.

To avoid hitting the runner with the ball, the throwing fielder should have a good line of sight with the receiver. The throwing fielder should avoid throwing over the runner. The fielder making the tag should try to do so with the ball in the glove and the other hand preventing it from popping loose.

The rotation for the fielders executing a rundown is shown in figure 6.34. Fielder 1 (F1) starts with the ball and runs toward the runner (R). After throwing the ball to F2, F1 runs in the direction in which the throw was made, running to the outside of the basepath, to be in position to help in the rundown should it continue. After the ball is thrown the infielder cannot stay in the basepath because the runner can force a collision and be called safe for obstruction by the infielder. F2 then tries to tag R but if unable to do so throws to F3 and then rotates in the direction in which the throw was made, running to the outside of the basepath as shown.

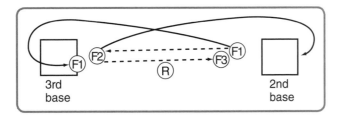

FIGURE 6.34 Rundown rotation to tag a trapped base runner.

THE THINKING INFIELDER

As you can see, you can't play the infield well without having your head in the game. On every pitch you need to know the possible plays that you may have to make. Your internal self-talk may go something like this if you're playing shortstop:

- "This batter likes to hit up the middle. I'll play my regular position, but as he begins to swing I'll shift over a step or two toward the middle."
- "If the ball is hit to my right, when I catch it I'll probably have to throw to third base."
- "If it's hit directly to me or to my left, I'll pitch it to the second baseperson to start a double play."
- "If it's hit to the pitcher, second baseperson, or first baseperson, I've got to cover second. Get there quickly."

Engage in that talk with yourself before the batter steps into the box to hit and then shift your concentration totally to the batter, watching the swing so that you can get a jump on the direction in which the ball is hit. Relax your mind for a moment between pitches. Then as the ball is being pitched, again rivet your attention on the batter.

One of the hallmarks of excellent defensive teams is how well they communicate with each other. Reminders of what each other has to do for certain defensive plays may be verbal, and others are subtle nonverbal gestures and looks that alert each other to possible plays. Each of you as infielders has a responsibility to communicate with teammates by reminding each other of such things as how many outs there are, who the relay person will be at second base, and who will take the relay from the outfield when the ball is hit up the middle. When there are two outs, be sure that all infielders know whether the pitcher is covering second base.

SUMMARY

- Catching the ball is an essential skill of the sport, but many conditions can make catching a ball difficult. Infielders must learn to catch hard-hit ground balls, throws wide of their mark, and soft tosses while on the run with a base runner charging at them.
- When ground balls are hit close to you, assume a good ready position and play the ball to catch it in line with the foot on the glove-hand side.
- Develop the skills to field balls to your right and left and to charge in on slow ground balls.
- Learn how to field balls that are in the sun, influenced by the wind, popped up near the fence, and hit high in the air and pursued by several fielders.
- Infielders use five types of throws to make various plays—overhand throw, sidearm throw, dart throw, underhand toss, and backhand flip. Know when to use each type of throw and practice each.
- Improve your throwing accuracy through regular practice and by not rushing your throws too much.
- Difficult throws to make include throwing while you're running, throwing to another fielder who is running, and the long throw to a base after a backhand catch.
- Tag runners by straddling the base and then use the two-hand tag if time permits or the sweep tag if it doesn't.
- The second baseperson and shortstop are responsible for the relay throw from the outfield, a play that requires good positioning and an accurate arm.
- Infielders have many different play situations, and they should know the responsibilities of each, when they are likely to occur in a game, and the decisions that they need to make almost instantly as the play unfolds.
- First basepersons can make many more catches at first by learning the proper footwork and when and how to stretch out for throws that are not on target.

- All infielders have the opportunity to execute double plays, which usually entails fielding the ball cleanly and throwing on target to a relay fielder, who must catch and relay the ball quickly and accurately to another fielder, who must catch the ball, all of it done in about 4 to 5 seconds.
- The rundown is a special play that requires coordination among infielders to eliminate confusion and minimize the number of times that the ball must be thrown before the runner is tagged out.
- Besides good fielding and throwing skills, infielders need to have excellent decision-making and communication skills.

CHAPTER 7

Outfielder Skills

So you are or want to be an outfielder. Playing the outfield is a terrific position in slowpitch softball because there is so much action. As an outfielder you'll know not only the joy of catching routine fly balls but also the challenges of snaring bullet line drives that are knuckling, leaping for fly balls at the fence, and diving for bloopers just past the infield. You'll be trying to catch fly balls on the run while avoiding collisions with teammates, and you'll have to make long and accurate throws to the infield to throw out runners. Playing outfield is a challenge, but it is exceptionally rewarding when done well!

FIELDING

First, we look at being ready to catch balls in the outfield, and then we share with you several cues to improve your "reading" skills—your ability to determine quickly where a batted ball will land. Then we look at a variety of fielding plays that you'll be asked to make as you play the game of slowpitch. Read about each of these plays next and then watch the DVD for this chapter to review them in action.

Ready Position

Being in the ready position in the infield is important because the ball can reach an infielder in less than a second. Outfielders have more time and thus don't need to assume the same ready position that infielders do. A comfortable stance that permits you to move quickly in any direction is what you want to take.

Perhaps more important than being physically ready to move to catch the ball should it be hit your way is being mentally ready. That is, you must keep your head in the game by knowing the game situation, adjusting your position for the probable play, and reading the batted ball so that you can get a quick start in moving toward its destination. Let's look at reading the ball now.

Reading the Batted Ball

A subtle skill that is seldom discussed or taught to outfielders is the ability to determine the flight of a batted ball and the optimal route to run to make the catch. Learning to judge the direction and depth of a batted ball, what we call reading the ball, is essential to getting a quick start in pursuit of the ball and running the most direct route to intercept it.

So how do players learn to read the flight of the ball? What are the cues that tell them where the ball will land? We don't fully know how players develop this skill, but obviously it comes with experience in the field and paying attention to the following cues:

- The location of the pitch as it is being hit is a cue. Inside pitches are more likely to be pulled, and outside pitches are more likely to be hit toward center field or the opposite field.
- The batter's stride provides information about which direction the ball will be hit. When batters open up in their swing (right-handed batters turn toward left field, and left-handed batters turn toward right field), they are more likely to pull the ball. When batters remain closed in their swing, they are more likely to hit up the middle or to the opposite field.
- The velocity of the bat swing is a cue about how hard the ball will be hit.
- The sound produced by the impact of the bat on the ball is a cue. Determining how hard the ball was hit used to be easier when we used wooden bats because of the consistent and distinctive sound that a well-hit ball made, but today with the variety of metals and synthetic materials used in bats, it takes a little more listening experience to recognize a sweet-spot hit from an off-center hit.
- Another cue is the early flight of the ball. As the ball leaves the bat, its angle of flight will tip you off about its probable location. Balls going up immediately are likely to be pop-ups; take a few steps in. Balls going down will be ground balls; come in. Balls in between are likely to be hit harder; continue to track the ball and move toward it.

These cues are just that—cues. They give you an approximate idea of where the ball is going so that you can get a quick start in running toward its probable location. As you're running you continue to monitor the flight of the ball, never taking your eyes off it, as you continuously adjust your running route to intercept it.

Catching Routine Fly Balls

A routine fly ball is one that allows you plenty of time to reach the spot where you will catch the ball. Don't meander to the location to catch the ball; get there and get set to catch it. The preferred position to catch a fly ball is slightly above your head and in front of your throwing shoulder. Put your throwing hand next to your glove and use it as insurance to prevent the ball from accidentally dropping out of your glove. This position, as shown in figure 7.1 and

FIGURE 7.1 Catching a fly ball when there's time to set up.

Defense→Outfielder Skills→Catching Fly Balls on the DVD, puts you in good position to transfer the ball to your throwing hand and make a quick release.

When runners are on base and the fly ball is hit far enough that the runners may try to advance, if you have time, position yourself two or three steps behind where the ball will come down and in line with the base to which you will throw. Then time your move to make the catch so that you maintain momentum to make the throw. Watch out that you don't look up to see the runner or start to make the throw before you catch the ball when making this play.

Catching Fly Balls on the Run

The preferred way to catch a fly ball is to move to the location of the ball, get set, and make the catch, but, of course, for many balls hit to the outfield you'll be catching the ball on the run. From the position you take before the ball is hit, to the first movements you make to run to the ball, and to the last stretch you make to catch it, each element can be critical in your reaching and catching the ball. When you fail to reach a ball by a step or two, ask yourself these questions:

- Did I read the ball location correctly so that I got a quick start in its direction?
- Did I pivot right or left quickly to start moving toward the ball?
- Did I hesitate to move, thinking that the adjacent fielder would catch it?
- Did I pace myself, thinking that I would reach the ball, but then realize that it was farther away and fail to reach it, even though I picked up my speed?
- Did I run a direct route or misjudge the location of the ball and have to make an adjustment along the way?

The best way to improve your outfield play is to analyze how you performed on these types of plays. You don't need a coach or teammate to tell you what you know, but you must be honest with yourself. Others may not have seen your late start to the ball or recognize that you weren't running all out, but you know. When you miss a ball by inches, ask yourself the previous questions. If the answer leaves room for improvement, work on making that improvement in practice and in the next game. Watch Defense→Outfielder Skills→Catching Fly Balls to help you improve.

OK, you got a good start, you're running fast, and you can see that you'll reach the ball. Now you must catch it. First, don't reach out with your glove until the very last moment to make the catch. When you reach out too early, you slow down. Second, as you're approaching the ball, continue to run smoothly, especially if you see that you need to slow down so that you don't overrun the ball. When slowing do not brake by landing on the heels of your feet. That technique causes your eyes to bounce so that that the ball looks as if it is jumping. Stay on the balls of your feet to decelerate and brake as smoothly as possible to keep your eyes steady.

Catching Balls in Front of You

As soon as you read that a ball will land in front of you, you charge forward quickly to make the catch. If it is a moderate- to high-fly ball, after you know that you can reach it you should let everyone know that you've got it. You want to avoid any collision with an infielder or your adjacent outfielders. Remember that the outfielder always has the right-of-way on balls hit between the infielder and outfielder because he or she is in a better position to catch the ball. If you know that you can't reach it, let the infielder who is coming out know so that he or she continues to pursue the ball.

On line drive hits in front of you the difficult decision is whether you should try to catch the ball in the air by making a shoestring catch or slow up and let the ball bounce. You'll want to have the game situation in mind as you decide whether to make the difficult catch in the air or let the batter have a hit. If you decide to catch it in the air, you'll want to do all you can to block the ball if you don't reach it when it takes that difficult short hop in front of you.

Diving

Whether the ball is hit in front of you or to one side or the other, at times you'll want to dive for it, which you should view as a desperation act. If you don't make the catch, the ball will likely get by you and go all the way to the fence for a sure triple or inside-the-park home run. If you do make the catch, though, you'll help the team win.

When you decide to dive for the ball, make a skillful dive so that you don't injure yourself. The technique for diving is the same one that infielders use, which we described in chapter 6, page 128 (you can also view this play in Defense→Outfielder Skills→Catching Fly Balls on the DVD). As an outfielder keep these guidelines in mind when you consider diving for the ball:

- Diving on pop-ups in front of you is safer because the ball won't go far behind you.
- Diving is safer when you know that a fellow outfielder is backing you up.
- Diving on balls hit along the foul lines is riskier because you won't have any backup.
- Dive for the ball when missing it won't cost you the game and when not catching it will cost you the game.

Catching Balls Over Your Head

If the ball is not hit too far over your head, you can run backward or backpedal to catch the ball without taking your eye off it. But if the ball is hit deeper than a few steps behind you, you'll want to pivot toward the side where you think the

FIGURE 7.2 Catching a ball hit over the outfielder's head. *(a)* Pivot toward where the ball is expected to be caught, and *(b)* reach for the ball over your shoulder to make the catch.

ball will descend and sprint to that location, as shown in figure 7.2. As you run keep your eyes on the ball so that you can make adjustments in your route as the ball approaches you. Try to get an angle on the ball so that you don't have to catch it directly over your head, which is a much more difficult catch to make. Therefore, try to take a route that maintains that angle.

Of course, the ball doesn't always travel straight because of the wind or the way that the bat sliced the ball. So you may start out pivoting to your left to pursue the ball but see that it is drifting to your right. Now you need to shift from running with your left shoulder toward the infield to running with your right shoulder toward the infield.

One way to switch is called the inside roll. You perform this action by turning toward the infield to change directions, as shown in figure 7.3. The advantage of the inside roll is that you don't have to take your eyes off the ball. The disadvantage is you have to slow down considerably to execute the switch and you risk tripping yourself.

FIGURE 7.3 The inside roll. *(a)* Running to the right, plant the left foot to break your speed, *(b)* then plant the right foot to serve as the pivot foot. *(c)* Swing the left leg around in a reverse pivot, and *(d)* stride out with the right leg to pursue the ball.

The outside roll is a faster alternative. You turn away from the infield and switch to look over one shoulder rather than the other shoulder (see figure 7.4). The disadvantage of the outside roll is that you lose sight of the ball for a moment, but you maintain more speed.

Now watch Defense→Outfielder Skills→Catching Fly Balls to review how to catch balls hit over your head.

FIGURE 7.4 The outside roll. *(a)* Break to the right, looking over your left shoulder. *(b)* To roll, plant the right foot at an angle and use it to pivot to turn to the right. *(c)* At the same time rotate your shoulders to the right and *(d)* quickly change from looking over your left shoulder to looking over your right shoulder as you pursue the ball.

FIGURE 7.5 Right-handed outfielder blocking the ball. Plant the left foot first, kneel with the right leg turned outward somewhat, and place the glove on the ground.

Fielding Ground Balls

How you catch a ground ball depends on where it is hit and how quickly you want to get the ball back into the infield. When you have sufficient time to get to the ball and do not need to hurry a throw into the infield, when the ball is moving fast, or when the field is rough, you should position yourself to block the ball as shown in figure 7.5. By taking this position you reduce the chance that the ball will get by you.

When you don't have sufficient time to block the ball by kneeling, especially if you're playing on uneven turf, then take the same ready position that infielders do to catch the ball. In figure 7.6a you see the conventional way by fielding the ball between the legs and in figure 7.6b you see the player fielding the ball in front of her glove-side foot. This position puts you in a good fielding position, reduces the risk of a bad bounce into your face, and increases the chance that you can block the ball with your foot if it scoots under your glove.

When you must get the ball into the infield quickly, you'll save time by using the one-hand scoop shown in figure 7.7. The most opportune time to make this play is on smooth turf where bounces are predictable and when you know that you have a backup outfielder. You should know the game situation to determine how much of a chance to take in making this play. Be especially cautious of rushing so much and looking up to see where you're going to throw that you forget to watch the ball into your glove.

Now watch Defense→Outfielder Skills→Fielding Ground Balls on the DVD to review.

FIGURE 7.6 Fielding position for an outfielder catching ground balls. (a) The conventional method and (b) the alternative position.

FIGURE 7.7 Outfielder making the one-hand scoop. Charge the ground ball by approaching it on your glove side to scoop it up.

Making Difficult Fielding Plays

Outfielders confront several challenging fielding situations, including line drives and less-than-ideal field and environmental conditions, which we examine now.

Line Drive Hit Directly at You

The line drive hit directly at you is the hardest play to read because you don't have a side perspective that helps you know how hard the ball is hit and whether it will continue on a straight path to you, dip down, or sail up over your head. Sometimes you can tell by the bat contact whether the ball has topspin or backspin. Remember that with topspin the ball will dive down in front of you and with backspin it more likely will lift up and sail over your head.

The adjacent outfielder may be able to help you get a perspective on it by letting you know quickly whether to come in or go back on the ball, but sometimes this hit comes so quickly that there's little time to receive help. If the ball looks as if it will drop in front of you, you have to decide whether to go for the catch or to play it on one or two hops. If the ball looks as if it will sail, you won't have time to run back much, so the best thing to do is to be prepared to jump.

The line drive hit directly at you when the ball is knuckling is without doubt the most difficult ball to catch. The flutter on the ball can cause you to stab at it, which often results in a miss. Instead, watch the ball carefully all the way to your glove and pray!

Windblown Balls

As you take the field each inning you should check the direction of the wind. If the wind is coming in from your position toward the infield, you can position yourself a little closer to the infield than usual. On high fly balls you'll know that the wind will push the ball back toward the infield. In addition, on topspin line drives and even looping line drives, the wind will push the ball down sooner. When the wind is blowing directly toward you, you'll want to play deeper in the outfield and you'll have to make long throws into the wind.

When the wind is blowing across the outfield in the direction of your adjacent outfielder, you'll want to communicate with your teammate to determine who should catch the fly ball. The batted ball may start out as a ball that you should field, but as it continues to drift, it may be best for the adjacent fielder to take it. You'll need to make this judgment as the play unfolds, but it's helpful if you and your fellow fielder have discussed the possibility in advance. Just as you need to let the adjacent fielder take a ball when it moves into his or her zone, you need to be prepared to catch a ball that drifts over to your zone.

When you're playing left field or right field and the wind is blowing across the field toward your foul line, you'll want to adjust your positioning by moving a little closer to the foul line. Then you should expect balls to drift away from you, so you must begin your chase early, moving in the direction of the wind even when the ball starts out directly at you.

Balls in the Sun

As with fly balls in the infield, good sunglasses can help. Using your glove or hand to shade the sun so that you can find the ball is the obvious thing to do (see figure 6.9 on page 129). If the ball is very high, then the adjacent fielder may have time to come over and make the catch from an angle that's not in line with the sun.

Rough Turf

We've already commented on adjusting your fielding technique to the quality of turf that you're playing on. It's a joy to play on a well-maintained outfield where the surface is even and the grass is cut short. Rough surfaces turn a game of skill into a game of chance, but by adapting to the conditions as discussed earlier you can increase the odds a bit in your favor. When the surface is rough and the ball bounces are unpredictable, put yourself in a position to block the ball.

Wet Grass

The toughest part of playing on wet grass is that hard-hit line drives skip off it, shooting by you before you can set up. The ball moves like a puck on the ice. By being aware of this probability you can adjust by setting up quicker and looking for the skip. Wet grass also means that it is harder to gain footing and to start and stop in the outfield. Well-studded shoes will help immensely, and then you need to try to run without making the sharp starts, stops, and cuts that you may normally make.

The Fence

We've seen outfielders who have no fear of the outfield fences, crashing into them at near full speed, and we've seen those who are extremely cautious about approaching the fence in pursuit of the ball. We recommend that you aim between those extremes. Play the fence to avoid injury but learn how to get to the fence quickly and make the catch.

When you judge that the ball is going to be close to the fence, run as fast as you can to the warning track (most fields have one), keeping your eyes on the ball, and then begin to slow down, reaching for the fence with your throwing hand. Then turn toward the infield to prepare for the catch, possibly having to jump for the ball (see figure 7.8 and Defense→Outfielder Skills→Catching Fly Balls on the DVD). Remember this: It's far easier to run to the fence, find it, turn around, and come back toward the infield to catch the ball than it is to turn short of the fence and backpedal to catch it.

FIGURE 7.8 When catching balls at the fence, reach for the fence with the throwing hand while you continue to watch the ball.

THROWING

Outfielders with strong and accurate throwing arms keep base runners from advancing extra bases. In this section we look at the best way to throw, throwing more accurately, and throwing to the correct place.

Overhand Throws

If you read chapter 6, "Infielder Skills," you know that the overhand throw is the preferred way for outfielders to throw because it generates the most velocity and is more accurate for long-distance throws. Once in a while an outfielder may have to use one of the other types of throws that infielders use, but that will occur infrequently.

Review page 131 in chapter 6 and study Defense→Infielder Skills→Types of Throws on the DVD to improve your ability to make strong and accurate overhand throws. The key points of the overhand throw are to grip the ball across the seams and to bring the arm straight over the top. Throw the ball in a straight line or nearly straight line rather than a looping rainbow. When runners see a rainbow, it signals them to advance another base.

If the throw is short to medium distance, use the one-step throwing method. Field the ball with your throwing-side leg forward and then take one step with your other foot to release the ball quickly, as shown in figure 7.9. For longer throws add a crow hop to your step to gain momentum to make a stronger throw. The crow hop is shown in figure 7.10. You can watch a demonstration of both the one-step and crow-hop throwing techniques on the DVD (Defense→Outfielder Skills→Overhand Throws).

If you do not have a strong throwing arm, take these steps to make it stronger. First, begin a strength-training program by consulting one or more of the strength-training references provided in appendix A. Second, throw more and in doing so remember the specificity principle: Practice in the way that you will play. So when you're warming up on the sidelines during practices and games, after 10 to 15 throws at 40 to 60 feet (12 to 18 m), gradually move back, throwing increasingly greater distances. You can't expect to make great 180-foot (55 m) throws in games when in practice you throw only 60 feet.

Trajectory

Observe a few slowpitch softball games and you'll see two trajectories on throws from outfielders. The first is a strong line-drive throw that may have a little arc to reach its destination. That's the preferred way to throw. The second, the rainbow, is a high, arcing throw that some outfielders will make because they want to throw the ball on the fly all the way to a base or perhaps because they don't know better. The rainbow throw takes longer to get to its intended receiver, and it signals base runners behind the base to which the ball is being thrown to advance because the ball cannot be cut off by a relay person. The trajectories of these two throws are shown in figure 7.11.

Accuracy

Maybe you've seen an outfielder who appears to have a rifle for an arm, but when he or she pulls the trigger you see that it's really a shotgun. Although the player's arm is strong, the throws spray all over. Just as you want to improve the strength of your arm so that you can generate more velocity on the ball, you want to develop your ability to throw accurately to be successful in outfield play. Remember the speed–accuracy tradeoff that we discussed regarding hitting in chapter 2. Strong, inaccurate throws don't stop base runners from advancing. Throws with a little less velocity but on target do result in outs and keep runners from advancing. Accuracy comes with practice and knowing where to throw, which we examine next.

FIGURE 7.9 One-step throwing method. (a) Field the ball with the throwing-side leg forward, then (b) take one step with the other foot to release the ball quickly.

FIGURE 7.10 The crow hop. (a) Field the ball on your glove side with the glove-side leg back and then (b) quickly hop forward by pushing up with the throwing-side leg and turn sideways to position yourself to throw. (c) Next, plant the throwing-side foot and stride forward with the glove-side leg to execute a powerful overhand throw.

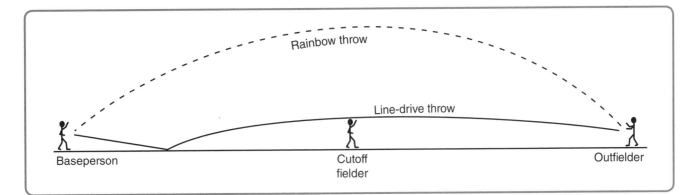

FIGURE 7.11 The trajectories of line-drive and rainbow throws from outfielders to infielders.

Where to Throw

You're playing left-center field with a runner on first base and one out. The batter hits a ground ball through the infield, which you field. As you look up, the runner on first is rounding second and heading for third. The batter–runner is rounding first. Do you throw to third to try to get the out, or do you play it safe and throw to second to prevent the batter–runner from advancing? The best outcome would be that you throw to third and get the runner out. The worst outcome would be that you throw to third, fail to get the runner out, and allow the batter–runner to reach second. How do you know where to throw? It's a judgment call on your part about the probability of throwing out the runner going to third versus keeping the batter–runner on first to retain the double-play possibility.

These are the kinds of decisions that you must make in the outfield, often under considerable pressure. Through experience in playing the game you'll learn just how far a runner can be from a base and how far you are from that base (knowing your throwing ability) to know whether throwing there is the smart play. Also, because you're watching the ball to field it, your fellow outfielders should be telling you which base to throw to. Likewise, after you catch the ball the relay infielder should be letting you know where to throw. So although in the end the decision is yours, you should be receiving help from your teammates.

Although no absolutes govern where to throw the ball, usually you will try to throw to get the lead runner out or prevent that runner from advancing to the next base. And if you can't do that, you try to get the trailing runner out or prevent him or her from advancing to the next base.

Another key principle is to get the ball into the infield quickly. Don't hold the ball because you don't know where to throw and definitely don't challenge the runner by holding the ball and daring him or her to try to advance on your awesome arm. Make sure that you know the game situation, especially the number of outs. An infrequent but annoying mistake occurs when an outfielder catches a fly ball and mistakenly thinks that it is the third out, letting a runner advance or worse score because he or she didn't throw the ball in quickly.

You can make the difficult decisions about where to throw easier if before each batter you review the likely or probable throws that you would make for various types of balls hit to you. You'll consider the game situation (inning, score, outs), the speed of the runners, and whatever you know about the batter. Your thinking might go something like this:

- "If the ball is a grounder, I'll charge it and look for a possible throw to home."
- "If the ball is a deep fly ball, I'll relay to the second baseperson."
- "If the ball is to my left I'll look to throw out the runner at second, but if it is to my right I'll try to throw out the runner at third."

Outfielders will have a few unusual opportunities to throw runners out. Consider these examples:

- When a ball is hit to you in right field and the batter is loafing to first, you may be able to charge the ball and throw the batter out at first.
- With a runner on first base, a short fly ball drops in front of you in right-center field. The runner can go only about halfway because he or she is

uncertain about whether you'll catch the ball. When it drops you pick it up quickly and throw to second for the force-out. Or, if you catch the ball you may be able to throw out the runner at first.

- You field a ball shallow in the outfield. The runner at a nearby base concludes that the play is over and turns away from you, but the umpire has not yet called time-out. With an alert infielder covering the base, you make a quick throw to catch the runner sleeping.

OTHER OUTFIELD RESPONSIBILITIES

Infielders like to tell outfielders how easy they have it. Just catch the ball and throw the ball. That's all there is to it! But outfielders know better. They have to do a lot of running, have difficult plays to make, and have additional responsibilities that we'll consider now.

Backing Up Plays

You want to back up your fellow outfielders because at times they'll miss fielding a ball. When you're the closest fielder to the player fielding the ball, you have the backup responsibility. Although you may have confidence in the sure hands of your teammate, and you're tired from all the running because this is your third game of the day, you can't shirk your responsibility. Sprint to a spot about 20 feet (6 m) behind the fielder to catch any balls that happen to slip by him or her. He or she will appreciate the help, and when a ball slips by you, you'll appreciate your teammate's support.

You also should be prepared to back up the infielder in front of you. Too often outfielders assume that infielders will catch the ball, so they do not move until they see the ball coming to the outfield. Those outfielders are not fulfilling their backup responsibilities. Anytime the ball is hit to the infielder in front of you, you should be immediately moving in for a possible backup play.

You also have responsibilities for backing up throws to the bases when the direction of the throw is such that an errant throw would bring the ball into your outfield area. Here are some common backup plays that you should anticipate and move to back up.

- **Right fielder.** The catcher, pitcher, or third baseperson throws the ball wide to first. It hits the sideline fence and rolls along the fence into right field.
- **Right fielder and right-center fielder.** The third baseperson or shortstop throws wide to second.
- **Right-center fielder and left-center fielder.** The catcher or pitcher throws errantly to second base.
- **Left-center fielder and left fielder.** The first baseperson or second baseperson throws wide to second base.
- **Left fielder.** The catcher, pitcher, or first baseperson throws inaccurately to third base.

Frankly, in slowpitch, outfielders rarely make the extra effort to back up those errant infield throws by anticipating them and moving into a position to retrieve

Right fielder backing up first base on an overthrow.

the ball quickly and minimize the damage from the overthrow. Without a doubt, it takes a lot more effort on top of a lot of running in the outfield anyway. But if you want to be excellent, backing up the infield is one of those little things that can make the difference between winning and losing a close game.

Communicating

As in the infield, good defensive team play requires effective communication in the outfield. Throughout this chapter we've noted when it is important for outfielders to communicate with their fellow outfielders and infielders. Let's look at these situations more closely now.

Positioning

Outfielders should not think of themselves as playing independent positions, but as being dependent on others to play effectively as a single large unit. How one fielder positions him- or herself influences the other positions. Thus all the outfielders must communicate and agree on how they will position themselves for each batter. To facilitate that communication, a person should be designated to coordinate the outfield positioning. The coach could do it from the sidelines, or an infielder could do it, but we think that the best approach is to designate an outfielder to coordinate positioning.

Deciding Who Will Catch Fly Balls

The batter hits a long fly ball deep between the left-center fielder and right-center fielder. Both are in pursuit, each intensely focused on the ball. Just as they are about to catch it they collide. Both players are down, fortunately with only bumps and bruises. The cause? A failure to communicate!

The batter lofts a high pop-up into shallow left-center field. The left fielder and left-center fielder both charge in, and the shortstop is racing out. No one calls for the ball, but each player catches a glimpse of the other fielders and hears them charging. All three stop to avoid the collision, and the ball drops in for a hit. Again, a failure to communicate!

Every team should have unambiguous communication rules regarding who will catch fly balls. Here are our recommendations:

- **Rule 1.** The fielder who is in the best position to catch a fly ball should catch it. That fielder should yell, "I got it" as soon as he or she makes that judgment. The adjacent fielder should then move into a backup position and avoid getting too close to the fielder catching the ball so as not to distract him or her.

- **Rule 2.** When both fielders have an equal chance to catch the ball or it is unclear who will be able to catch it, the fielder who first declares, "I got it" has the green light to catch the ball, with the one exception stated in rule 3.

- **Rule 3.** The outfielder who is assigned priority may overrule or call off the outfielder without priority by declaring, "I got it." Who is the priority outfielder? The coach should establish the priorities among the outfielders, but if he or she doesn't you and your fellow outfielders can establish who the priority fielders are. For example, if most of the outfielders are right-handed and therefore catch with the left hand, and given that catching with a forehand is generally considered easier than catching with a backhand, and also considering that often the best fielding outfielders are in left and left center, a sensible priority would be that the outfielder to the right when facing the infield has priority over the outfielder to the left. So this rule means that the left fielder can call off the left-center fielder, the left-center fielder calls off the right-center fielder, and the right-center fielder calls off the right fielder. Another possibility is to assign priorities based on the coach's judgment about who the strongest outfielders are. For example, you could give the left fielder priority over left-center fielder and give the right-center fielder priority over the left-center fielder and right fielder. The key point here is to establish priorities for which outfielders may overrule other outfielders on fly balls.

- **Rule 4.** Outfielders always have priority over infielders in catching fly balls. The reason for this rule is obvious; outfielders are in a better position to make a catch coming in than infielders are going out.

Now let's apply these rules to a pop-up hit directly over second base in shallow center field. The left-center fielder, right-center fielder, shortstop, and second baseperson all have a chance to catch the ball.

- **Scenario 1.** The second baseperson sprints out and yells first, "I got it." The outfielders see that the second baseperson is in a good position to catch it and don't overrule him or her, so they take up backup positions in case the ball is missed.

- **Scenario 2.** The shortstop runs out for the ball and yells, "I got it," but the left-center fielder sees that he or she can catch the ball and yells, "No, I got it." The shortstop immediately gives way and lets the left-center fielder make the catch.

- **Scenario 3.** The right-center fielder calls for the ball. Both infielders immediately peel off and look to back up the play. Suddenly the left-center fielder yells, "I got it." If, as suggested above, the left-center fielder is the priority fielder, then the right-center fielder immediately moves out of the way and relinquishes the catch to the left-center fielder.

Throwing to the Infield

Each outfielder has the responsibility to help the fielding outfielder know where to throw the ball. To avoid giving mixed messages, the outfielder backing up the play or the outfielder closest to the fielding player should have the sole responsibility for instructing the fielder where to throw. Those instructions may be to hit the relay infielder, preferably using his or her name, or to throw to a specific base.

Judging the Depth of a Hit

We noted how difficult it is to know how deep some balls are hit, especially those hit directly at you. The adjacent fielder who has the side perspective can help the fielding outfielder with the depth of the ball by instructing him or her to charge in or sprint back. If the fielder is going back, the adjacent fielder is responsible for helping the fielding player know how close he or she is to the fence.

Game-Situation Reminders

As a game moves on or when you play multiple games in one day, you may lose your concentration. Thus all outfielders should remind each other of the game situation, information about the batter, and possible plays that may occur. Here are some possible communications:

- "We've got one out and a runner on first."
- "There are two strikes on the batter. If the ball is in foul territory, let it drop so that the runner can't advance."
- "She is really fast. Get the ball to second in a hurry."
- "This guy usually hits the ball down the line."
- "Watch the wind. It's really pushing the ball toward right."

Knowing the Rules

Of course, you need to know the few rules that apply to outfield play. A major one is to know whether a third-strike foul is an out. In most leagues and tournaments it is. So knowing that, if you're playing left field or right field you don't want to catch a third-strike foul when runners are on base because they can then advance.

When there is no fence along the foul lines, a line is often drawn about 20 to 30 feet (6 to 9 m) in foul territory and parallel with the foul line. This line is the out-of-bounds demarcation. You should know what the consequence is if you catch a ball within foul territory but then cross over the out-of-bounds line. Usually the rule is that the ball is dead and each base runner advances one base. If you don't catch the ball, the ball is dead and runners do not advance.

The other rule to know is what happens when the ball gets stuck in a fence or goes under a fence. You should hold up your hands immediately so that the umpire can make a judgment about the positions that the runners get when the ball is stuck or goes under the fence.

SUMMARY

- Improve your ability to judge the flight of the ball by reading the cues provided by the batter.
- When you can be stationary, catch fly balls slightly above your head and in front of your throwing shoulder.
- When you are running to catch fly balls, run smoothly and reach for the ball at the last moment. If you need to slow down as you reach the ball, avoid braking by a heel–toe foot strike. Stay on the balls of your feet.
- Learn to judge whether to try to catch a line drive hit directly at you or to let it bounce and catch it on one or two hops.
- Learn when it is worth diving for a ball, and when it is, how to dive safely.
- Practice catching balls over your head by turning to the right or left when running back and learn how to execute an inside and outside roll to shift running positions.
- When time permits, field ground balls by taking a blocking position. When you do not have time, use the running one-hand scoop to field the ball.
- Take extra precautions when fielding windblown balls, balls in the sun, balls landing on wet grass and rough turf, and balls hit near the fence.
- When throwing from the outfield you should use the overhand throw predominantly, and you should work in practice to improve your accuracy.
- Knowing where to throw the ball requires good judgment and assistance from your teammates, who should tell you where to throw while you are focusing on catching the ball.
- Know the opportunities to throw runners out from the outfield in unusual situations.
- Remember that you have backup responsibilities not only to your fellow outfielders but also to the infielders.
- Communicating with your fellow outfielders and infielders improves your team defense and prevents collisions. Establish communication rules regarding who will catch fly balls.
- Know the rules that pertain to playing the outfield.

CHAPTER 8

Defensive Strategies and Tactics

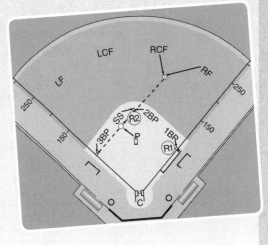

After defeating a considerably younger team for the Vintage Softball Championship in Honolulu, Hawaii, we were visiting with our opponents in the parking lot when one of their players commented, "You can sure tell that you guys have played together before." He recognized and appreciated the defensive team play of our Florida Legends team. When a ball was hit to the outfield, our outfielders made accurate throws to the relay person, who was correctly positioned to throw the ball to keep the runners from advancing an extra base. Our pitcher covered first base on balls hit to the first baseman and backed up the appropriate base on other plays. And when the opportunity presented itself, we were in position to execute double plays.

Playing in a local league, on the other hand, with a runner on first and a ground ball hit to right field, our right fielder threw a looping ball, a rainbow, toward third base in attempt to get the runner from first out, but because the throw was high and not accurate, there was no chance to get the runner. And guess where the batter ended up? On second base, of course, because he saw that the second baseman or shortstop could not cut off the throw. The poor throw not only failed to put out the leading runner but also let the batter gain an extra base and removed the chance to get a force-out at second base.

Defensive team strategies are about using the available information, either before or during the game, to make decisions that minimize the opportunity for the opposing team to score. The idea is to play the percentages so that they are in your favor. Strategies or tactics will not always work, but the odds are that they will.

Good execution of defensive tactics forces the offensive team to combine several hits to score a run by not letting runners advance more than what the hit earned. Poor defensive tactics permit the offensive team to take extra bases and take away the force-out at second and third base.

In chapter 6 we covered many defensive decisions that players should make for each infield position, and we did the same in chapter 7 for outfielders. Here in chapter 8 we'll look at how the team works together to play smart team defense. We'll focus on various defensive team strategies, tactical positioning of the defense, executing relays and cutoffs, the tactics of double plays and some other special defensive plays, and coordinating communication.

The factors to consider as your team contemplates defensive team strategies include the following:

1. The defensive ability of your players and the positions to which they are assigned
2. The offensive abilities of your opponents, considering both their strengths and weaknesses
3. The playing field, especially the distance to the fences
4. The environmental conditions (wind, rain, and so on)

Based on these factors here on some examples of defensive strategies that your team may adopt:

- The offensive team has good place hitters but little power. Your team strategy will be to have the outfielders play shallower than usual, accepting that a few extra-base hits may occur in exchange for catching more line-drive fly balls.
- The offensive team does not run well, so the infield will play a little deeper in double-play situations.
- The offensive team has two home-run hitters. Your strategy will be not to throw them strikes in hopes that they'll chase bad pitches or to walk them intentionally in critical game situations.
- The offensive team hits up the middle frequently. Your team decides to play five infielders, one playing up the middle, and only three outfielders.

POSITIONING

One of the important strategies of a team is the assignment of players to particular positions, which is the coach's responsibility, and the positioning of those players in various game situations. We'll not discuss player assignments, but in this section you'll learn some useful guidelines for positioning defensive players.

Players in general know the location or zone for the position they play. Too often, though, fielders do not consider how their position relates to and complements the adjacent positions to compose a team defense. In a sport known for being a game of inches, poor positioning occasionally costs a team a win, and often the team doesn't even recognize that better positioning could have prevented the loss. Study the guidelines that follow to help you and your team adjust your defensive positioning.

Playing Straightaway

Without consideration to other factors, theoretically the defensive team should be spaced about equally around the infield and outfield, what we call playing straightaway, as shown in figure 8.1. For youth softball, playing straightaway is playing closer to home because the bases are only 60 feet (18 m) apart and the batters do not hit the ball as far.

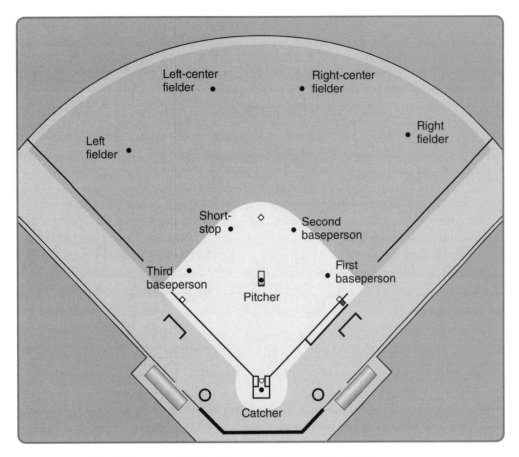

FIGURE 8.1 Straightaway defensive positions on the field.

Be aware of keeping the spacing between you and your fellow fielders equidistant when positioning yourself, in both the infield and the outfield. Also, left and right fielders and first and third basepersons should be aware of their location in relationship to the foul lines.

When playing straightaway many first and third basepersons tend to position themselves too close to the foul lines to prevent giving up the extra-base hit down the line. In doing so, however, they create large openings in the 3-4 and 5-6 holes. Left and right fielders may also position themselves too close to the foul lines, although we see that less often. Remember that the foul line is your ally; any ball hit outside that line can't be a hit. In addition, when batters have two strikes they are less likely to risk hitting near the foul lines. Thus, defensive players have a greater chance of catching balls by positioning themselves farther away from the foul lines when playing straightaway.

In our opinion many outfielders play too deep because they dislike being burned by batters who hit the ball over their heads. We suspect that they play too deep because they are not as adept at fielding balls behind them as they are balls in front of them. The consequence of playing too deep is that many more fly balls drop in front of them for hits, balls that would have been outs had the outfielders not been playing so deep. Besides being able to drop in more hits in front of the outfielders, batters turn singles into doubles and runners on the bases advance at least two bases rather than one because outfielders need more time to field the ball.

Because first and third basepersons want to protect against the extra-base hit and because outfielders have a neurosis about the ball being hit over their heads, these players position themselves for the exceptional play, not the probable play. Doing so is a mistake. For first and third basepersons the odds are that they'll make more outs by moving away from the foul lines. Likewise, outfielders can make more outs by not playing too deep. So a key principle when playing straightaway is to position yourself for the probable play, not the exceptional play.

Making Adjustments

From the straightaway positions your team will want to make adjustments to their positions by considering at least the following variables. Of course, these adjustments are based only on educated guesses about where the batter is likely to hit the ball. It's not uncommon to see a cat-and-mouse game going on between a savvy batter and clever fielders. Each watches what the other is doing. But like a gambler, you're looking to play the odds in your favor.

The Batter

- **Left- or right-handed batters**. Many if not most batters hit the ball more frequently to the side that they bat on (right-handed batters pull the ball toward the left side of the field), and usually they hit the ball harder and farther to that side.

- **Hitting power**. How close or deep you play will depend on the known or estimated power of the batter.

- **Hitting location history**. If the batter usually hits to the same location, you'll want to shift in that direction, but if the batter sprays the ball to all fields you'll want to play straightaway.

- **Running speed**. If the batter is fast the infield may need to play in a step or two, and if the batter is slower they may be able to drop back a couple of steps.

- **Bat used**. If the batter uses a high-tech bat, outfielders will want to play deeper than when the batter is using something less.

Game Situation

- **Base runners' locations and number of outs**. These two variables are major factors in determining the position of the infielders, as we'll discuss in the following sections.

- **Inning and score**. The later the inning and closer the score, the greater the need is to keep runners from advancing or scoring.

Environment

- **Wind speed and direction**. These conditions especially influence the depth of the outfielders.

- **Temperature and humidity**. Remember that balls travel farther in hot and humid conditions.

- **Wet or dry surface**. When the infield is muddy it's harder to move, and when the outfield grass is wet the ball tends to skip.

Defensive Player Ability

- **Speed and quickness**. Your positioning needs to take into account your speed and quickness.
- **Throwing speed and distance**. The depth that an infielder plays must be within his or her range to throw out the batter–runner.

As you can see many factors influence positioning. Some should be considered with each batter, and others might be considered only occasionally. Now let's look at some team defensive alignments for common combinations of these variables, keeping in mind that players in each position may make minor adjustments within these alignments based on personal ability and other information.

When to Play Straightaway

- **Infielders and outfielders**. When you know nothing about the batter, when it's early in the game with no one on base, and when the playing environment is normal.

When to Play Deeper

- **Infielders**. When you have superior speed and throwing ability but are not in double-play situations; and when you have two outs and a runner on first or runners on first and second, creating a potential force-out play at second or third.
- **Outfielders**. When you know that the batter has good power, and when the wind is blowing strongly toward the outfield.

When to Play Closer

- **Infielders**. When the batter has good running speed to first and no force-out is in play at second or third base, when you have a double-play situation, and when the game-winning run or inning-limit run is on third base and you must throw the runner out at home.
- **Outfielders**. When the batter lacks power or has a history of punching the ball into the shallow outfield, when the winning run or inning-limit run is on second or third with less than two outs, when the batter has excellent speed and will likely try to reach second base on a hit ground ball, and when you have good speed and ability to go back to field balls hit over your head.

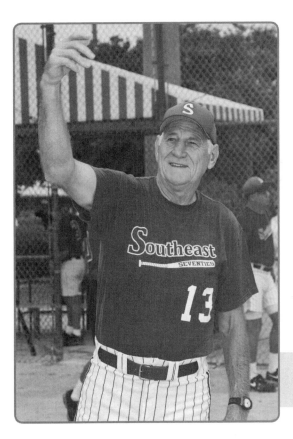

A coach moving his outfielders closer to the field.

When to Shift Right or Left

- **Infielders and outfielders**. When a right-handed batter comes to bat who is known to hit to left field, everyone shifts to the left. With a left-handed batter who hits to right field, everyone shifts to the right. When you know that a power hitter always hits to his or her strong side (right-handed hitter to left field), you may want to shift a weak-side infielder to the strong side. In addition, you will want to shift the outfielders so that three of them are on the strong side and only one is on the weak side. Even if this shift doesn't get the batter out, it may encourage the batter to abandon his or her strength and try to hit to the weak side, resulting in less damage than a home run.

- **Infielders**. When you know that a batter consistently hits a favorite hole, you'll want to shift positions to squeeze that hole smaller. For example, if a batter consistently hits the 5-6 hole, the third baseperson and shortstop should each take a step or two into the hole as the ball is being pitched. At the same time the pitcher should take a step or two toward the third-base side to protect the 1-6 hole.

RELAYS AND CUTOFFS

With a runner on first the batter hits a deep line drive to right-center field. The ball careens off the fence, but the right-center fielder quickly retrieves it and throws a strike to the second baseperson, who has positioned him- or herself in shallow right-center field. The second baseperson relays it to the catcher to get the runner out at home. This is an example of a well-executed defensive play. We'll refer to the relay player, who is always the second baseperson or shortstop, as the person who catches a thrown ball from an outfielder and relays it to an infielder at one of the bases.

Now let's slightly alter the play just described. As the second baseperson makes the throw home from his or her short outfield position, the pitcher, who is lined up between the second baseperson and catcher in the infield, hears the catcher yell, "Cut, three!" The pitcher cuts off the throw home and throws to the third baseperson to get the batter–runner out. This excellent defensive play happened not by chance but because the catcher saw that they would not get the runner out at home, that the batter–runner was trying to take an extra base on the throw home, and that the pitcher was in the correct cutoff position.

These two examples of defensive plays are a joy to watch because of the teamwork involved, yet they happen infrequently in slowpitch because most teams don't practice relays and cutoffs beyond the basics. If you want to play better slowpitch softball then your team needs to study this section and devote some well-organized practice time to executing successful relays and cutoffs.

In the cutoff plays that we review next the pitcher is always the cutoff player, whose purpose is to cut off a relay throw and redirect the ball to another base to make a play on a trailing runner. Although we prefer the pitcher as the cutoff player in all defensive plays, if your pitcher is not adept at making cutoffs and relays to the bases, then the first baseperson can be the cutoff player. The only adjustment needed is for the pitcher to cover first base for a possible throw to that base.

To execute these relays and cutoffs, both the infielders and the outfielders need to have a sense of time, an internal clock, to know how far the batter and base runners are likely to advance based on the time taken to field the ball and relay it into the infield. Here are some guidelines for competitive men's softball. For women, youth, and seniors you may need to add a few more seconds to each play mentioned here:

- It takes batters from 3 to 5 seconds to run from home to first base and about 6 to 8 seconds to run from home to second base.
- It takes base runners about 3 to 4 seconds to advance one base and 6 to 7 seconds to advance two bases.
- It takes about 3 to 4 seconds for a ground ball to reach outfielders playing 250 feet (75 m) from the plate.
- It takes from 5 to 7 seconds for outfielders to reach a ball that goes to the fence and another 3 to 4 seconds to pick it up, throw it to the relay fielder, and have the fielder catch it.
- It takes from 3 to 5 seconds for a moderately high fly ball to travel from the bat to an outfielder positioned 250 feet (75 m) from the plate.

Besides having a good sense of time as plays unfold, each defensive player needs to make quick decisions about where to move to, where to throw the ball, and when to cut and relay the ball to another base. Through simulated practice using base runners and from actual competitive play, all defensive players can develop this sense of time and good decision-making skills.

The following scenarios cover the various relay and cutoff situations that your team will want to execute to play good team defense. Remember that your primary goal is to keep the leading runner from advancing any extra bases and that your secondary goal is to do the same with any trailing runners. The key variables in making successful relays and cutoffs of balls hit to the outfield are

- the location of where the ball is hit,
- the location of the runners on base, and
- whether the ball is a base hit or caught fly ball.

In table 8.1 we list the more common defensive plays based on these variables, and in table 8.2 we show the abbreviations used in the figures that illustrate these plays. Although none of these plays is that difficult to execute, in the heat of a game it takes cool heads by players who have practiced these defensive relays and cutoffs over and over to make the right defensive moves.

In describing the defensive play for each offensive action listed in table 8.1, we'll diagram the play for a ball hit to one location in the outfield and then describe the defensive adjustments when the ball is hit to other locations. Our descriptions of these plays are based on adult men players who have average throwing ability. Women, younger people, and elite players will need to adjust these defensive plays to their abilities. Read about each play and then watch the DVD to see the following plays marked with an icon in action.

TABLE 8.1 Common Defensive Relays and Cutoffs

Offensive action	Runners on base	Target base for relay
Single	None	2B
Double	None	3B
Triple	None	H
Single	R1	3B
Double	R1	H
Triple	R1	H
Fly out short	R1	2B
Fly out deep	R1	3B
Single	R1 & R2	H
Double	R1 & R2	H
Triple	R1 & R2	H
Fly out short	R1 & R2	3B
Fly out deep	R1 & R2	H
Single	R1, R2, & R3	H
Double	R1, R2, & R3	H
Triple	R1, R2, & R3	H
Fly out short	R1, R2, & R3	H
Fly out deep	R1, R2, & R3	H

TABLE 8.2 Abbreviations and Symbols Used for Team Defense Diagrams and Text

Description	Symbol	Description	Symbol
DEFENSE		**OFFENSE**	
Pitcher	P	Batter–runner	B
Catcher	C	Base runner at first	R1
First baseperson	1BP	Base runner at second	R2
Second baseperson	2BP	Base runner at third	R3
Third baseperson	3BP	**OTHER SYMBOLS**	
Shortstop	SS	First base	1B
Left fielder	LF	Second base	2B
Left-center fielder	LCF	Third base	3B
Right-center fielder	RCF	Home	H
Right fielder	RF	Location of base hit	⊘
		Location of relay player	O
		Path of thrown ball	- - - - - -
		Path of defensive player	———

SINGLE, NO ONE ON BASE

Hit: Line drive over the head of 3BP and into left field for a solid single. See figure 8.2 for an illustration of how to make the relay to 2B.

Defensive goal: Keep B at 1B and relay the ball to 2B.

Fielding the ball: LF quickly fields the ball and throws it to the relay player. If time permits, LCF moves to back up LF.

Relay: SS is the relay person and moves to the outfield in a direct line between where LF is fielding the ball and the anticipated throw to 2B. The distance that SS goes out depends on how deep the ball is hit and the strength of the fielder's throwing arm. 2BP, who is covering 2B, tells SS what to do with the ball:

1. Don't cut; let it come through to 2B.

2. Cut and throw to 2B.

3. Hold the ball and run it into the infield.

If the ball is not hit too hard and the fielder is close to the infield, SS doesn't need to provide

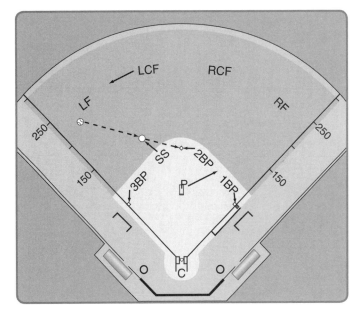

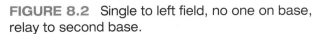
FIGURE 8.2 Single to left field, no one on base, relay to second base.

a relay to 2B. In that case he or she should just peel off and let the outfielder throw directly to 2BP, who is covering 2B. If the ball is hit deep, then SS not only needs to go deeper but also needs to make a quick decision about whether to concede 2B and therefore line up to relay the ball to 3B.

Other defensive positions: 2BP covers 2B, and 1BP and 3BP move to their bases on balls hit to either side or up the middle. P backs up the throw to 2B. As mentioned in chapter 6, too often you'll see 1BPs watching this play and not moving to the bag. Smart base runners observe this and realize that they can round the base much farther because there is no threat of a throw back, which gives them an advantage in running to second should the ball be bobbled in the outfield. So be sure that your 1BP always moves to the base on this play.

Hits to other locations: A hit to the right side is played the same way, but now the relay player is 2BP and SS covers 2B. When the ball is hit into the middle, SS and 2BP should work out in advance who will be the relay person, the choice going to the person with the strongest or most accurate throwing arm.

DOUBLE, NO ONE ON BASE

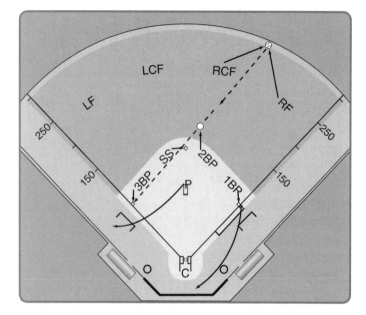

FIGURE 8.3 Double to right-center field, no one on base, relay to third base.

Hit: Hard hit to deep right-center field that hits the fence on one hop for a sure double. RCF races to retrieve the ball and get it back into the infield as shown in figure 8.3.

Defensive goal: Hold B to a double and relay the ball to 3B.

Fielding the ball: RCF and RF both run after the ball, and whoever gets to the ball first yells, "I got it," which in this example is RCF. Then RF determines the location of the batter–runner and tells RCF where to throw the ball.

Relay: 2BP is the relay person and comes out to short right-center field, about equidistant between the ball and 3B, and in line between the ball and 3B. 3BP tells 2BP what to do with the ball:

1. Don't cut; let it come through to 3B (this would take an exceptional throw by RCF).
2. Cut and throw to 2B or 3B (much more likely).
3. Hold the ball and run it into the infield.

Other defensive positions: 3BP covers 3B. SS covers 2B. After 1BP sees that B has secured 2B and there is no play at 1B, he or she can move toward home to back up a play there should an overthrow be made on a play at 3B and B attempts to score. P backs up 3B.

Hits to other locations: When the ball is hit to the left side of the outfield, the relay play is the same except now SS is the relay person and 2BP covers 2B.

TRIPLE, NO ONE ON BASE

Hit: Deep fly ball to left field landing just inside the foul line and rolling to the fence. It looks to be a triple. LF is in pursuit as illustrated in figure 8.4.

Defensive goal: Hold B to a triple and relay the ball to H.

Fielding the ball: LF is alone in fielding a ball near the foul line. The only throw from this position is to the relay player.

Relay: SS is the relay person, coming out to about the 150-foot (45 m) mark or halfway between the ball and home, and, of course, in line between the ball and home. C lets SS know what to do with the relay throw:

1. Cut and throw to 3B.
2. Cut and throw to H.
3. Cut and hold, running the ball back into the infield.

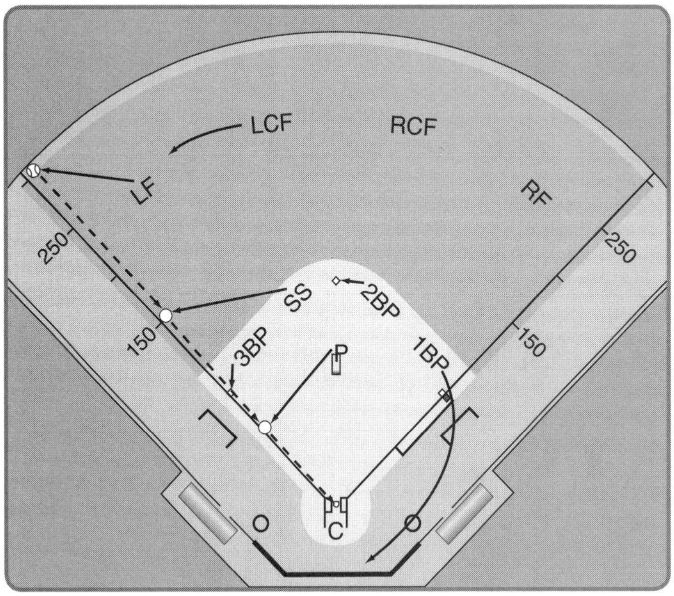

FIGURE 8.4 Triple to left field, no one on base, relay home.

P positions him- or herself to be the cutoff player, positioned in line with SS and home and about 50 feet (15 m) out from home, as shown in figure 8.4. If B tries to go home, then SS throws home through P. C tells P what to do with the throw:

1. Don't cut; let it come through.
2. Cut and relay to home (because the throw is off line or weak).
3. Cut and throw to 3B (because B rounded 3B but on the strength of the throw stopped and is trying to return to 3B).

Other defensive positions: 1BP backs up H, 2BP covers 2B in case B retreats, and 3BP goes to 3B.

Hits to other locations: If the ball is hit to center field or the right side, the relay to H is essentially the same, except that 2BP becomes the relay person for balls hit to the right side and SS covers 2B.

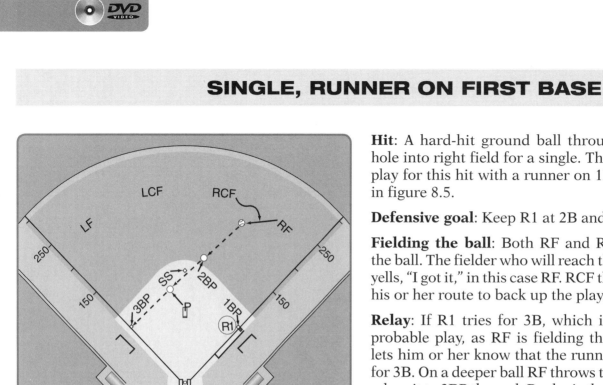

FIGURE 8.5 Single to right field, runner on first, relay to third base.

Hit: A hard-hit ground ball through the 3-4 hole into right field for a single. The defensive play for this hit with a runner on 1B is shown in figure 8.5.

Defensive goal: Keep R1 at 2B and B at 1B.

Fielding the ball: Both RF and RCF charge the ball. The fielder who will reach the ball first yells, "I got it," in this case RF. RCF then adjusts his or her route to back up the play.

Relay: If R1 tries for 3B, which is the most probable play, as RF is fielding the ball RCF lets him or her know that the runner is trying for 3B. On a deeper ball RF throws to 2BP, who relays it to 3BP through P, who is the cutoff and is positioned about one-third of the way toward 3B from 2B (see figure 8.5). P tells 2BP what to do with the relay throw. On a shallow base hit RF throws to 3B on a line through P, omitting 2BP from the play. 3BP will let P know one of the following:

1. Let the ball come through to 3B (no cutoff).
2. Cut the ball and relay it to 3B (the throw is off line or doesn't have enough speed to reach 3B).
3. Cut the ball and throw back to SS, who is covering 2B for a possible play on B, who is trying to advance an extra base when the throw is made to 3B. The key here is that RF throws a line drive to 3B, which freezes B from trying to advance to 2B.

If R1 does not try to reach 3B, RF will throw the ball to 2BP, the relay person, who is positioned on the edge of the grass and lined up between the ball and 2B. Or RF may throw the ball directly to SS covering 2B. Because R1 has secured 2B and is not attempting to run to 3B, the only possible play for 2BP or SS to make is a quick toss to 1BP at 1B if B rounded 1B too far or turns his or her back to the ball to return to 1B.

If a play is likely at 2B, for example, on a blooper single when R1 is uncertain that the ball will be caught by the outfielder and cannot immediately run to 2B, the outfielder throws directly to 2B and 2BP gets out of the way. SS takes the throw at 2B, looking to get a force-out on R1, or if R1 rounded 2B but decides not to run to 3B, SS looks to tag out R1 coming back to the base.

Other defensive positions: 1BP and 3BP cover their bases.

Hits to other locations: For shallow hits to the left side of the outfield with a runner on 1B, the defensive play options are similar. LF and LCF both charge the hit ball, and SS is the relay person, taking a position just beyond the infield and lined up between the ball and 3B. If the ball is fielded quickly and a play at 2B is possible, the backup outfielder lets the fielding outfielder know that and the outfielder throws directly to 2BP covering 2B.

If R1 tries to advance to 3B, the outfielder throws through SS to 3BP, who is covering 3B (see figure 8.6). Because the ball is hit shallow, usually the outfielder can throw directly to 3B but he or she should still throw through SS. 3BP tells SS to do one of the following:

1. Let it go through without a cut.

2. Cut and throw to 3B (probably because the throw is off line).

3. Cut and throw to 2B (an attempt to get B trying to advance on the throw to 3B).

For hits to the left side of the outfield, P backs up 3B in case of an overthrow.

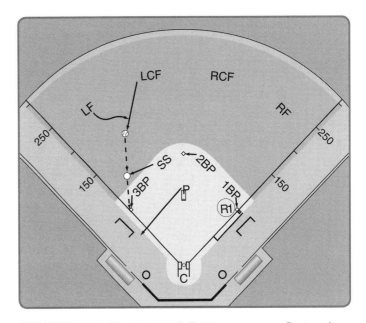

FIGURE 8.6 Single to left field, runner on first, relay to third base.

DOUBLE, RUNNER ON FIRST BASE

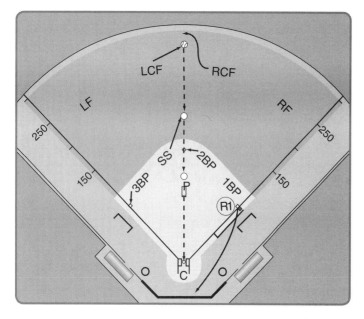

FIGURE 8.7 *Double to center field, runner on first, relay home.*

Hit: Medium fly ball in the gap between LCF and RCF for a double. With a runner on 1B, see figure 8.7 on how to defend this situation.

Defensive goal: Keep R1 at 3B and B at 2B.

Fielding the ball: LCF is the first to reach the ball, preventing it from rolling through to the fence. RCF backs up the play and lets LCF know where to throw the ball.

Relay: SS is the relay person in this example, but it could be 2BP just as easily if that's the decision made in advance between SS and 2BP or the coach. SS is lined up between the ball and H and is in shallow center field, the depth determined by the throwing ability of LCF and SS. P is the infield cutoff and is positioned just above the pitching box. LCF throws to SS, and P tells him or her what to do with the ball:

1. Cut and throw to H (throwing through P).
2. Cut and throw to 3B, attempting to get B taking an extra base.
3. Cut and throw to 2B, attempting to get B returning to 2B.
4. Don't cut; let the ball come to P.

If the throw from SS is to H, C tells P what to do with the ball:

1. Cut and hold the ball (no play at any base).
2. Cut and throw to 2B or 3B to get B.
3. Cut and throw to 3B to get R1.
4. Cut and throw to H to get R1.
5. Don't cut; let the ball come through to home.

Other defensive positions: 1BP backs up home, 2BP covers 2B, and 3BP covers 3B.

Hits to other locations: If the ball is hit anywhere on the left side of the outfield, the defensive play is the same. If the ball is hit to the right side, 2BP is the relay person and SS covers 2B.

TRIPLE, RUNNER ON FIRST BASE

Ball hit down the first-base line that rolls to the deep corner of right field in foul territory. R1 will score easily, and B will have a standup triple and can possibly score if the relay is misplayed. Therefore, this defensive play is identical to a triple with no runners on base (see Triple, No One on Base, page 185).

FLY OUT, RUNNER ON FIRST BASE, LESS THAN TWO OUTS

Hit: Fly ball to any outfield position with less than two outs and a runner on first base.

Defensive goal: Catch the ball and keep R1 from advancing to 2B (or 3B, on extremely deep fly balls).

Fielding the ball: The first objective, of course, is for the fielder to catch the ball for the out, and if time permits, to position him- or herself to make a quick, strong throw to 2B.

Relay: When the caught fly ball is shallow, R1 is not likely to try to advance to 2B, the exception being when the fielder is running away from 2B in an effort to catch a pop-up. Then R1 may have a good chance to advance because the fielder must stop, turn, and set up to throw. On caught shallow fly balls the ball is thrown in directly to the person covering second base. No relay throw is needed.

When the ball is hit deeper, depending on the speed of R1 and the throwing ability of the outfielder, the outfielder will throw through the relay player to 2B. SS, of course, is the relay person for the left side, and 2BP covers 2B. 2BP is the relay player for the right side of the outfield, and SS covers 2B. The player covering 2B will let the relay person know what to do with the ball:

1. Don't cut; let the ball come through to 2B (this option is preferred because with a reasonably fast runner, there is usually not enough time for a relay).

2. Cut and throw to 2B.

3. Cut and throw to 1B (R1 started for 2B and decided to return to 1B).

4. Cut and hold the ball.

On deep fly balls, more than likely you'll concede 2B to R1, and therefore the relay person will go out deeper and line up between the ball and 3B. The 3BP will let the relay person know what to do with the ball.

Other defensive positions: 1BP covers 1B, 2BP covers 2B when SS is the relay person, SS covers 2B when 2BP is the relay person, and 3BP covers 3B. P backs up the throw to 2B.

SINGLE, RUNNERS ON FIRST AND SECOND BASE

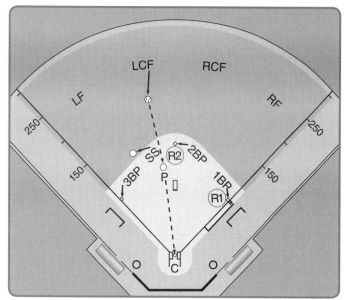

FIGURE 8.8 Single to left-center field, runners on first and second, relay home.

Hit: Line-drive single off the glove of SS that rolls out to LCF in shallow left-center field (see figure 8.8). R1 and R2 both advance a base, and R2 is threatening to go home.

Defensive goal: Keep R2 at 3B or throw R2 out at H and keep R1 at 2B.

Fielding the ball: LCF fields the ball in shallow left-center field and throws it to P.

Relay: Because the ball is shallow SS is not needed as a relay player. P is the infield cutoff and is positioned between the ball and H, about 50 feet (15 m) from H. The LCF throws to P if R2 attempts to score and throws to 2BP at 2B if R2 holds at 3B. If the throw is to P, C tells P what to do with the ball:

1. Don't cut; let the ball come through to C.
2. Cut and relay to H.
3. Cut and throw to 3B.
4. Cut and hold.

Other defensive positions: 1BP, 2BP, and 3BP each cover their respective bases.

Balls hit to other locations: If the base hit is deeper than shallow outfield, the possibility of getting R2 out at home is almost nil. Thus the defensive play is to keep R1 at 2B and B at 1B. In this situation SS sets up as the relay player for a throw to 3B if R1 attempts to advance to that base. LCF throws to or through SS to 3B, and 3BP tells SS what to do with the ball:

1. Don't cut; let the ball come through to 3B.
2. Cut and relay to 2B.
3. Cut and hold.

In this play P backs up 3B.

If the ball is hit to the right side of the outfield, then the play is executed the same way except that 2BP is the relay player and SS covers 2B.

DOUBLE, RUNNERS ON FIRST
AND SECOND BASE

The ball is hit between RCF and RF, and B is a fast runner. B most assuredly will have a double, R2 will score, and R1 will most likely reach 3B without a play. If the relay is not executed correctly, R1 will attempt to score. So the defensive team's goal is to keep R1 from scoring. The relay for this play is the same as the relay for a double with a runner on 1B (see page 188).

TRIPLE, RUNNERS ON FIRST
AND SECOND BASE

The ball is hit in the direction of the RCF but takes a bad hop and goes to the fence. R1 and R2 score easily, and B is assured of a triple and possibly an inside-the-park home run if the relay is misplayed. Therefore, this defensive play is identical to a triple with no runners on base (see Triple, No One on Base, page 185).

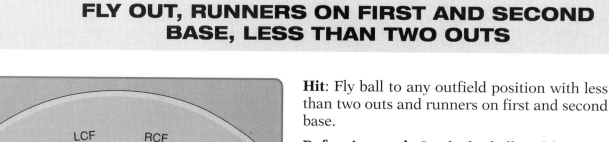

FLY OUT, RUNNERS ON FIRST AND SECOND BASE, LESS THAN TWO OUTS

FIGURE 8.9 Fly out to short right field, runners on first and second with less than two outs, relay to third.

Hit: Fly ball to any outfield position with less than two outs and runners on first and second base.

Defensive goal: Catch the ball and keep R2 from advancing to 3B (or H on deep fly balls).

Fielding the ball: Foremost, the fielder needs to catch the ball for the out. Then, if possible, the fielder should position him- or herself to make a quick, strong throw to 3B.

Relay: When the caught fly ball is shallow, R2 is less likely to try to advance to 3B. On caught shallow fly balls to the left side, the ball is thrown directly to 3B. No relay throw is needed. On shallow balls on the right side (see figure 8.9), P is the infield cutoff. 3BP tells P to make one of the following plays:

1. Don't cut; let the ball come through to 3B.
2. Cut and relay to 3B (because the throw is weak or off line).
3. Cut and relay to 2B for a play on R1.
4. Cut and hold.

When the ball is hit to the left side and caught deeper, SS determines whether the outfielder has a good chance of getting R2 out at 3B or whether the better play is to throw to 2B, to get R1 out if he or she decides to run or to discourage R1 from trying to advance to 2B. For this defensive play, SS is the relay person lining up for the throw to 3B or 2B (that's why SS needs to make the call about where the outfielder should throw).

If the ball is caught on the right side of the outfield at medium depth, R2 will easily advance to 3B on the tag, so the throw should be made to 2B through 2BP, the relay person, who is lined up between the ball and 2B (see figure 8.10). SS covers 2B and lets 2BP know what to do with the ball:

1. Don't cut; let the ball come through to 2B (this option is preferred because with a reasonably fast runner there usually is not enough time for a relay).

2. Cut and throw to 2B.

3. Cut and throw to 1B (R1 started for 2B and decided to return to 1B).

4. Cut and hold the ball.

On deep fly balls, you'll likely concede 2B to R1 and 3B to R2. So the defense sets up the relay for a throw H, as shown in figure 8.8 on page 190.

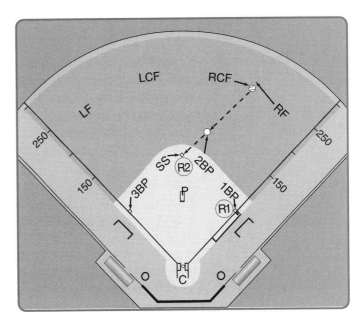

FIGURE 8.10 Fly out to medium right-center field, runners on first and second with less than two outs, relay to second.

SINGLE, BASES LOADED

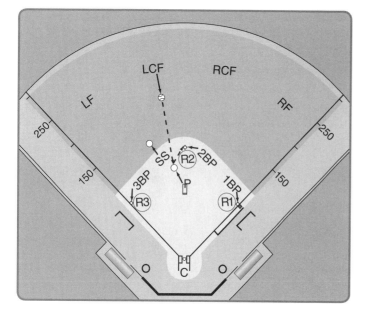

FIGURE 8.11 Single to left-center field, bases loaded, relay home.

Hit: Ground ball single through the 1-6 hole.

Defensive goal: Keep R2 from scoring and R1 from advancing to 3B.

Fielding the ball: LCF wants to field the ball as quickly as possible because all base runners are advancing.

Relay: SS is the relay for a possible throw to 3B. 2BP covers 2B, and P lines up between the ball and H for a possible throw to H. As the ball is being fielded, LCF or the adjacent outfielder makes the decision about where LCF should throw the ball.

R2 could be trying to score, and R1 may be advancing to 3B. LCF or a teammate makes the decision about where to throw based on (1) wanting to get the leading runner out, and (2) the probability of being successful in getting an out. If the throw is to 3B through SS, 3BP tells SS what to do with the ball. If the throw is to H through P, C tells P what to do with the ball. In figure 8.11 we show the throw going to H, but P cuts the ball off and throws to 2B to get B out.

Other defensive positions: 1BP covers 1B, 2BP covers 2B, and 3BP covers 3B.

Balls hit to other locations: If the ball is hit to the right side of the outfield, then 2BP becomes the relay for a throw to 3B and SS covers 2B.

DOUBLE, BASES LOADED

The ball is hit to straightaway center field between LCF and RCF for a sure double. R3 and R2 will undoubtedly score and thus this play becomes identical to Double, Runner on First Base (see figure 8.7 on page 188).

TRIPLE, BASES LOADED

The batter hits a line drive to left field. As LF is about to catch the ball he looks up to see where the runners are and the ball goes through his legs. LCF is coming over to back up the play and chases the ball almost to the fence. All base runners will score easily, and B will make it to 3B and may score if the relay is not executed well. Therefore, this defensive play is identical to a triple with no runners on base (see Triple, No One on Base, page 185 and figure 8.4).

FLY OUT, BASES LOADED, LESS THAN TWO OUTS

The defensive play here is determined entirely by how deep the ball is when caught and the throwing ability of the outfielder and relay or cutoff persons. On a shallow fly ball a throw home may be worthwhile. This play has no relay person, but P lines up in the infield for the cutoff.

As the ball is hit deeper, the probability of getting R3 out decreases, and throwing to 2B or 3B may make better sense, depending on where the ball is caught, to keep a runner from advancing or to get an out. If the ball is caught at medium depth on the right side, a throw to 2B to hold R1 at 1B is the percentage play. If the ball is caught at medium depth on the left side, a throw to 3B is the most likely play.

If the ball is caught deep, unless the outfielder has an outstanding arm, you'll concede one base to all three runners and then be concerned about R2 trying to score and R1 going to 3B. Thus, you'll set up the defensive relay for a throw to home as described for a Double, Runner on First Base (see page 188, figure 8.7).

INFIELD PLAYS

We covered the common plays made by individual infielders in chapter 6. Now we look at common and less common double plays and some other special plays among the infielders.

Common Double Plays

A well-executed double play is not only great fun to execute but also is a back-breaker to the offense. The conventional double plays that your team will want to master always begin with a runner on first base:

- B hits a ground ball to P, who throws to 2B for a relay throw to 1B for the double play. The conventional coverage of 2B is that 2BP takes the throw from P when a right-handed batter is batting because a right-handed batter will more likely pull the ball, and SS covers 2B when a left-handed batter is batting. Remember the exception to this coverage discussed in chapter 6, page 151.

- B hits a ground ball to SS, who throws to 2BP covering 2B, and 2BP relays the ball to 1BP. If SS is close to 2B, he or she may run to the base and then throw to 1B.

- B hits a ground ball to 2BP, who throws to SS covering 2B, and SS relays the ball to 1BP. If 2BP is close to 2B, he or she may run to 2B and then throw to 1B.

- B hits a ground ball to 3BP, who throws to 2BP covering 2B, and 2BP relays the ball to 1BP.

- B hits a ground ball to 1BP, who throws to SS covering 2B, and SS relays the ball back to 1B (if he or she is able to cover the base after fielding the ball) or to P, who breaks toward 1B anytime a ground ball is hit to the right side. This play is the most difficult of the conventional double plays. When 1BP fields the ball close to 1B he or she can execute this double play by first stepping on 1B and then throwing to SS at 2B, who then has to tag R1 for the out because the force-out was removed.

To review some of these conventional double plays watch Defense→Infielder Skills→Second-to-First Double Plays on the DVD.

Less Common Double Plays

Here are some less common double plays with a runner on 1B that alert infielders can execute. You can watch animations of them on the DVD at Defense→Defensive Strategies and Tactics→Less Common Double Plays→With Runner on First Base.

- Any infielder catches a line drive for an out and then makes a quick throw to a base where the runner failed to tag up.

- 1BP plays in close, on or near the direct line between 1B and 2B. When a ground ball is hit to 1BP he or she catches it before R1 can get by 1BP, tags R1, and steps on 1B for a quick double play.

- 2BP plays in close to the direct line between 1B and 2B. When a ground ball is hit to 2BP he or she fields it before R1 can get by, tags R1, and then throws to 1B. If R1 stops or tries to evade 2BP, 2BP throws to 1BP for the force-out and then 1BP throws to SS covering 2B, who tags out R1.

With runners on 1B and 2B, infielders like to turn double plays that get the lead runner out. Here are double plays for doing so:

- 3BP plays close to 3B. When a ground ball is hit to him or her, 3BP steps on 3B and throws to 2B if there is time or to 1B.
- 3BP is positioned away from 3B. When a ground ball is hit to him or her 3BP runs toward R2 to tag him or her and then throws to 2B. Smart runners will stop when they see 3BP trying to tag them, so then 3BP throws to 2B to force out R1. 2BP then throws to P or SS, who is covering 3B, to tag R2, who continued running after he or she saw the throw to 2B.
- SS plays in closer in the infield and charges a ground ball hit to him or her to field it in the baseline between 2B and 3B. If SS fields the ball before R2 passes, SS tags R2 and pitches the ball to 2BP at 2B for an easy double play. If R2 is past SS on his or her way to 3B, SS throws to 2B for a conventional double play.
- Any infielder can field the ball and throw it to 2B for the start of a conventional double play, but if the relay player sees that R2 is not running quickly to 3B, he or she can throw to 3B to get the lead runner out rather than throw to 1B.

When the bases are loaded all the double plays discussed earlier are possible, depending on where the ball is fielded. Nevertheless, the most desirable play is to get R3 out trying to score and then an additional out. Here are some possibilities:

- Ground ball to P, who throws to C, who relays it to 3B preferably or to 1B if R2 would be safe at 3B.
- Ground ball to 3BP, who throws to C, who throws to 3B preferably or to 1B. If 3BP is not too far from 3B, he or she should step on 3B and then throw home. If there is no commitment line, C must tag R3 for the out. If there is a commitment line, 3BP makes sure that R3 crosses it and then throws to C for the force-out. This is the most damaging double play in the game.
- Ground ball to 1BP, who executes the same play that 3BP did, preferably stepping on 1B and then throwing to C.

Here are two more double plays that can be made when the batter or runners are not hustling:

- Beginning with R1 and R3 or with bases loaded and with no one out, a ground ball is hit to any infielder, who relays it to 2B for the start of a conventional double play. 2BP or SS, whoever is covering 2B, sees that R3 is not hustling home and throws to C for a nifty double play.
- The following play happens amazingly often: B hits a pop-up and in total frustration stands at home looking at the ball. If a runner is on first (no infield fly rule is in effect), the fielder can choose to let the ball hit the ground, scoop it up, and throw to either SS or 2BP at 2B, who then relays

to 1B for a double play. To make this play work, the fielder makes it look as if he or she is going to catch the ball but at the last moment pulls the glove away. The fielder must anticipate how the ball will bounce so that it does not dart away. This play often stirs up controversy. Umpires may rule the batter safe because the fielder intentionally dropped the ball. That ruling is correct if the ball is a line drive, but it is not correct on a pop-up when there would have been no chance for a double play if the batter had bothered to run to first. The play—letting the ball drop, not touching it with the glove or body until it hits the ground, and then executing the double play—is not only legal but smart. The opposing team sometimes will accuse you of unsportsmanlike play for letting the ball drop, but it is not unsportsman-like; it is a good tactic. If the opposing team wishes to dispense criticism, they need look no further than the batter standing at home.

Now watch animations of these unconventional double plays at Defense→Defensive Strategies and Tactics→Less Common Double Plays→With Runners in Other Locations on the DVD.

The execution of double plays, often done in less than 3 seconds, requires not only good motor skills but also good decision making. When there is one out, you want to execute the easiest double play to end the inning, usually a conventional double play. In some situations infielders need to decide quickly whether they will have time to turn a double play or whether they would do better by getting a force-out on the leading runner. For example, when an infielder has to move some distance to field the ball or bobbles the ball momentarily, a double play is usually impossible so a throw to get the leading runner is the better play. When no one is out, you want to turn a double play that gets the leading runner and any other runner or the batter.

Two More Special Plays

Here are two other special defensive plays that require teamwork. Read the descriptions and then watch the animations at Defense→Defensive Strategies and Tactics→Two More Special Plays on the DVD.

- Beginning with R1 and R2, a ball is hit in the 5-6 hole. SS makes a nice backhand stop on the ball, but momentum takes him or her toward the 3B foul line. Stopping and throwing to 2B in time to get R1 would be difficult. Thus, the preferred place to throw is to 3B. If 3B did not go after the ball, he or she should be covering 3B to receive the throw from SS, but if he or she did attempt to field the ball, P must cover 3B. Just as P should break toward 1B on ground balls hit to the right side, he or she should break toward 3B when ground balls are hit to the left side.

- When the winning run or inning-limit run is on third with less than two outs, the batter will likely try to hit a sacrifice fly. One possible defensive maneuver is to walk batters to load the bases so that a force-out is available at any base. Next, an outfielder comes into the infield and takes a position in the middle but shaded to the side to which the batter is expected to hit. The other outfielders come into shallow outfield, close enough that they can throw out the runner from third base at home on a fly ball. Next, the pitcher tries to get the batter to hit a ground ball to the infield by throwing short or flat. This defensive play often doesn't work, but every once in a while the shift is successful.

ELEVENTH FIELDER

As players get older they lose some of their mobility. Thus in some men's and women's senior softball leagues and tournaments an 11th fielder is added. We'll call this fielder the middle fielder (MF), although in some places the term *rover* is used for this player. The age at which an MF is used varies widely in local leagues, but it usually begins at the 50-to-60 age range. In national tournaments the MF is added to the 65 and older teams, although the MF is not used with the 65 Major Plus teams (the top national teams). The MF is used at all levels of play in the 70 and over age groups.

Most senior teams play the MF as a middle infielder, playing to the side of 2B that the batter is expected to hit (see figure 8.12). On occasion, however, we've seen teams play five outfielders equidistant around the outfield. Teams often select their best infielder to play the MF position, someone who can go back to catch pop-ups and has a strong arm to throw runners out from this position or when making relay throws from the outfield. Because the MF is predominantly positioned as a middle infielder, we next describe our recommended approach to using this fielder in defensive play.

Position

With right-handed batters, play three infielders on the left side, somewhat evenly spaced between 2B and 3B. We call this a shift left. With left-handed batters, shift MF to the right side, spacing three infielders evenly between 1B and 2B, or what we call shift right. If you know that a batter tends to hit to the opposite field a high percentage of the time, shift in the direction in which the batter is known to hit. If a batter is known to place hit all over the field, shift to the batter's dominant side (for right-handed batters shift left), but do not shift as much toward the left side as you would do with a batter who is predominantly a pull hitter.

The pitcher (P), after delivering the ball, takes one step to the opposite side of where MF is positioned. So if you have a right shift on, P takes one step (but only one) to the 3B side of the infield and is ready to field the ball.

As noted earlier, most teams have MF play directly behind the pitcher behind 2B and then break right or left based on a read of the pitch location and the batter's footwork. This cat-and-mouse game with batters may work for some MFs, but we recommend that MF take a position and stay set, ready to move right or left when the ball is hit.

In terms of depth, with less than two outs MF positions him- or herself close enough on the infield that he or she can be in position to help execute double plays. With two outs and a runner on 1B, all infielders drop back several steps to increase their range and get the force-out at 2B. If P is mobile and a good fielder, P can cover 2B so that all the infielders can play much deeper.

Base Coverage for Infield Hits

When you use a left shift with a runner on 1B and the ball is hit to 3BP, SS, or MF, 2BP is responsible for covering 2B. With less than two outs 2BP needs to play close enough to 2B to reach the base quickly so that he or she can execute the relay part of the double play. If the ball is hit to the right side of the field, MF will cover 2B and relay the ball to 1B.

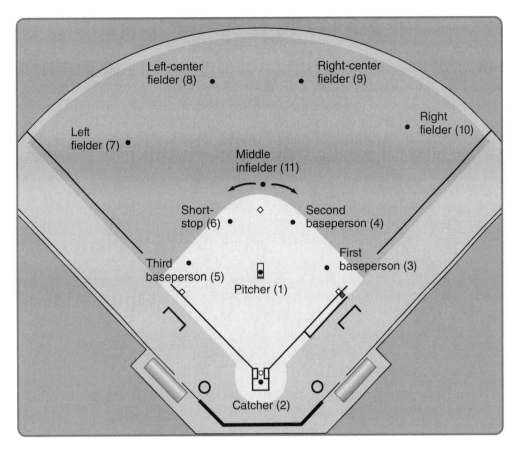

FIGURE 8.12 Positioning with 11 defensive players.

When you have a right shift on with a runner on 1B and the ball is hit to the 1BP, 2BP, or MF, SS is responsible for covering 2B for a force-out or to turn a double play. If the ball is hit to the left side of the field, MF will cover 2B for the force-out or double play.

When the ball is hit to P, MF usually takes the throw at 2B. But if you have a left shift on, for example, and the ball is hit between P and MF, MF may be breaking to field the ball, not knowing whether P will catch it. In this situation 2BP must cover 2B. And the opposite is the case when you have a right shift on. If the ball is hit between P and MF, SS needs to be ready to cover the base. Watch Defense→Defensive Strategies and Tactics→Infield Hits With 11 Defensive Players on the DVD to see animations of these plays.

Relays and Base Coverage for Outfield Hits

Regardless of which way the infield is shifted, when a ball is hit to left field or to left-center field, SS positions him- or herself for a possible relay to 3B if such a throw may be likely. SS also is the relay person for a throw home from left field. MF positions him- or herself for a relay throw to 2BP, who is covering 2B. If the ball is hit to left-center field and the play is likely to be at home, MF is the relay person.

If the ball is hit to right field, 2BP takes the relay throw from RF for a play at 2B. 2BP also is the relay person for RF throwing home. If the ball is hit to RCF, MF will be the relay for the throw to 2B or 3B or H. Watch Defense→Defensive Strategies and Tactics→Outfield Hits With 11 Defensive Players on the DVD to see animations of these plays.

COORDINATING COMMUNICATION

Most slowpitch softball teams struggle to make relays and cutoffs along with the less common infield plays described earlier because no one is in charge of the defense and each player just tries to do what he or she thinks is best. The consequence is confusion on the field. So to make good defensive plays consistently your team needs a defensive leader or captain who is on the field, preferably in the infield. Often it is the pitcher or shortstop, but it could be any of the infielders. An outfielder has difficulty coordinating defensive play because of the distance from the infield.

The defensive captain has the following responsibilities:

- Adjust the positions of the defensive players based on the game situation and the batter.
- Call out the defensive play to be executed when options are available on the play. For example, the captain calls the relay setup for a throw to third base or home.
- Remind players of the game situation and possible plays to be made.
- When defensive players fail to execute a play correctly, review with them how the play should be done.
- Ensure that the correct players are communicating the appropriate information during a play and that other players are quiet.

Obviously, good communication is essential for coordinating the defensive plays. For each defensive play, a person is designated for communicating a decision to a fellow player. Three things go wrong with this communication process.

1. The player designated to communicate forgets to do so.
2. The person being told what play to make doesn't listen.
3. Other players start yelling instructions, creating confusion about what to do.

Coordinated defensive play requires discipline—discipline to meet your responsibility to communicate when you're the designated person to do so, discipline to follow the directions of your teammate, and discipline to remain quiet when you are not the designated communicator. For teams to communicate successfully, each player has to have an attitude of acceptance to the messages. You may know that there are two outs, and your teammate's reminding you of that may be a bit annoying, but you should hear it with the understanding that it is being said to help you. And at times you will need the reminder. Excellent teams communicate, helping each other to play the game better.

SUMMARY

- Develop your defensive team strategies based on your team's defensive abilities, the offensive team's hitting and running abilities, the playing field, and the environmental conditions.

- Know how to position yourself defensively based on the team strategy and in relation to your teammates.
- Adjust your positioning based on the batter's hitting record or tendencies, the game situation, the environment, and your speed and throwing ability.
- Learn the specific responsibilities for your position in executing the many relays and cutoffs.
- To execute defensive plays, develop a sense of time and good decision-making skills through continual practice and game experience.
- By being aware of the many special double-play possibilities, infielders can execute them when the opportunity presents itself.
- When playing with a middle fielder, each player must learn who is responsible for infield relay throws at second base and relay throws to the various bases from the outfield.
- The coach or defensive captain is responsible for coordinating communication and making team tactical decisions.

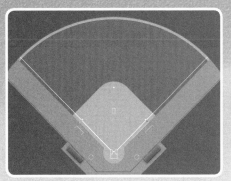

PART III

PREPARATION

If you're new to the sport of slowpitch softball or it's been a long time since you've played, you'll want to read this section carefully. Even experienced players will find it helpful to review the four chapters of this section to prepare better for future play.

Is your bat certified for competition? Do you know what it means that a bat has a rating of BPF 1.20? Do you know what is meant by a softball that has a 44 COR and 375 compression? You can find the answers to these questions and much more in chapter 9, "Field and Equipment." In chapter 10, "Physical Preparation," we'll provide you with enough information to get you started on a fitness program that will prepare you for the intensity of softball that you plan to play. The fitter you are, the better you'll play and the more you'll enjoy the game, and you'll have a better chance of avoiding injury as well.

After you've established a reasonable level of proficiency in the offensive and defensive skills covered in parts I and II, you'll come to realize that the only obstacle to greater success in the sport will be your mind. Chapter 11, "Mental Preparation," will focus on helping you control your emotions, improve your concentration, and build and maintain your self-confidence. In chapter 12, "Softball First Aid," you'll learn how to diagnose, treat, and rehabilitate those minor injuries that inevitably come with playing slowpitch softball. We'll also help you recognize when you have a more serious injury and should seek medical help.

CHAPTER 9

Field and Equipment

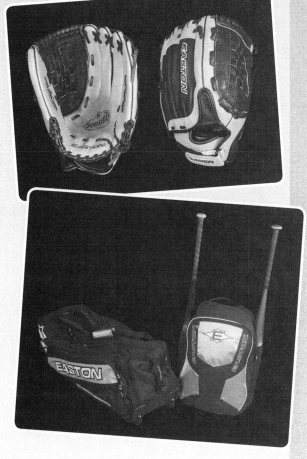

In this chapter we're going to help you prepare for your career in slowpitch softball. We'll give you the basics about playing fields and help you pick out the right bat from the many models that are available. When you hear fellow players talking about the coefficient of restitution and compression of balls, you'll be able to join in the conversation. We'll help you select the right fielding glove, uniforms, and practice equipment. In short, this chapter is full of all the nonplaying information that will help prepare you to play and enjoy the game more.

PLAYING FIELD

If you play lots of softball you'll experience a variety of facilities—from a single field in a local park to exquisite multifield complexes complete with many amenities. Along the way you'll see the results of planning, maintenance, and budgets. Each affects the type of softball experience that both players and fans will have.

Softball fields vary in orientation, infield surface coverings, outfield grasses, quality of drainage and irrigation, fences, lighting, dugouts, bleachers, and, of course, restrooms, but we'll not cover those items in this guide. Instead, we'll focus on the one relatively constant similarity—the dimensions of the field that you'll be playing on.

Figure 9.1 is a diagram of the basic field dimensions for adult players. As you can see, the bases are 65 feet (20 m) apart for men, women, and youths 14 and older. The pitching distance is 50 feet (15 m) for adults, measured from the front of the rubber to home plate. The backstop should be between 25 and 30 feet (7 and 9 m) behind home plate, and the minimum outfield fence distance is usually 300 feet (91 m) for men, sometimes longer; 265 to 275 feet (81 to 84 m) for women; and 275 feet for coed.

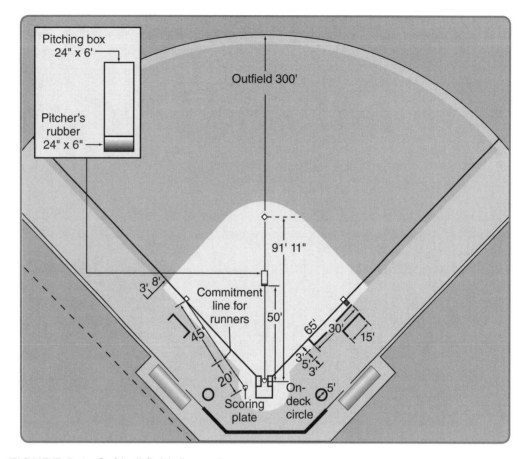

FIGURE 9.1 Softball field dimensions.

In most of the newer softball fields you'll find a warning track, which has an interesting beginning. According to legend, a track was built in Old Yankee Stadium around the field for use in track and field events, but outfielders discovered the track warned them that they were approaching the fence. And so the warning track was born. Initially made of dirt and fine gravel, today the 10- to 15-foot-wide (3 to 4.5 m wide) path is made of various composite materials.

The batter's box, home plate, and the catcher's box are all shown in figure 9.2. Slowpitch softball organizations use batter's boxes of slightly different sizes, but the norm is a box that is 7 feet (2.10 m) long by 3 feet (1 m) wide on each side of home plate (and the strike mat if one is used). Strike mats vary in size between 17 and 21 inches (43 and 53 cm) wide and 32.5 and 35 inches (83 and 89 cm) long. See table 5.1, pages 114–121, for specific strike mat dimensions for each national slowpitch softball organization.

In recent years many organizations have adopted the pitching box as another safety measure for pitchers. As shown in figure 9.1, the box extends behind the pitching rubber, allowing a greater distance between the batter and pitcher, giving the pitcher more time to react. The box varies in depth from 3 feet to 8 feet (1 m to 2.4 m) among the various slowpitch softball organizations, but the most common depth is 6 feet (1.8 m). Pitchers can release the ball anywhere inside that box.

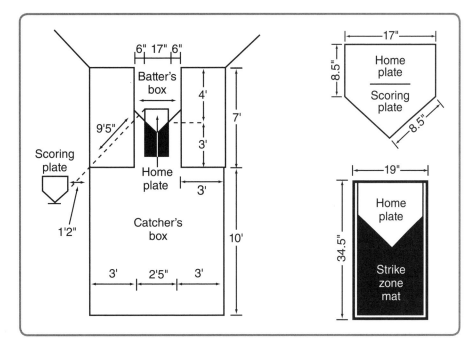

FIGURE 9.2 Batter's box, home plate, and catcher's box dimensions.

EQUIPMENT

As in most sports, you can begin to play slowpitch by making a modest investment in equipment, but as you play the game more you will likely decide to invest in a more expensive bat, a better glove, and shoes that give you more traction. You might even want to get a batting glove and a bag for all your equipment. In this section you'll learn all about the various kinds of equipment used to play the sport so that you can make informed decisions when purchasing your equipment.

Bats

Ask any player what the most important piece of equipment is in slowpitch softball, and he or she will most likely say, "Bat." As with most sports, technology has had an effect on slowpitch softball. The bats used today are technological wonders compared with the wooden bats of yesteryear. In this section we describe the basic characteristics of bats, bat composition, and bat certification issues. Then we will give you some guidelines for purchasing a bat.

Bat Metrics

Bats can be up to 34 inches (86 cm) long and weigh up to 38 ounces (1,077 g), although most bats used today are in the range of 26 to 30 ounces (737 to 850 g). Bats have three distinct parts: the barrel, the taper, and the handle. As you can see in figure 9.3, the handle is about 12 inches (30 cm) long and covered with a safety grip. Then the thin handle begins to flare out for a length of about 6 inches (15 cm) to join the 2 1/4-inch-diameter (5.7 cm) barrel that is between

Handle · Taper · Barrel

FIGURE 9.3 The three main parts of the bat.

12 and 14 inches (30 and 36 cm) long. The safety grip can be made from cork, nonplastic tape, or composition material. Other parts of the bat include a rubber, vinyl, or plastic end cap if the bat is not a one-piece construction, and a safety knob at the end of the handle. Detailed rules regarding the specifics of the safety grip and safety knob exist, so before you begin to customize your bat, make sure that what you're adding to the bat is legal according to your local or national softball organization.

Bats are either balanced or end loaded. End-loaded bats have more weight at the barrel end, and balanced bats have the weight more equally distributed along the entire barrel. Swinging a 27-ounce (765 g) balanced bat will feel lighter than swinging an end-loaded bat of the same weight. Power hitters generally prefer end-loaded bats, and place hitters usually prefer the feel of a balanced bat.

Bat Composition

Bats were initially made of wood, but in 1969 Easton introduced the first aluminum bat. These thin-walled hollow bats were appealing to players because of their lighter weight and flex. Lighter weight meant that players could swing the bat with greater speed, and as you know speed is part of the equation for hitting balls farther. Moreover, when bat meets ball, these bats compress and then spring back in a trampoline-like motion, causing the ball to jump off the bat with greater speed. The early single-walled bats were limited in durability because the aluminum alloys were not always strong enough to keep the bats from cracking or denting. Using improved alloys, single-walled bats are still made today and used by some players.

In 1993 the titanium bat made its appearance. Because titanium is a stronger alloy

Bats and other equipment on display at a national tournament.

than aluminum, these bats could be made with thinner walls than those in aluminum bats, which increased the trampoline effect of the bat. Batters could hit balls nearly 10 miles per hour (16 kph) faster, resulting in an increased distance of 40 to 50 feet (12 to 15 m). These bats were great for batters, but not so great for the safety of the fielders. Consequently, slowpitch softball organizations uniformly banned their use.

About the same time that the titanium bat was released, DeMarini released the first double-walled aluminum bat, and it became an immediate hit. The bat was constructed with two thin aluminum tubes, one inside the other, creating a giant sweet spot. With this bat players routinely hit the ball harder and farther than they could with other legal bats.

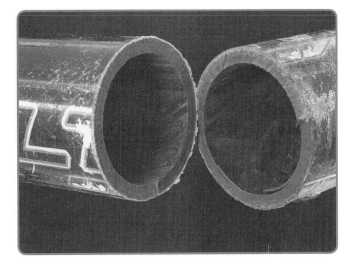

FIGURE 9.4 Cross-section of a composite bat.

In the mid-1980s graphite bats appeared in the marketplace, but they did not perform as well as aluminum bats and soon disappeared. In the late 1990s composite bats made out of carbon fiber, glass, or Kevlar began to appear (see figure 9.4). At first they did not perform as well as aluminum bats, but they gradually improved.

The now famous Miken Ultra composite bat hit the marketplace in 2002 and was an extremely hot bat, just like the titanium bats of the early 1990s. This original Ultra bat was banned from slowpitch because of its rocketlike performance, which increased the chance of injury to pitchers and other infielders. Not to be deterred, however, Miken came out with another composite bat, the Ultra II, which has been and continues to be one of the most popular bats sold.

A unique characteristic of composite bats is that they have a break-in period before the bat provides the greatest force to the ball. As the carbon fibers and resins begin to break up during initial use, the trampoline-like effect of the bat increases, which in turn makes the ball go farther. It's generally thought that a composite bat is broken in after a couple of hundred hits. Another characteristic of composite bats is that they break fairly easily, sometimes even before they've been fully broken in. And they are more vulnerable to breaking in temperatures below 60 °F (16 °C).

Here is a summary of the differences between aluminum and composite bats:

- Composite bats generate slightly greater batted-ball speeds. According to one study, ball speed coming off a composite bat was 5 to 10 miles per hour (8 to 16 kph) faster than ball speed coming off a double-walled aluminum bat.
- Composite bats have a break-in period, and aluminum bats do not.
- Vibrations are less intense in composite bats than in aluminum bats.
- Composite bats usually seem lighter to swing than aluminum bats of the same weight because of the balance point of the bat.
- Composite bats seem to be more forgiving when a ball is not hit on the sweet spot.
- Composite bats break more easily.

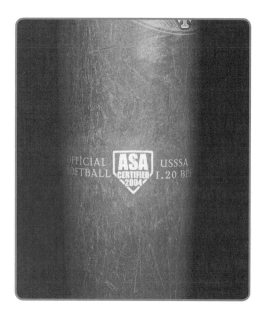

FIGURE 9.5 Bat certification marks.

Bat Certification

The softball bat that you play with must be marked with the words "Official Softball" for it to be legal, and it will need to have certification marks on it (see figure 9.5). Bats are certified because national softball organizations want to regulate the upper limit of speed with which balls are hit for the safety of the players.

In 2000 the Amateur Softball Association (ASA) established a policy for assessing bat performance by measuring batted-ball speed. The organization decided that for a bat to be ASA certified, the speed could be no greater than 85 miles per hour (137 kph). The testing procedure used, which is complex and beyond the scope of this book, was seriously flawed, so a more realistic testing procedure was adopted in 2004, along with a new standard of batted-ball speed. Now bats with a batted-ball speed not exceeding 98 miles per hour (158 kph) receive ASA certification.

The ASA updated its testing procedure again in 2009 for composite bats. Recognizing what slowpitch softball players have known for years—that the bats have a break-in period—ASA now simulates 1,000 swings before testing any composite bat toward the 2004 standard.

How do these regulations translate for the bat or bats that you use? If you're playing in a league or tournament sanctioned by the ASA, then your bat must have either an ASA 2000 or ASA 2004 certification mark on it if it is a bat manufactured before 2008. If it is a 2009 or later composite bat, it must have a 2009 certification on it. In addition, your bat must not be listed on the ASA nonapproved bat list.

Other organizations use a different method for testing bats called bat performance factor, or BPF. Bats must be marked with a BPF of 1.20 or less, although in 2010 this was increased to 1.21 or less by a number of senior softball organizations. This method of testing is more indirect than the ASA method and is generally regarded as not being as useful as the batted-ball speed method.

World Softball League rules stipulate that ASA 2004 bat certifications will be used in its tournaments unless the tournament is declared a 1.20 BPF event. Although certification is predominantly a safety issue, some softball purists also feel that the bat restrictions help to restore balance to the game between offense and defense.

Altered Bats

Unfortunately, not everyone agrees with the bat certification regulations. So a few players look for a way to gain an unfair advantage in their hitting by altering their bats, by what's called doctoring or juicing the bat. These practices are illegal, and we condemn them. We include this list of illegal alterations only to make you aware of the things that you, or anyone else, should not do to your bats.

1. It is illegal to take an unapproved or uncertified bat and repaint it to look like an approved bat.
2. It is not legal to change the bat's balance, either by adding weight to the end of the bat or by moving weight from the handle to the end of the barrel.
3. It is illegal to shave the interior walls of the barrel. The decreased thickness of the barrel wall increases the trampoline effect of the bat.

You should be aware of one additional practice considered bat doctoring by the ASA: It's called accelerated break-in. Rather than waiting for the bat to break in naturally after several hundred hits, a bat can be artificially broken in by rolling or compressing it. In both cases the composite fibers are broken, making the bat less stiff. This process increases the trampoline effect, causing the maximum allowed ball speed to be exceeded. Although these procedures do not add or redistribute the weight of the bat, they tamper with a product that was certified based on its original construction according to the ASA.

Players caught cheating can be banned from play for up to 10 years and have been subjected to significant monetary loss from lawsuits filed by bat manufacturers and bat-certifying organizations. Managers are also subject to suspension, and games played with altered bats are forfeited. The penalties for using doctored bats are severe, as they should be. Not only is it cheating; it disrespects the game.

Buying a Bat

Now you're ready to buy a bat. We won't recommend specific bats for you to buy, but we will tell you that Anderson, Combat, DeMarini, Easton, Louisville Slugger, Miken, and Worth are all respected leaders in the field, producing bats used by millions of slowpitch softball players around the world. Follow these guidelines and you'll likely be happy with your purchase.

- Select the right bat weight for you. Reread pages 16–18 in chapter 1 to help you.
- Determine whether you prefer the feel of a balanced bat or an end-loaded bat.
- Decide how serious you are about playing. If you're playing once a week in a recreational league, you don't need an expensive, high-performance bat. If you're playing tournament ball, then you'll probably want the best-performing bat you can find.
- Consider your budget when buying a bat. Bats range in price from under US$100 to over $300 for some high-performance bats.
- Decide whether you prefer a single-walled or double-walled aluminum bat, or a composite bat. If you will be playing when the temperature is below 60 °F (16 °C), you may not want to purchase a composite bat.
- Make certain that the bat you select is certified for use in the leagues or organizations in which you'll be playing. Most organizations will post any bat regulations on their Web sites.

We recommend that you don't just walk into a sporting goods store to purchase a bat or order one from a catalog or Web site. If you're already playing, ask your teammates whether you can try out their bats and why they selected the bats that they use. If you're not on a team, go watch some local games and see what bats are popular. Ask some of the players to let you swing their bats and tell you why they selected that bat.

Balls

You wouldn't think that there could be so many variations to the small object known as a softball, but there are. The only common denominator is that every softball is round! Beyond that, they can vary in size, color, stitching, speed, and hardness.

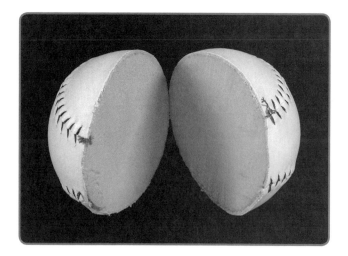

FIGURE 9.6 Interior of a softball.

Ball Metrics

Official softballs are smooth seamed, even surfaced, and, of course, round. The ball has a center core made out of one of the following substances: a silky fiber called kapok, a mixture of cork and rubber, a polyurethane mixture, or other approved materials (see figure 9.6). The ball is either hand or machine wound with a fine twisted yarn and is then covered with latex or rubber cement before the two-piece cover made of leather or synthetic material is sewn to the ball using a waxed cotton or linen thread.

The size of the ball varies according to the division of play. An 11-inch (27.9 cm) ball (weighing between 5 7/8 and 6 1/8 ounces [between 167 and 174 g]) is used in women's play, and a 12-inch (30.5 cm) ball (weighing between 6 1/4 and 7 ounces [between 177 and 198 g]) is used in men's play. In coed play an 11-inch ball is used when a woman bats, and a 12-inch ball is used when a man is up to bat.

Different color stitching and different color balls are used by various organizations. Although white balls were the norm for years, optic yellow balls have become increasingly popular because they are easier for players to see. Worth, Dudley, and Trump are among the most prominent ball manufacturers.

COR and Compression

You may have heard players and officials talking about the COR and compression of balls, discussing various numbers that meant nothing to you. And, of course, you didn't want to ask and appear stupid. Actually, many players don't fully understand what these numbers mean. So let's find out.

COR, short for coefficient of restitution, is a measure of the loss of speed of a ball bouncing off an immovable object like a wall. Here's how it works. A ball is projected at a solid wall at 90 miles per hour (145 kph), and let's say that it bounces back at 42 miles per hour (68 kph). Thus the speed is reduced by 47% (42 divided by 90 = .47), and so that ball is labeled as having a .47 COR. The higher the COR is, the speedier the bounce back is and the more lively the ball is.

Compression measures the hardness of a softball. It is a measure of how many pounds of force are needed to compress the ball 1/4 inch (0.6 cm). When it takes 375 pounds of pressure per square inch (2,600 kPa) to compress a ball 1/4 inch, the ball receives a compression rating of 375. If it takes 525 pounds of pressure per square inch (3,600 kPa) to compress a ball 1/4 inch, its compression rating is 525. Generally, a 525 compression ball will go farther than a 375 compression ball will, but it also depends on the type of bat used to hit the ball. Low-compression balls don't do as well with more flexible bats.

The various organizations use different combinations of COR and compression, and you'll see balls from .44 COR 375 compression to .47 COR 525 compression and various combinations in between. The COR and compression ratings are often printed on the ball.

So why do different organizations use balls with different COR and compression? Various combinations of COR and compression lead to more or less lively balls. The less lively balls allow for more reaction time by the defense and limit the number of out-of-the-park home runs hit in a game. More lively balls often lead to higher game scores.

Fielding Gloves

Besides your bat, your glove is probably the most important piece of equipment that you use to play slowpitch softball. You'll want a good glove that is broken in so that it is flexible but not an overused rag that collapses when you don't catch the ball perfectly in the pocket. It should feel comfortable on your hand—not too short, not too long, and not too heavy. Gloves vary in length, but generally infield gloves are 11 3/4 to 12 3/4 inches (30 to 32 cm) long and outfield gloves are 12 3/4 to 14 inches (32 to 36 cm) long.

Traditionally, infielders, especially shortstops and second basepersons, have tended to use smaller gloves so that they can get the ball out of the pocket faster to make relay throws, whereas outfielders usually use larger gloves with deeper pockets because they often reach for fly balls. But we think that overall a bigger glove is more advantageous than a smaller one because it allows you to field any type of ball more easily.

Unlike baseball and fastpitch softball, specialized catchers and first-base mitts are not typically used in slowpitch softball, although they can be. (Gloves have fingers, and mitts do not.) The rulebooks of all slowpitch softball organizations specify the exact dimensions of gloves and the colors of gloves that are unacceptable.

Besides the size of the glove and which hand it will fit on, you'll want to consider other qualities or characteristics of gloves when making a decision to purchase one (see figure 9.7).

- **Material**: You can choose between leather, treated leather, or synthetic materials. Leather is the most durable, and synthetic material is the least expensive. Treated leather usually is more flexible and therefore easier to break in.

- **Open or closed web**: An open web allows players to get the ball out faster; a closed web provides additional support for catching the ball.

- **Glove pockets**: Shallow pockets are used more often by infielders; deeper pockets are preferred by outfielders.

- **Open- or closed-back glove**: Open-back (or conventional) gloves have an open space across the back around the wrist and are used most often by infielders; closed-back gloves provide a little more support and are more often used by outfielders.

- **Wrist adjustments**: Located on the backs of gloves, this wrist strap (often Velcro) keeps the glove tight on the player's hand.

- **Price**: Gloves vary in price from under US$100 to upward of $400. Paying more doesn't necessarily get you more. Many good gloves are available for under $100.

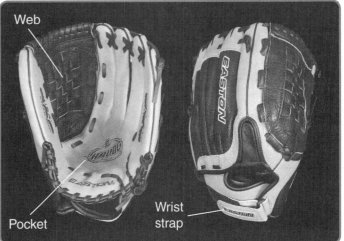

FIGURE 9.7 Parts of the glove.

Well-known glove manufacturers include Akadema, Easton, Louisville Slugger, Mizuno, Nokona, Rawlings, Wilson, and Worth. No hard and fast rules govern which glove is best for you. See what other players are using and try on several before making your decision. Your choice comes down to what feels good and what is in your price range.

Treated gloves break in easily, but untreated leather gloves often require 1,000 catches or more before they're broken in. Usually the better the leather is, the longer it takes. Special glove oil or conditioner should be used to coat the glove lightly, beginning with the palm area and then moving outward until the entire glove is covered. Some experts recommend putting the oil on a cloth rather than on the glove directly so that the glove doesn't become saturated. Keeping a softball in the pocket of the glove, especially when new, also helps to shape it. Make sure that you keep your glove away from water and don't apply any direct heat to it to dry it out.

Batting Gloves

Another type of glove that you might want to invest in is a batting glove, or a pair of batting gloves. These gloves are designed to help you get a better grip on the bat, especially when your hands are sweating, and to reduce the vibration that you'll feel from the bat, especially in cold weather. But batting gloves are worn for other reasons, too. Some players wear one under their fielding glove to keep the sweat off it, whereas others wear them to protect their hands when sliding.

Most players wear only one glove while batting, but some prefer a glove on each hand. If you wear a single glove, you usually wear it on the bottom hand on the bat, the arm and hand that produces most of the power in the swing. So if you bat right-handed, you wear the glove on your left hand.

The glove should fit snugly, but not tightly, on your hand, and there should be no loose material when you grip the bat. Most players wear gloves made of a single layer of leather to get a better feel on the bat, but some prefer a slightly padded glove (see figure 9.8). The additional padding protects particularly vulnerable areas, such as the area inside your thumb, and can decrease the stinging sensation from the bat. Many companies produce quality batting gloves, ranging in price from about US$17 to $50 per pair.

Ball Bags

You'll likely want to invest in some type of a ball bag to transport your equipment to and from the field. The size and type of bag that you get depends on what you want to carry and how you want to carry it (see figure 9.9). The traditional bags can be carried over your shoulder or wheeled to the field, using a set of small wheels on the underside of the bag. Many bat bags have pockets for two or more bats and flexible inserts that can be moved around with the aid of Velcro strips to make sections of various sizes. Some

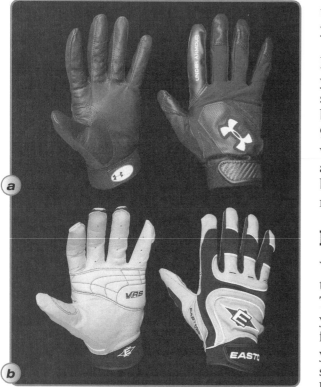

FIGURE 9.8 *(a)* Unpadded and *(b)* padded batting gloves.

have zippers with conveniently placed D-rings, allowing you to lock your bag when flying to tournaments. In recent years, bat backpacks have become popular for those who have less to carry. Most of the major bat manufacturers make a variety of bat bags, varying in price from about US$25 to over $100.

Shoes and Socks

Molded cleats or turf shoes are the shoes normally seen on slowpitch softball fields (see figure 9.10), but some players wear running shoes or cross-trainers. The advantage of cleats or turf shoes is that they generally give you better footing, which is especially important in running the bases and when playing on wet grass or moving from the infield to the outfield to make a play.

The shoe uppers are made from leather, canvas, mesh, or synthetic materials. The bottoms of the shoes will be rubber or some type of a molded plastic. Turf shoes have a series of small nubby protrusions that cover the entire bottom of the shoe. Another type of sole is made by Tanel, who has created a 360° circular cleat pattern that is advertised as providing "torque reducing pivot-ability." Shoes with metal cleats are not permitted in slowpitch softball.

Most of the shoes come in a variety of colors, and as with other athletic shoes you can find high tops, mid-cut, or low-cut shoes to meet your needs with prices ranging from US$20 to over $100. Regardless of what type of shoe you buy, make sure that you get a good fit that offers firm arch support to avoid podiatric problems.

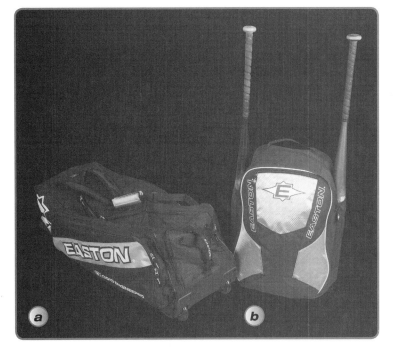

FIGURE 9.9 *(a)* Ball bag that can be carried over the shoulder or rolled on wheels and *(b)* backpack.

FIGURE 9.10 *(a)* Turf shoes and *(b)* molded cleats.

When trying on shoes, wear the socks that you'll wear when you play. Socks come in all varieties—crew socks or low cuts, white or colored, and thick or thin. Some do a better job of wicking moisture, whereas others claim to be better shock absorbers. As with shoes, comfort is the first thing to consider when purchasing socks.

Protective Equipment

A wide variety of protective equipment is available for softball players. We'll cover the main ones in this section, from head to toe.

- **Helmets or facemasks**. Unlike baseball or fastpitch softball, batters in slowpitch don't wear head protection, nor do catchers. Increasingly, however, pitchers are wearing helmets or facemasks to protect themselves from line drives or errant bounces. If you're in the market for a helmet, comfort comes first; otherwise you won't wear it. Then look for sufficient padding, strong construction, light weight, good ventilation, unobstructed vision, and ease of adjustment (see figure 9.11). Two of the more popular helmets or masks are made by Worth and Markwort Sporting Goods, the maker of Game Face. Prices vary between US$30 and $80.

- **Mouth guards**. For players who want to protect their teeth but don't want to wear something as large as a helmet, a mouth guard is the perfect answer. A mouth guard not only protects the teeth from direct blows but also acts as a buffer between the teeth and the tongue and lips, and between braces and cheeks, limiting injury that can occur to soft tissue. Several types of mouth guards are available, the least expensive being a stock mouth guard that comes preformed and ready to wear. Another type of mouth guard is one that you boil to soften and then bite into to provide a more customized fit than the stock guard. Both types of mouth guards can be purchased at sporting goods stores, and they are less expensive than the custom-made guards that dentists can provide. The latter will fit you the best but will cost you more.

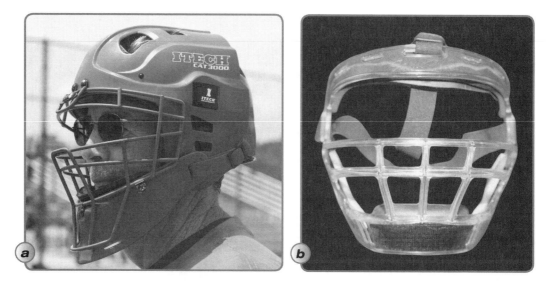

FIGURE 9.11 *(a)* Helmet; *(b)* facemask.

- **Sliding and compression shorts**. Sliding shorts are worn underneath your uniform shorts or pants and offer protection to the legs and buttocks from abrasions that may occur during slides. Many styles have extra padding on the side and buttocks panels and come in a variety of comfortable, moisture-wicking materials (see figure 9.12). Some sliding shorts for men also have a cup, or protector, pocket. With balls coming off the bat so quickly, pitchers and other infielders may feel safer if they wear this piece of protective equipment, either as part of sliding or compression shorts or in an athletic supporter. Some women's sliding shorts have a special pelvic protector to provide additional protection. Compression shorts not only provide protection for sliding but also provide warmth and support, minimizing injury to the groin, hamstrings, and thighs. You can spend as little as US$10 or as much as $40 to find shorts that are right for you.

FIGURE 9.12 Sliding shorts.

- **Braces, wraps, and pads**. Attend a few softball games, especially senior softball games, and you'll see a wide variety of braces, wraps, and pads. For nearly any part of the body, from elbows to forearms, wrists, hands, groins, thighs, knees, calves, ankles, and feet, a product offers some type of support for whatever your ailment or need. Sporting goods stores devote entire sections to these mostly elastic or neoprene products that claim to take pressure off an injured area, keep it warm, aid in the recovery process, or protect against future injury.

Most, but not all, purchases of these products are made after a self-diagnosis rather than a doctor's specific recommendation. Players with significant knee problems, usually some type of ligament or cartilage injury, may wear a more substantial brace than those made of elastic or neoprene. Made out of some type of lightweight aluminum or carbon composite material, with padding added for comfort, these braces may be worn as an alternative to surgery or as additional support after a knee is surgically repaired. You'll want to consider wearing kneepads if you like to go down on your knees to field ground balls. Longer pads cover both the knee and several inches below it to protect the lower legs when sliding. Shorter kneepads similar to what volleyball players wear to protect their knees against floor burns are another option.

FIGURE 9.13 Soccer-style shin guard.

- **Shin guards**. Some pitchers wear shin guards to protect themselves from balls hit up the middle. Most players who want this protection wear either a fastpitch molded plastic shin protector or some type of a strap-on guard, neither of which is made specifically for slowpitch play but will do the job. Another option, which doesn't offer as much protection, is to wear soccer shin guards underneath high socks to keep them in place (see figure 9.13).

- **Sweat bands**. Players who sweat a great deal frequently wear cotton bands that absorb moisture. Wrist bands range in width from 1 to 4 inches (2.5 to 10 cm) and help keep sweat from getting into the glove or onto the bat grip, and a head band worn beneath the cap helps keep sweat from dripping down the forehead into the eyes. Do-rags are popular with a few players (especially those with no hair) because they cover the entire head. Besides keeping sweat from dripping from underneath the cap, they provide protection from the sun when wearing mesh caps.

Uniforms

The color and style of uniforms is usually left to the manager or sponsor to decide, but sometimes players have a voice in the matter. Uniforms can vary dramatically between league and tournament play, but in most leagues all players must wear identical shirts, each having a unique number on the back. In tournament play, hats or visors, pants or shorts, and jackets might make up the remainder of the uniform. We'll discuss each of these components briefly in this section, directing specific comments to tournament play as needed.

Our number-one piece of advice for those buying uniforms is to keep it simple! You'll see many teams who have different color combinations for different days of a tournament. For the first day they wear white shirts, and on the second day they wear red shirts. They may or may not switch the color of their pants or shorts. Although this may look attractive, it has limitations that you should consider. First, players forget. Inevitably, someone shows up wearing the wrong shirt, even though they were reminded what shirt to wear the day before. The second problem is that more than likely you don't have another shirt to change into if you happen to play back-to-back games on a hot day. With your second shirt being of a different color, you can't change unless the entire team does.

The solution to these limitations is simple. Especially for tournaments, buy each player two or three of the same color shirt (and shorts or pants). That way, players can switch out shirts so that they always have a dry shirt when playing more than one game in a day.

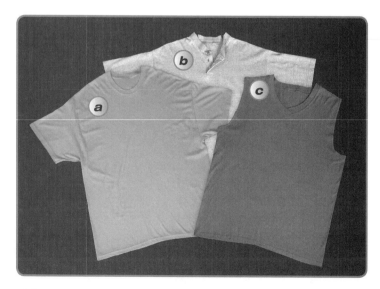

FIGURE 9.14 *(a)* T-shirt, *(b)* Henley, and *(c)* sleeveless vest shirt styles.

- **Shirts**. Shirts come in several styles (see figure 9.14), including T-shirts, the popular Henley shirts (collarless shirts with a 4- to 6-inch-long [10 to 15 cm long] placket, usually having three buttons), or sleeveless vests (worn over T-shirts, which can be changed as needed). Shirts made with moisture-wicking material are popular among players, but uniform shirts are also made from 50–50 polyester and cotton, 100% polyester mesh, and heavier 100% cotton. Most shirts are short sleeve, although some women prefer to play in a sleeveless top. In cooler weather, players often choose to wear a long-sleeve shirt underneath their uniform shirt for additional warmth. All shirts must be the same color and must have 6–inch (15 cm) numbers on the back between 0 and 99. The team name is usually on the front of the shirt.

- **Pants or shorts**. You'll see both shorts and long pants worn during softball games. Players on the same team can choose to wear either shorts or pants in any game; the whole team does not need to wear one or the other. The style and color of the pants and shorts should be identical (i.e., same color, same color braid, and so on), but in leagues and low-key tournaments, this rule is often not enforced. Most shorts and long pants are made from polyester, although a polyester mesh or moisture-wicking material is also used (see figure 9.15). The most popular shorts and pants have tunnel belt loops, two set-in pockets, double snaps on the front, and a brass zipper. Nylon or heavyweight polyester are used for the best-made shorts and pants.

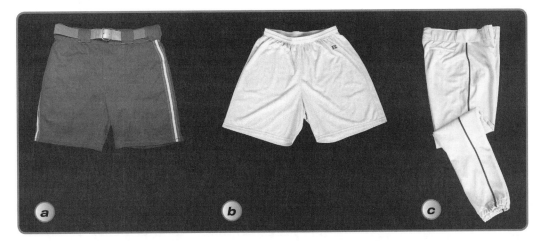

FIGURE 9.15 *(a)* Polyester shorts, *(b)* mesh shorts, and *(c)* polyester pants.

- **Jackets**. You'll likely need some type of a jacket when playing softball, depending on what part of the country you live in. Probably the most common jackets you'll see are nylon pullovers with snaps on the placket. They come in both short-sleeve and long-sleeve versions and are available in a variety of colors to complement any uniform. You also see players with jackets that zip or snap, are made with or without pockets, and have linings for cooler days.

- **Hats, caps, and visors**. Manufacturers offer a wide variety of styles, colors, and fabrics (see figure 9.16). For years, wool was the fabric of choice, but in recent years many teams have gone to a soft mesh material because it is cooler during the hot months. Sweatbands on the inside of hats help absorb moisture and keep players cooler. Visors have become popular in recent years. Players of both sexes wear them, but clearly women wear them more frequently. They are made from many of the same fabrics as the hats are, and they generally have Velcro closures.

FIGURE 9.16 Hats and visors come in a variety of fitted and adjustable styles and materials.

Hats and visors can be ordered from the companies that provide the team uniforms, from local sporting goods stores, or from companies that can embroider the hats and visors with the team name or logo. Prices range from under US$5 to as much as $15, depending on the style, quantity purchased, and whether the item is embroidered or not.

FIGURE 9.17 Pitching screen.

TRAINING AND PRACTICE EQUIPMENT

Let's look at various training and practice aids that you may find helpful.

- **Pitching screens**. One of the most useful pieces of equipment that a team can have is a pitching screen, which is used to protect the pitcher during batting practice. Several different screens are available, but one we highly recommend is the Pitch Safe™ Pitching Screen. It's simple to use, durable, and not too costly. And best of all, these screens are portable, so they can be transported easily. The screen, measuring 76 inches (193 cm) tall and 38 inches (96.5 cm) wide and weighing 20 pounds (9 kg), is lined up just in front of the pitcher's box (see figure 9.17). The pitcher is positioned directly behind it, stepping to the side of it to release the ball and then immediately back behind it after releasing the pitch. Without a doubt, this type of protection has saved many pitchers from serious injury.

- **Weighted or specialized bats**. Players in the on-deck circle use a variety of methods to loosen up before stepping up to the plate. The most common include swinging a much heavier bat than normal, swinging two or more bats, adding some type of weight to the bat, or swinging a unique batlike device. At one time players commonly used donut weights, but they are no longer legal because of the chance that they will fly off the end of the bat and injure someone. One attachable bat weight that is legal is the Pow'r Wrap made by Grand Enterprises West. It is placed over the barrel of the bat, weighs 24 ounces (680 g), and is made of recycled polycarbonate plastic. Another popular device used for warming up is made by Schutt and is called the Dirx Warm-Up Bat. It has an adjustable-weight bat that allows you to simulate your bat by moving a weight along a metal rod so that it feels balanced or end loaded. Most models come in various weights, ranging from 80 to 130 ounces (2.3 to 3.7 kg). Although many players use weighted bats, we believe that they are not beneficial and are contrary to the principle of specificity discussed in part I.

  Another device that players might use before the game or in practice is the Chute Trainer made by Atec. It's a parachute-like device that attaches to the bat to increase bat resistance, intended to improve bat speed and power in a game.

- **Batting tees**. Another popular device is the batting tee. Players can work on refining their swing by hitting off these tees and then return to hitting pitched balls.

- **Weighted balls**. Players sometimes warm up with weighted balls that weigh from 12 to 16 ounces (340 to 450 g). These heavier balls can help warm up shoulder and arm muscles before a game as well as help players strengthen or rehabilitate muscles following injury. But these weighted balls can also cause injury by overstressing the muscles and may adversely influence throwing accuracy when players resume throwing a regular softball.

SUMMARY

- Slowpitch is played on fields with 65-foot (20 m) basepaths and fences ranging from 275 feet (84 m) for women to about 300 feet (91 m) for men. The pitcher is 50 to 58 feet (15 to 18 m) from home plate when the ball is released.

- Your bat can be either balanced or end loaded. The average weight is between 26 and 30 ounces (737 and 850 g), and the bat can measure no more than 34 inches (86 cm) in length.

- Double-walled aluminum and composite bats are the most popular bats among serious players.

- All bats must meet minimum certification requirements to be used in leagues or tournaments.

- Softballs have both a COR and compression measure. The COR influences the speed of the ball and varies between .44 and .47, whereas the compression measures how hard the ball is and varies between 375 and 525 pounds per square inch (2,600 to 3,600 kPa).

- Fielding gloves are made from leather or synthetic materials and measure 11 3/4 to 12 3/4 inches (30 to 32 cm) long for infielders and 12 3/4 to 14 inches (32 to 36 cm) for outfielders. They have an open or closed web, shallow or deep pockets, and open or closed backs with wrist adjustments.

- Molded cleats or turf shoes will give you the best footing while playing softball.

- Batting gloves and ball bags are two accessories that you may want to invest in if you're a serious player.

- Protective equipment ranges from mouth guards and facemasks for pitchers and infielders to sliding shorts and braces, wraps, and pads worn by any player.

- The minimum uniform for league play is identical shirts with different numbers on the back. Short-sleeve moisture-wicking shirts are the most popular, and players can wear either shorts or long pants depending on their preference. Jackets and hats or visors round out the typical uniform worn by both men and women.

- Pitching screens should be used in batting practice whenever possible to protect the pitcher.

- Weighted bats, batting tees, and weighted balls are all training devices that players use to help them prepare to play. But you should evaluate whether they indeed are helpful based on the principle of specificity discussed in chapter 2.

CHAPTER 10

Physical Preparation

Slowpitch is far from being the most demanding sport in terms of physical conditioning, but if you've been inactive you'll want to do some conditioning before taking up the game. If you play recreational slowpitch softball during the summer season in a local league but don't work out during the off-season, then before you leap out on the diamond and pull a muscle, you'll want to do some cardiovascular and muscular conditioning. And if you're a serious slowpitch softball player who participates in tournaments, but you don't work out regularly, you can improve your game and health with a well-planned year-long conditioning program. In this chapter you'll learn the benefits of a well-designed fitness program, the components of physical fitness, and the physical demands of slowpitch softball. We'll also explain the principles of fitness training and provide you with some solid advice about good nutrition and hydration for softball players.

BENEFITS OF FITNESS

People are considered physically fit when they can meet the physical demands of their sport to perform up to their ability. Compared with sports like basketball, soccer, rowing, and wrestling, softball is at the low end of the physical demands to play the game well. Nevertheless, a weekend tournament in which you play six or eight games when the heat index is well over 100 °F (38 °C) can be demanding, and a reasonable level of fitness is essential.

Although playing softball will help improve your fitness level if you've been inactive, to be really fit to play softball, you'll need to supplement your playing

This chapter is abridged and revised from Rainer Martens, *Successful Coaching*, *Third Edition*, Part IV, "Principles of Physical Training," Human Kinetics, 2004.

Improve your fitness to play better and live longer.

© Human Kinetics

with other conditioning activities. Many of our softball friends observe that one of the benefits of playing softball is that it motivates them to keep in shape, and almost all of them supplement their playing with some form of aerobic exercise and strength training. So don't expect to play yourself into shape; get yourself into shape to play.

There are many good reasons why you should improve your fitness to play softball:

- You'll perform better. The evidence is clear that players in better physical condition perform better, or we might say that they are able to play closer to their potential.
- You'll experience less physical and mental fatigue when playing multiple games.
- You'll recover quicker after strenuous practices and games.
- You'll have far less muscle soreness.
- You'll reduce your chances of injury and will recover quicker from many types of injuries.
- You'll play with greater self-confidence knowing that you're prepared.
- And last, you'll enjoy the game more as a result of performing better and feeling less fatigued.

Now those are good reasons to get into shape. But wait before you drop this book to get your workout clothes on; we have even more good news. Improved physical fitness along with good nutrition is a recipe for these additional benefits:

- You have a much better chance of avoiding disease, especially diseases associated with inactivity such as obesity and type 2 diabetes.
- You'll have a higher quality of life by maintaining your ability to function independently.
- You have a higher probability of living longer. If you love life—and softball—you need no more reasons than this.

So get fit and stay fit, not only to play softball better but to live longer and better.

COMPONENTS OF FITNESS

You probably know that physical fitness includes two major components:

- energy fitness, or what is sometimes called cardiovascular or aerobic fitness, and
- muscular fitness.

Let's learn a little bit more about these two types of fitness now.

Energy Fitness

Our bodies have two energy systems, anaerobic and aerobic, that fuel our muscles and remove carbon dioxide and other wastes. The anaerobic system is for immediate and intense bursts of activity and is the energy system that you use to sprint from home to second base, to race across the outfield to snare a line drive, and to hit a towering home run. The fuel for the anaerobic system is stored in the muscles, is available for immediate use, and does not require oxygen to burn the fuel (*anaerobic* means "without oxygen"). But this fuel supply is limited and thus can produce energy for only about 2 minutes of intense activity before the aerobic system takes over (see figure 10.1).

The aerobic system is for more enduring and less intense activity. It is your source of energy when jogging or having a lively (not standing around) practice session. The aerobic system uses the carbohydrates and fats stored in our bodies combined with oxygen (*aerobic* means "with oxygen") to produce glucose, which is converted to the fuel that your muscles need to work. Fat is the major source of fuel for the aerobic system, supplemented with a limited supply of carbohydrate. About 80% of the energy needed to play slowpitch softball comes from the anaerobic system, and the other 20% comes from the aerobic system.

Muscular Fitness

Muscular fitness is composed of five components, and you'll need all five to play softball to the best of your ability.

1. **Muscular strength** is the maximum amount of force that a muscle can generate in a single effort. You learned about the importance of strength in hitting in chapter 2.

2. **Muscular endurance** is the ability of muscles to contract repeatedly or to sustain a continuous contraction involving less than maximum force. Muscular endurance, which applies more to hitting than defensive play, is typically less important in slowpitch softball because of the recuperation time available between turns at bat.

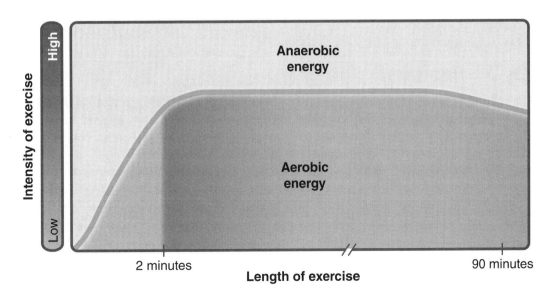

FIGURE 10.1 Sources of energy.

Adapted, by permission, from R. Martens, 2004, *Successful coaching*, 3rd ed. (Champaign, IL: Human Kinetics), 270.

© Human Kinetics

Through strength training you can increase your power to hit better.

3. **Muscular power** is speed and strength combined, or the ability to exert muscular strength quickly. Power is vital in hitting and to a lesser extent in throwing. When you increase strength or speed you increase power.

4. **Speed** is the ability to move the body or parts of it very quickly. Of course, we all know that speed is a great asset in softball, not only in base-running but in fielding as well. A popular myth is that speed is inherited and can't be trained, but it can, and we'll give you a reference to learn how.

5. **Flexibility** is the range of motion through which the joints of the body are able to move. Less flexibility limits movement and increases the risk of muscle strains and tears. Too much laxness puts joints at greater risk of sprains and dislocations. Without intervention, we lose flexibility as we age, but you can maintain reasonable flexibility with a good stretching program.

Fitness Demands of Slowpitch Softball

In table 10.1 you can compare the estimated energy and muscular fitness demands for slowpitch softball with a few other sports. Although slowpitch softball is not the most physically demanding sport, a reasonably good aerobic foundation and at least moderate levels of muscular fitness are helpful in playing the game at an optimal level.

Are You Ready to Be Active?

If you've been sedentary for the last 6 months or more and you now want to begin playing slowpitch softball in a local league, read and answer the questions in figure 10.2 on page 230. This questionnaire is widely used to screen people when they are beginning to participate in physical activity after a month or more of inactivity. If you answered yes to any of the questions, you are advised to seek a medical opinion about your health condition before you begin to play.

We wish we had space to describe for you a comprehensive fitness test that determines your energy and muscular fitness levels, but that would require another small book. Nevertheless, we encourage you to ascertain your fitness level before you undertake a fitness training program and then retest yourself after 6 months and 1 year.

TABLE 10.1 Estimated Energy and Muscular Fitness Demands for Slowpitch Softball Compared With Other Sports

Sport	ENERGY FITNESS		MUSCULAR FITNESS				
	Aerobic	Anaerobic	Flexibility	Strength	Endurance	Speed	Power
Softball hitting	L	H	M	M	L	H	H
Softball fielding	L	M	M	L	L	H	M
Softball baserunning	L	H	M	M	L	H	M
Basketball	M–H	H	M	M	M–H	H	M
Football linemen	L	H	M	H	M	M	H
Football running backs	M	H	M	H	M	H	H
Football receivers	M	H	M	M	M	H	M
Golf	L–M	L	M–H	L–M	L–M	L	M
Soccer (other than goalkeeper)	H	H	M	M	H	H	H
Tennis	M–H	M–H	M–H	M	M–H	H	H
Volleyball	M	M–H	M–H	M	M	M–H	H

L = low, M = moderate, and H = high.

So if you're serious about becoming fitter to play softball and living a healthier life, we have an outstanding general fitness program to recommend to you. It's the American College of Sports Medicine's (ACSM) Fitness Program. ACSM is the world's leading health and fitness organization. Its members are sport scientists, health and fitness experts, and sports medicine doctors. These people are real experts, not celebrities touting fad programs.

ACSM's experts have developed a fitness test that you can take at home with the help of a family member or friend. For each test item you can evaluate your results by looking at comparable scores for your sex and age. Then, using your fitness test results, you're guided into an exercise program appropriate for your current fitness level and you are shown how to do the various exercises recommended. The program is scientifically sound, easy to understand, and a sensible way for you to improve your general fitness.

The ACSM Fitness Program is presented in *ACSM Fitness Book*, *Third Edition*, published by Human Kinetics. Thousands of people have used this inexpensive reference to get them started with a quality fitness program. If your fitness level is fairly good but you want to improve a component of your fitness, see the references in appendix A for resources for improving strength, speed, power, flexibility, and aerobic fitness.

PAR-Q & YOU

Physical Activity Readiness
Questionnaire - PAR-Q
(revised 2002)

(A Questionnaire for People Aged 15 to 69)

Regular physical activity is fun and healthy, and increasingly more people are starting to become more active every day. Being more active is very safe for most people. However, some people should check with their doctor before they start becoming much more physically active.

If you are planning to become much more physically active than you are now, start by answering the seven questions in the box below. If you are between the ages of 15 and 69, the PAR-Q will tell you if you should check with your doctor before you start. If you are over 69 years of age, and you are not used to being very active, check with your doctor.

Common sense is your best guide when you answer these questions. Please read the questions carefully and answer each one honestly: check YES or NO.

YES	NO		
☐	☐	1.	**Has your doctor ever said that you have a heart condition <u>and</u> that you should only do physical activity recommended by a doctor?**
☐	☐	2.	**Do you feel pain in your chest when you do physical activity?**
☐	☐	3.	**In the past month, have you had chest pain when you were not doing physical activity?**
☐	☐	4.	**Do you lose your balance because of dizziness or do you ever lose consciousness?**
☐	☐	5.	**Do you have a bone or joint problem (for example, back, knee or hip) that could be made worse by a change in your physical activity?**
☐	☐	6.	**Is your doctor currently prescribing drugs (for example, water pills) for your blood pressure or heart condition?**
☐	☐	7.	**Do you know of <u>any other reason</u> why you should not do physical activity?**

If you answered

YES to one or more questions

Talk with your doctor by phone or in person BEFORE you start becoming much more physically active or BEFORE you have a fitness appraisal. Tell your doctor about the PAR-Q and which questions you answered YES.

- You may be able to do any activity you want — as long as you start slowly and build up gradually. Or, you may need to restrict your activities to those which are safe for you. Talk with your doctor about the kinds of activities you wish to participate in and follow his/her advice.
- Find out which community programs are safe and helpful for you.

NO to all questions

If you answered NO honestly to <u>all</u> PAR-Q questions, you can be reasonably sure that you can:

- start becoming much more physically active — begin slowly and build up gradually. This is the safest and easiest way to go.
- take part in a fitness appraisal — this is an excellent way to determine your basic fitness so that you can plan the best way for you to live actively. It is also highly recommended that you have your blood pressure evaluated. If your reading is over 144/94, talk with your doctor before you start becoming much more physically active.

DELAY BECOMING MUCH MORE ACTIVE:
- if you are not feeling well because of a temporary illness such as a cold or a fever — wait until you feel better; or
- if you are or may be pregnant — talk to your doctor before you start becoming more active.

PLEASE NOTE: If your health changes so that you then answer YES to any of the above questions, tell your fitness or health professional. Ask whether you should change your physical activity plan.

<u>Informed Use of the PAR-Q</u>: The Canadian Society for Exercise Physiology, Health Canada, and their agents assume no liability for persons who undertake physical activity, and if in doubt after completing this questionnaire, consult your doctor prior to physical activity.

No changes permitted. You are encouraged to photocopy the PAR-Q but only if you use the entire form.

NOTE: If the PAR-Q is being given to a person before he or she participates in a physical activity program or a fitness appraisal, this section may be used for legal or administrative purposes.

"I have read, understood and completed this questionnaire. Any questions I had were answered to my full satisfaction."

NAME _____

SIGNATURE _____ DATE_____

SIGNATURE OF PARENT _____ WITNESS _____
or GUARDIAN (for participants under the age of majority)

Note: This physical activity clearance is valid for a maximum of 12 months from the date it is completed and becomes invalid if your condition changes so that you would answer YES to any of the seven questions.

CSEP SCPE © Canadian Society for Exercise Physiology

Supported by: Health Canada Santé Canada

continued on other side...

FIGURE 10.2 Physical activity readiness questionnaire.

DESIGN OF A PHYSICAL TRAINING PROGRAM

We'll begin by introducing you to the seven principles of fitness training. We'll follow that with a look at the anatomy of a workout and the decisions that you need to make in planning your fitness training program.

Seven Training Principles

The ACSM Fitness Program is based on seven cardinal principles of fitness training. Even if you don't start with the ACSM Fitness Program, having an understanding of these key principles of fitness training will help you develop and modify your own fitness training program.

1. **Overload**. To improve your fitness level, you need to do more than what your body is used to doing. As you demand more, within reason, your body adapts to the increased demand. You can increase the intensity of the exercise (e.g., running faster) or the duration of the exercise (e.g., running longer), or both.

2. **Specificity**. The best way to develop fitness for slowpitch softball is to train the energy systems and muscles as closely as possible to the way that they are used in our sport. Thus the best way to train for running the bases or chasing down fly balls in the outfield is to practice that type of sprinting but then to apply the overload principle, by increasing either the intensity or the duration. For example, to improve the fitness of your throwing arm, you would increase the frequency with which you throw and the distance that you throw the ball.

3. **Progression**. To improve your energy and muscular fitness, you must steadily increase the physical demands on those systems, that is, overload them. If the overload, however, is too great or increased too quickly, you will not be able to adapt and may even break down (overtraining). If the demand is insufficient to overload the energy systems or muscles, you will not achieve a higher fitness level. Therefore, the right progression in overloading these systems is a vital part of a well-designed fitness program.

It's best to train by doing the activities specific to softball, such as sprints in running the bases.

4. **Diminishing returns**. If you're not in good shape your fitness level will improve rapidly when you first begin training, but as you become fitter the diminishing returns principle becomes law. The amount of improvement diminishes as you become fitter, and to go to the next higher level of fitness, you'll need to train much harder. Keep this principle in mind so that you have realistic expectations about improving your fitness levels.

5. **Variation**. This principle has two meanings. One is that several hard days of training should be followed by an easy day to give your body a chance to recover. This principle also means that you should vary the exercises to avoid overstressing parts of the body and to maintain motivation by increasing interest. For example, you may usually jog for aerobic fitness, but you could also swim or bike.

6. **Reversibility**. You know this principle: Use it or lose it. When you quit training, those hard-won fitness gains slip away all too quickly. If you play a lot of softball and discontinue supplementing your play with your training program, your fitness levels will decline as the season progresses.

7. **Moderation**. All things in moderation! Training is a slow, gradual process. Don't beat yourself up by overtraining. Listen to your body; it will tell you when you're training too much. You will enjoy your sessions more and stick with a training program longer by working at it steadily, gently coaxing your body into superior condition.

Anatomy of a Workout

With these fitness principles in mind, and by doing a little more reading, you can design your own workout program, which consists of three parts.

- The warm-up phase takes 5 to 10 minutes. Begin with slow aerobic activities such as jogging and gradually increase the intensity. Then stretch the muscles that you'll be using after warming up the muscles, not before.

- Assuming that the warm-up didn't wear you out, you now engage in the training program. One day you may work on improving your aerobic and anaerobic conditioning, and the next day you might work on training the muscles for strength and power.

- After the training phase you should cool down with a stretching program. Muscles tighten up after repeated use, and you want to stretch them out to their regular length while they are warm. Stretching is also thought to reduce muscle soreness, but the evidence isn't clear on that benefit. Although it is widely accepted that stretching is helpful after intense exercise, it's not so easy to do in softball. The game ends, and the social activities begin. Stopping to spend 10 minutes to stretch is difficult to discipline yourself to do, but in our opinion it's worth it.

In designing your own fitness program you have six decisions to make:

1. Choice of exercise
   – Is it aerobic (long-distance running) or anaerobic (sprinting) training?
   – Is it lower-body or upper-body exercises?
   – Is it moderate weights or heavy weights?
   – Are the exercises done slow or fast?

Stretching after the game helps alleviate muscles tightening up.

2. Order of exercises
– Do you do energy training one day and muscular training the next?
– Do you alternate muscle groups or exhaust one group?

3. Intensity of exercise
– Do you train at low, moderate, or high intensity?

4. Volume of exercise
– How long is the training period?
– How far do you run, swim, or bike?
– How many repetitions do you do?

5. Frequency of training
– Do you train once or twice a day?
– Do you train every day or every other day?

6. Length of rest period
– How much time do you allow yourself to recover between sprints or lifts?
– How much time do you allow between workouts?

With the help of the resources listed in appendix A and from knowledgeable friends or personal trainers, you can develop a fitness program that will help you play better slowpitch softball.

NUTRITION

Eat to Win was the title of a popular book some years ago, and although eating correctly will not guarantee that you win games, it will guarantee you a healthier life. You have a choice. You can fuel your body with high-octane, healthy foods

FIGURE 10.3 My Pyramid.
U.S. Department of Agriculture

that will provide you with the energy that you need to play your best, or you can consume low-octane fuels that will slow you down and possibly bring you to a complete stop. In this section we'll give you some healthy eating tips. You probably know these things, but you may appreciate a reminder.

The Athlete's Diet

The athlete's diet should consist of 55 to 65% carbohydrate, 25 to 30% fat, and 15 to 20% protein. This is not a special diet; it's what the U.S. government recommends as a healthy diet for the entire population. This well-balanced diet will provide the energy that you need to play softball all day long and then go dancing at night.

Follow the My Pyramid shown in figure 10.3 to help you make good daily food choices and to select the appropriate servings from each food group. To put the pyramid to work for you, go to the following Web site to download a brochure that will tell you what foods make up each food group, what a serving size is for each food, and how to track the calories that you consume and likely burn in a day. It's all free from the U.S. government at www.health.gov/dietaryguidelines/dga2005/document/default.htm.

See the box on the next page where we've summarized for you seven rules for eating right based on the U.S. government's dietary guidelines. Follow these rules and you'll be a healthier athlete.

Nutritional Supplements

Many high school, college, and professional athletes take nutritional supplements, legal ones, not because of some dietary deficiency but because they've heard that supplements may give them a competitive edge. The unregulated nutritional supplement business makes claims that various supplements will increase muscle tissue, improve muscle energy supplies, and increase the rate of energy production in the muscles. By and large, those claims are false or unproved. In this section we look at some of the more common supplements used by athletes.

Most athletes do not need nutritional supplements if they eat a well-balanced diet, but too many of us do not always eat healthy. Vitamin supplements are reported to be taken by 75% of college and professional athletes. Extensive training, however, doesn't increase the need for more vitamins than what is obtained by eating a balanced diet. If you have a vitamin deficiency as identified by a qualified health care professional, then a supplement may help.

Creatine is the second most widely used supplement by athletes, after vitamins. Scientific evidence shows that creatine increases power and speed in short-duration, high-intensity sports like softball. Taken in dosages of 20 grams per

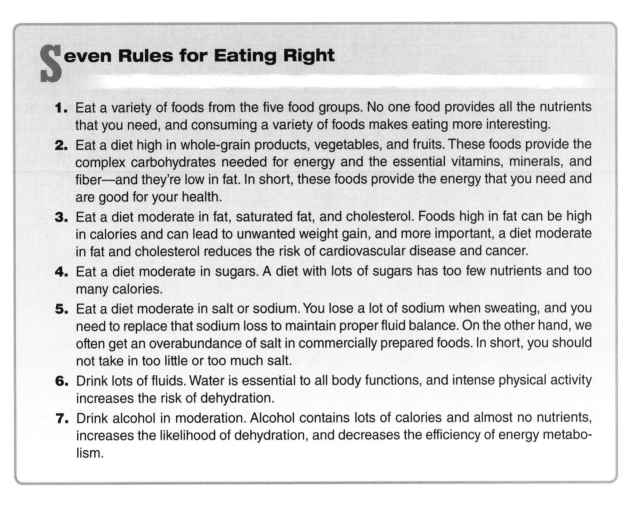

Seven Rules for Eating Right

1. Eat a variety of foods from the five food groups. No one food provides all the nutrients that you need, and consuming a variety of foods makes eating more interesting.

2. Eat a diet high in whole-grain products, vegetables, and fruits. These foods provide the complex carbohydrates needed for energy and the essential vitamins, minerals, and fiber—and they're low in fat. In short, these foods provide the energy that you need and are good for your health.

3. Eat a diet moderate in fat, saturated fat, and cholesterol. Foods high in fat can be high in calories and can lead to unwanted weight gain, and more important, a diet moderate in fat and cholesterol reduces the risk of cardiovascular disease and cancer.

4. Eat a diet moderate in sugars. A diet with lots of sugars has too few nutrients and too many calories.

5. Eat a diet moderate in salt or sodium. You lose a lot of sodium when sweating, and you need to replace that sodium loss to maintain proper fluid balance. On the other hand, we often get an overabundance of salt in commercially prepared foods. In short, you should not take in too little or too much salt.

6. Drink lots of fluids. Water is essential to all body functions, and intense physical activity increases the risk of dehydration.

7. Drink alcohol in moderation. Alcohol contains lots of calories and almost no nutrients, increases the likelihood of dehydration, and decreases the efficiency of energy metabolism.

day spread out over the day in four doses of 5 grams each, creatine increases muscle by as much as 20%. If creatine is supplemented with strength training, it improves strength significantly. Creatine appears to be safe, but we don't know the long-term effects on the body.

Caffeine, the popular stimulant found in coffee and chocolate, has been shown to improve performance in endurance events, but not in sports like softball. Some recent evidence suggests that caffeine reduces muscle pain arising from strenuous exercise. Two to three cups of regular coffee is the recommended amount. By the way, it's a myth that coffee dehydrates you by causing you to urinate more.

Many other supplements are promoted to and taken by athletes. If you wish to learn more about the effectiveness and safety of nutritional supplements, consult the references listed in appendix A.

What and When to Eat Before the Game

Follow these guidelines about what to eat before competing in softball:

- Every day eat the athlete's diet to fuel and refuel your muscles.
- Avoid high-fat proteins like cheese, steak, hamburgers, and peanut butter.
- Eat foods that you usually eat and that you know digest easily.

Bananas and apples are good foods for eating between games.

- Limit foods with high sugar content. They may give you a sugar high, which will be followed by a sugar low.
- Choose carbohydrate with low to moderate glycemic ratings (raises the blood sugar levels at a slower rate). Apples, yogurt, oatmeal, bananas, bean soup, and lentils are examples of low and moderate glycemic foods.

Allow the following times for food to digest before practicing and competing:

- 1 hour for a small snack
- 1 hour for a blended or liquid meal
- 2 hours for a small meal
- 3 hours for a large meal

If you tend to get nervous or very excited before competition and don't tolerate food well, don't eat. But eat well the day before and have a bedtime snack.

Nutrition During Tournaments

Nutrition is especially important when you play in tournaments lasting 2 or more days. Many players just eat what's available, often from concession stands that offer hot dogs, chips covered with cheese, hamburgers, and candy bars. Or they eat nothing between games.

You can do better. Your goal during these events is to eat to meet the energy demands of the sport, maintain good hydration, and keep blood sugar levels even. Sports drinks and bars, fruits of all types, and juices are good snacks between games. If you have at least a couple of hours between games, we recommend an easily digested snack or light meal.

HYDRATION

Dehydration is a common problem in slowpitch softball because games are often played when the temperature and humidity are high. Heat exhaustion and the far more serious heatstroke are insidious illnesses; they can sneak up on you if you don't drink the right fluids in the correct amounts before, during, and after playing in the heat.

You may have experienced some of the following effects of dehydration:

- Your performance suffers.
- Your heart rate and body temperature rise.
- You feel physically and mentally fatigued, which increases the risk of injury.

If you become too dehydrated you'll experience heat exhaustion. And if you don't get immediate medical attention, heat exhaustion can become heatstroke, which is life threatening. See chapter 12, "Softball First Aid," pages 265–266, about how to provide an emergency response to a player who is suffering heat exhaustion and heatstroke.

You are more likely to become dehydrated on sunny days when the air temperature and humidity are high and the wind is calm. Recognizing dehydration is the first step in prevention. The signs of dehydration are thirst, dry lips and mouth, flushed skin, irritability, headache or dizziness, apathy, feeling weak, muscle cramps, infrequent urination, dark yellow or brown urine, and nausea. Thirst does not develop quickly enough to be an effective indicator of dehydration. By the time you notice that you're thirsty, you could already be dehydrated.

Prevent yourself and your teammates from becoming dehydrated by following these guidelines:

- Drink 16 ounces (480 ml) 2 hours before playing in games or strenuous practices.
- Drink 4 to 8 ounces (120 to 240 ml) 10 minutes before playing.
- Drink 4 to 8 ounces (120 to 240 ml) every 20 minutes during the game or practice.
- Drink 16 ounces for every pound (1 L for every kg) of weight lost after the game.

Can you drink too much? Yes, too much water dilutes the body's sodium levels, creating an electrolyte imbalance. So, what should you drink? Sports drinks are the preferred choice when exercising for more than an hour. They replace not only water but also carbohydrates needed to fuel the muscles and electrolytes. Water is an excellent choice for shorter periods of exercise that are not likely to deplete carbohydrates and electrolytes. Fruit juices, which are rich in nutrients, are good refreshment beverages. Because they are absorbed a little more slowly into the body than sports drinks are, they're better as a postexercise drink. Soft drinks contain water and sugar, which help to fuel the muscles, but they provide no other nutrients. They're acceptable but not optimal for rehydration. Diet soft drinks contain water without any nutrients. They too are acceptable but not optimal. Beer and alcoholic drinks in general impair rehydration, are a poor source of nutrients, and do not help recover for the next exercise event. Sorry!

SUMMARY

- Improving your fitness has many benefits, not the least of which is helping you perform better and live longer.
- The two major components of physical fitness are energy fitness (cardiovascular fitness) and muscular fitness.
- Energy fitness involves the training of the anaerobic (without oxygen) energy system and the aerobic (with oxygen) system.
- Muscular fitness involves training for strength, endurance, power, speed, and flexibility.
- Slowpitch softball does not require as much fitness as many other sports, but better fitness will help you play better.
- Test your physical fitness using the ACSM fitness test to determine the level of training at which you should begin.
- Keep in mind the seven principles of training as you plan and engage in your fitness activities.
- Know the three phases of a workout and the six decisions that you need to make in planning your workout.
- Eat the athlete's diet by eating 55 to 65% carbohydrate, 25 to 30% fat, and 15 to 20% protein, and follow the seven rules for eating right.
- Most supplements have little or no scientific evidence to support claims that they improve performance or health, but a few do.
- Follow the recommended guidelines on what to eat and when to eat before playing softball.
- You'll play better when your body is sufficiently hydrated, but you can easily become dehydrated when playing softball when the temperature and humidity are high.
- Avoid dehydration and heat illnesses by recognizing the signs.
- Prevent dehydration by drinking sufficient fluids before and during the game and drinking sports drinks or water.

CHAPTER 11

Mental Preparation

This we know to be true. Great athletes work hard to develop not only superior physical skills but also tremendous mental skills. Nothing is more frustrating and disappointing than to spend thousands of hours developing your softball skills but then in competition not being able to execute them because of a lack of emotional control, inability to concentrate, or lack of self-confidence. But it doesn't have to be that way. Just as you can learn to hit, throw, and catch, you can learn to be emotionally ready, mentally focused, and positive about yourself and team. In this chapter we'll help you prepare mentally to play up to your physical potential.

MENTAL READINESS TEST

Take a few moments to respond to the nine questions that follow to determine your mental readiness to play competitive softball. As you consider each item think about how others would rate you. Then rate yourself as honestly as you can on the five-point scale.

1. Your motivation to succeed

1	2	3	4	5
Low				High

2. Your mental toughness (ability to perform in pressure situations)

1	2	3	4	5
Weak				Strong

3. Your confidence in yourself

1	2	3	4	5
Low				High

4. Your ability to control your emotions (anxiety, fear, anger)

1	2	3	4	5
Poor				Excellent

5. Your attitude when the team is losing

1	2	3	4	5
Negative				Positive

6. Your cooperativeness with your teammates

1	2	3	4	5
Low				High

7. Your acceptance of coaching

1	2	3	4	5
Low				High

8. Your ability to maintain concentration

1	2	3	4	5
Low				High

9. Your ability to let go of mistakes and refocus on the game

1	2	3	4	5
Low				High

Now that you've thought about these mental attributes let's dig deeper into your mental preparation by first considering what we know about the state of mind when athletes experience their peak performances. Then we'll look at the mental issues identified in the questionnaire that you just completed and help you get started with a mental training program, including specific examples to improve your hitting.

EXPERIENCING FLOW

Have you had games in softball when everything went right, when you were totally focused on the game, when you knew that you were strong and in control? Have you experienced an almost euphoric state when your body and mind work together effortlessly, when you are so absorbed in the task at hand that you exclude all other thoughts and emotions? We call this being in flow. Sometimes it's referred to as being in the zone, or having a peak experience. It's a state of mind when you're totally absorbed in the game, neither anxious nor bored. You are not thinking about the past or the future. You are not evaluating yourself. Your mind is not wandering off thinking about other matters in your life.

You know that the game will be challenging, but you have a sense of confidence that you can meet the challenge. You feel in control, confident, focused, motivated, and alert, but you're not aware of these feelings because you're absorbed in the moment. When the game ends, regardless of the outcome, you have a great sense of pleasure; it's the intrinsic reward of participation in sport. It's the high that you get when playing softball well; it's the fun in fun. When you're in flow, hitting and fielding in slowpitch is easy.

If you've not experienced flow in softball, perhaps you have in another sport or activity. It's a memorable experience. In working with elite athletes we've heard them exuberantly describe the flow experience, and after they've experienced it they seek to experience it again. But flow is often elusive. It's not something that you can just demand to happen. You can't force it, but you can create the mental conditions that optimize the potential to experience flow and play your best softball. Here are some of those conditions:

- You are more likely to experience flow when you perceive that your ability and that of your team is equal to the challenge of the competition.
- You let yourself become absorbed in the game and rid yourself of distractions. You focus on the present, not the past or future. You develop the ability to center your attention completely on what you need to do in the game.
- You lose your self-consciousness. You have no room in your mind for self-praise or self-criticism.
- You develop the ability to stay relaxed physically and alert mentally.
- You develop routines or rituals in preparation for playing. They increase your ability to center your attention and are a source of confidence.
- You feel in control of your actions.

In figure 11.1 you can see that your performance is best when you're in the flow state. If you are not sufficiently psyched up, if you're not focusing intently on hitting or fielding, then your performance will be short of what it could be. On the other hand, if you're too psyched up or psyched out, then your performance will also suffer.

A brief aside: As former sport psychologists we're sometimes asked about psyching out our opponents. We didn't come to understand what psyching out really meant until we learned about flow. Being in flow is being psyched up, and you cannot psych out someone unless the person is first psyched up. Thus psyching out someone is simply disrupting that person's state of flow, which is usually done by getting that person to

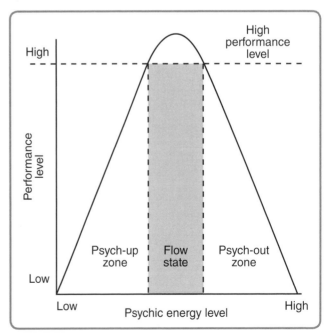

FIGURE 11.1 Optimal mental state for playing your best—the flow state.

Adapted, by permission, from R. Martens, 1987, *Coaches guide to sport psychology* (Champaign, IL: Human Kinetics), 100.

think about what he or she is or is not doing. It's an attempt to shift the person's attention from the activity being performed to how he or she is doing the activity. It's crawling into the person's mind, as explained beautifully in this verse:

> *A centipede was quite happy*
> *Until a frog in fun*
> *Said, "Pray which leg comes after which?"*
> *This raised her mind to such a pitch,*
> *She lay distracted in a ditch,*
> *Considering how to run.*
> *—Author unknown*

We often hear sports analysts talk about mental toughness, which to us means the ability to resist the internal or external forces that disrupt flow. Mentally tough athletes don't mentally beat themselves up over mistakes; they look at mistakes as learning opportunities. Mentally tough athletes don't let others psych them out. Through their mental preparation they have the mental skill to keep their mind focused on the task at hand.

So flow is the state of mind that we all try to achieve when playing softball. Nevertheless, we can't expect to be in that state every moment when we're playing. In the next section we'll look at psychological factors that prevent you from experiencing flow. Then in the following section we'll help you get started with some mental training so that you can achieve flow more often.

COMMON MENTAL PROBLEMS

The heading "Common Mental Problems" implies that most athletes are head cases and need a shrink, but that's not at all the case. Unfortunately, much of what sport psychologists do is misunderstood. We try to help people develop mental skills, just as your coach helps you with the physical side of the game if you're lucky enough to have a coach. Yet we know of no athlete, including ourselves, who has not experienced these three mental problems:

- Difficulty controlling our emotions, be it anxiety arising from fear of failure or anger from some perceived injustice.
- Inability to maintain focus on the task at hand because our attention shifts to internal or external factors that distract us and break up our concentration.
- Lack of self-confidence (diffidence) caused by unrealistic goals or a sudden slump during which time our self-worth crashes like the market of 2008.

So let's get a better understanding of these three common mental problems, the ways in which they disrupt flow, and methods that we can use to overcome them.

Emotional Control

We begin by looking at anxiety, and then we'll examine anger. These complex emotions can be destructive to any softball player if they are not controlled.

Anxiety

This insidious emotion robs more players of their physical energy, victories, and enjoyment than any other emotion. It can destroy your self-confidence by leading you to believe that you are incompetent. Anxiety can deny you the joy of demonstrating the skills that you have mastered through countless hours of practice. And it most certainly will deprive you of experiencing the ecstasy of flow.

In softball, anxiety is usually caused by your uncertainty that you will be able to perform as expected and then by you worrying about the consequences of not performing well when the outcome is important to you. Now notice that the cause of anxiety is not the impending game itself, but your perception of the game and its outcome. Your negative thoughts lead to anxiety, so the good news is that you can learn to control those thoughts. Doing so may not be easy to do, but it's doable. We'll describe those steps in a moment.

When you experience anxiety your mind is preoccupied with worry and thus cannot be fully focused on your hitting or fielding the ball. Anxiety causes muscles to tighten so that they don't move as quickly or smoothly in executing the motor skills of the sport. Anxiety causes your attention to narrow, often too far, with the consequence being that you miss cues in the environment to which you should have attended. The result of these negative effects of anxiety is poor performance.

You should recognize that being excited, pumped up, motivated, energized, or whatever term you wish to use, is not the same as anxiety. Being up is positive energy; being anxious is negative energy. Sure, an anxious thought may come into your mind when you're pumped up to play, but you quickly dismiss it because you have the mental skills to do so.

Anger

Everyone becomes angry at times; it's a normal human emotion. You rise up from picking something up off the floor and hit your head on the table. Your first response is anger, and you may impulsively reach out and hit the table (although you recognize that doing so is stupid). You may get angry in softball when

- you perceive that you've been wronged by your opponents, the umpire, or even your own teammates,
- you are physically threatened or harmed and you judge that the person who harmed you meant to do so,
- you make a mistake, or
- you fail to reach a goal that is important to you.

Although we all get angry, people differ widely in what they do with their anger. When people perceive that someone else has caused their anger, some retaliate through physical violence. Others employ verbal abuse. When we're angry with ourselves we may mistakenly direct our anger at those near us, or we may just beat ourselves up mentally, sometimes seething with contempt for our stupidity for making a mistake or our failure to achieve a valued goal. Yet most people deal with anger more constructively. After the initial emotional feeling of anger, which is usually associated with heightened tension, higher blood pressure, an increased heart rate, and a huge increase in energy, rational people seek to understand the cause of the anger and then try to deal with it in socially acceptable ways.

Softball, of course, has rules that punish players who cannot control their anger, and thus some players learn to redirect their anger by kicking dirt, throwing their gloves, or pounding on the fence. Other players keep the anger boiling inside, seething about the event that precipitated their anger. Their inability to let the anger go usually hurts their performance because they are unable to focus on the game. As with the emotion of anxiety, they cannot enter the state of flow when their mind is occupied with angry thoughts. We'll look at how you can manage your anger better shortly.

Attentional Control

To play softball well, you need to focus on what you're doing. But in a game that takes about an hour you are not going to keep your attention riveted on the game the entire time. For example, as you prepare to bat you may go through a routine that prepares you physically, and you mentally rehearse hitting the ball. Then as you step into the batter's box you shift your attention entirely away from any internal thoughts to focusing totally on the ball about to be pitched. That's the way it's supposed to work, but if you're anxious or angry your mind is at least partially occupied with thoughts about failure or retaliation, and you can't fully focus on hitting. Chatting with others, thinking about a family problem, worrying about work, or contemplating any other matter when you should be thinking about hitting, fielding, throwing, or running reduces your focus and hurts your performance.

Attention problems occur not only because of distractions but also because you've practiced the skill so much that you can do it reasonably well without giving it your full attention, or what we call concentration. You've become apathetic in applying your focus to the task at hand.

A key to successful play is to concentrate totally on the task at hand.

We'll give you an example. You know that to be a good hitter you need to watch the ball. Now that's profound! Of course, you must learn the mechanics of a good swing, but that's not hard to do. To be a really good hitter, to hit the ball well consistently, you must not just watch the ball—you must focus intensely on it. Yet many batters don't. After years of practice and playing, hitting becomes so easy that you don't have to concentrate on watching it. You see the ball, but you don't focus intensely on it. As we mentioned in chapter 2, another mistake is that batters look where they want to hit a split-second before making contact. The result is inconsistency in hitting. Good solid hits are interspersed among pop-ups and easy ground outs. But when you concentrate intensely on the ball, watching it all the way until you make contact, you have the ability to make minor adjustments in your swing *as you swing* so that you contact the ball squarely.

Here's another example of shifting our attention at the wrong time. With a runner on first, the ball is hit slowly to you at shortstop. Will you have a play at second base, or should you throw to first? As you look up to see where the runner going to second is, you don't see the last hop of the ball and you miss it. You need mental skill to control what you watch and when to shift your attention.

We have so many things going on in our lives that putting them aside when we step onto the diamond to play softball is a challenge. We can become so caught up thinking about past events or future plans that we're not mindful of the here and now. At times, of course, you need to think about the past and the future, but not when you're batting, fielding, or running the bases. You can't experience flow when you're thinking about the past or future; you must be focused on the here and now.

So an important mental skill is the ability to focus on or attend to the correct things during the game and to be able to turn on the intense concentration needed to execute the physical skills that you've mastered. Refocusing your attention on the game after making a mistake, especially a costly error that hurts the team, is especially challenging. A quality of mentally tough athletes is their ability to refocus after making an error. Just how good are you at focusing your attention on what matters during the game and maintaining concentration (the intensity of your focus) for the time required? We'll discuss shortly how to improve your mental focus.

Self-Confidence

Many athletes believe that self-confidence is essential to winning. Part of the American sport creed is that athletes should always think that they will win. To think otherwise is sacrilegious. If you don't think that you can defeat the other team, then you are thinking like a loser, which then makes you a loser.

It is this mistaken belief about self-confidence that often leads to a lack of self-confidence (called diffidence) or to overconfidence. True self-confidence is an athlete's realistic expectation about achieving success. It's not what athletes hope to do, but what they realistically expect to do. The relationship between self-confidence and performance is shown in figure 11.2. As you would expect, athletes who are optimally self-confident perform better than those who are diffident or overconfident.

Self-confident players set realistic goals based on their own abilities, and they play within themselves. That is, they understand themselves well enough to feel successful when they reach the upper limits of their ability, and they

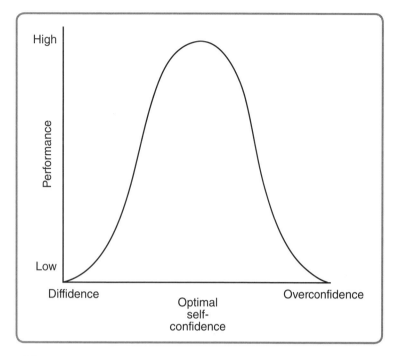

FIGURE 11.2 The relationship between self-confidence and performance.

Reprinted, by permission, from R. Martens, 1987, *Coaches guide to sport psychology* (Champaign, IL: Human Kinetics), 152.

don't attempt to achieve goals that are unrealistic for them. A mistake does not shatter the self-confident player; a loss does not become a tragedy.

Diffident players, on the other hand, fear failure so much that they are easily intimidated and play with trepidation. They become psychological prisoners of their own negative self-images. The self-doubts of diffident athletes become devastating self-fulfilling prophecies. They expect to fail, which in turn leads to actual failure. As you would expect, these players experience a lot of anxiety.

Overconfident athletes have their own problems. Actually, you can't be overconfident if the confidence is well founded in your abilities. When we talk about athletes being overconfident we really mean that they are falsely confident; their confidence is greater than their competencies warrant. Some athletes actually believe that they are better than they are; others act confident on the outside but on the inside are diffident.

Self-confidence is a reflection of a person's self-worth. People who experience success become more self-confident, feel more worthy, and are more motivated to pursue excellence. Those who experience failure, especially early on, become more diffident and feel less worthy.

The single biggest mistake that athletes in any sport can make is judging their self-worth based on winning or losing. The outcome of a game is determined only in part by any one player. Opponents, teammates, officials, environmental factors, and lady luck all play a role in determining who wins and who loses. Instead of evaluating yourself based on winning or losing, you should evaluate yourself based on your own performance—the things that you can control.

In slowpitch softball, evaluate your hitting on how well you made contact with the ball and your placement of it. Judge your fielding by examining how well you got in position to catch the ball, watch the ball, and make the stop. Those things are under your control.

Setting goals for yourself and then evaluating how you did in achieving those goals is an important part of developing a healthy self-confidence and maintaining a positive sense of self-worth. Here are five basic goal-setting principles:

- Set performance goals, not outcome goals. The outcome (winning and losing) is not completely under your control.
- Set challenging, not easy, goals.
- Set realistic, not unrealistic, goals.
- Set specific, not general, goals.
- Emphasize individual goals over team goals.

The last principle often raises eyebrows. Coaches especially are more inclined to feel that team goals should have priority over individual goals. There is no *I* in *TEAM*, they point out. But team goals tend to be vague. They diffuse responsibility and often are outcome goals that are not fully under the control of the team or individual players. In team sports, however, team goals can be valuable to help individual players work together as long as individual goals are clearly set. Setting a goal for the team to bat .500 in the next tournament is not useful without having each player set a realistic but challenging goal for his or her own hitting.

In summary, you want to be a self-confident player, to have realistic expectations about your abilities and thus set realistic goals. Diffidence and false confidence breed anxiety, which, as you know, impairs performance. Confident athletes evaluate themselves based on their own performance goals because they are in control of their own performance and are not in control of the outcome of the game. Diffident and overconfident athletes, however, are more likely to judge their self-worth based on winning and losing, which has many negative consequences for them. We'll now see how to solve this problem along with controlling your emotions and attention.

DEVELOPING YOUR MENTAL SKILLS

Think of mental skills just as you do the physical skills required to play softball. You want to control your mind to

- eliminate all anxiety by having no worries that distract you from your play;
- respond constructively to anger and get rid of it quickly so that you can refocus on playing;
- focus your attention on the right cues by avoiding distractions and knowing how to shift your attention at the right time;
- be able to concentrate intensely;
- be self-confident, not diffident or overconfident, by evaluating your self-worth based on your performance, not the outcome of winning or losing.

We will briefly introduce you to the mental skills of controlling your self-talk, using imagery as a mental tool and role playing as a means to practice. You develop these mental skills in much the same way that you have developed your physical skills:

1. You need to understand what the skill is—what you need to learn, which we explained earlier.
2. You need to evaluate how skillful you are now and whether you would benefit by improving these mental skills.
3. You need to practice developing these skills, alone at first, then in practice sessions, and finally in contests. We'll get you started and give you some references for more complete descriptions of these techniques.

Self-Talk

Come clean! Could you be a better softball player if you were more in control of your emotions, better focused, and more self-confident? Probably! Do you believe that what you say to yourself influences how you behave—and how you perform? Surely you do, otherwise why are you talking to yourself! Are your thoughts mostly positive and constructive, or are they more negative and unconstructive? Evaluate your positive and negative self-talk by placing a checkmark next to the items in the following list that are true for you.

Positive Thought Patterns

- ☐ You're optimistic; you consistently see the good side of things.
- ☐ You're realistic and try to be objective.
- ☐ You focus on the present, not the past.
- ☐ You see problems as challenges rather than threats
- ☐ You view successes as replicable and failures as surmountable.
- ☐ You think about what you need to do in the game, not the outcome of the game.
- ☐ You think about things you can control.
- ☐ You separate your performance from your self-worth.

Negative Thought Patterns

- ☐ You are critical of yourself.
- ☐ You tend to exaggerate the negative consequences of events.
- ☐ You overgeneralize, forming conclusions based on an isolated incident.
- ☐ You blame others for the team's failures.
- ☐ Things should or must be just the way you want them.
- ☐ You see things in polarized terms—they're black or white, good or bad.
- ☐ You believe that you should be competent in every aspect of the game at all times.
- ☐ You fear failure, dwelling on the consequences if you don't succeed.
- ☐ You think that life should always treat you fairly.

Step back now to think about what your responses tell you. Could you improve your performance by thinking more positively and less negatively? You don't need to admit it to anyone but yourself, but if you're inclined to think negatively you can choose to change that pattern of thinking. As we've said, first you need to become aware of these negative thoughts. You can do so in a couple of ways:

- Use imagery (we'll discuss that more later) to recall your thinking when you played well and poorly. Write down those thoughts.
- Keep a postpractice and postcompetition log, something like a diary, to record positive situations, your emotions, and your positive thoughts. Then do the same for negative situations.

It's not a fancy psychological technique, but you can program yourself to use more positive thoughts by writing down how you would like to respond in what you've seen as negative situations in the past and then practicing positive responses. You can initially practice by imagining negative situations and seeing yourself respond positively, and then you can practice it when at practice and during games. Work at catching yourself thinking negatively and tell yourself to stop. Then dispute the negative thinking with more rational thoughts.

Constructive self-talk can help you rid yourself of anxiety by disputing the value of worrying and focusing on the opportunities that you have to play the game. Well-planned self-talk can help you quickly dissipate events that anger you. Before hitting or fielding, use self-talk to remind you of what you need to focus on. Then as play begins turn off that voice in your head and turn your full attention to the ball or what you have to do. And most important, use constructive self-talk to evaluate your performance and avoid evaluating your self-worth based on the outcome of the game.

Imagery

Many athletes now use imagery to help them prepare mentally for competitive events. Imagery is an experience similar to a sensory experience (seeing, feeling, hearing), but it occurs in the absence of the usual external stimuli. Imagery is more than just visualizing (seeing) an experience in your mind's eye, although visualization is usually the dominant sense. Imagery can involve any or all of the senses.

When you experience reality you learn to attach various emotional states or moods to those experiences. You feel anxiety as you anticipate playing an important game; you experience joy when winning it or dejection when losing it. You also can experience those emotions when you vividly image certain situations that you have come to associate with those states of mind. This important dimension of imagery makes it a powerful tool for developing mental skills.

As discussed in the self-talk section, you can use imagery to help make yourself aware of your mental state or feelings as you participate in softball, and then you can rehearse the appropriate mental skills through your mind's eye. You can feel the emotions of anxiety and anger by vividly recalling moments when you experienced those emotions, and then you can practice seeing yourself responding to those situations more effectively. One technique for doing so is to relax yourself physically through deep breathing. That method works for some, and others find it more effective to call upon an image of a place where they have felt calm, relaxed, and worry free. They then quickly replace the anxious feelings with the nonanxious image and practice this substitution repeatedly.

You can also practice focusing your attention through imagery. You can create distractions in your mind and then see yourself pushing those distractions aside to focus on the task at hand. One of the things that doesn't work in trying to maintain the right focus is to be thinking about what your focus is when you need to focus. You must work to clear you mind, to attend totally to the here and now. You can practice what we call mindfulness by focusing your full attention on an object—for example, a softball—for as long as you can. Initially, the period may be short, but with practice you can increase your attention on the ball. Go ahead and try it!

Imagery is a useful way to practice thinking constructively about yourself. You can use imagery to see yourself performing well and then rewarding yourself for doing so. You can use imagery to see yourself making an error, analyze what you did wrong, and then refocus yourself on the game in front of you. You can visualize threats to your self-worth and then challenge those with constructive images.

Although imagery is a powerful tool for developing psychological skills, putting this tool to use takes some work. As with your motor skills, you'll need to practice, practice, and practice. The more vivid your images are and the more you can control them, the more benefit you'll get from imagery training. To practice effectively, you want to do the following:

- Initially practice in a quiet setting. Then as you become more adept at imagery you can practice almost anywhere, such as the on-deck circle just before you hit.
- Be relaxed but attentive.
- Be motivated to practice developing these skills.
- Have a reasonable expectancy of the outcome. Don't expect immediate improvement. With time, just as with learning the physical skill of hitting, you'll see improvement.

Role Playing

You can practice developing mental skills through role playing, but to do so you'll need a trusted friend or two. Here's an example of how it works. In preparation for the 1984 Olympic Games the first author, who was the sport psychologist for the U.S. Nordic ski teams, had each skier participate in a mock interview to simulate what might occur after their events in Sarajevo. The interviewer was a reporter for a popular ski magazine, and he knew the history of the athletes well. He probed the psyche of each athlete by asking questions that he believed would expose the athletes' vulnerability.

When one skier was asked repeatedly about choking in big events, you could quickly see his anger rising. He became quite emotional even though he knew

Learn to control your anger when confronting umpires.

that the activity was only role playing. We spent a lot of time with that skier and others practicing how to control their emotions when asked probing questions by reporters.

You can role-play a bad call by an umpire and practice controlling your anger. You can role-play controlling your anxiety when a teammate yells at you not to hit into a double play as you step in to bat (which is really a dumb thing for teammates to say). You can have someone create all types of distractions while you focus on your pitching.

In summary, it all comes down to controlling your mind. To do so, you need to become aware of your emotions and thoughts, identify a better response than the one you're making if it's not satisfactory, and then practice those responses through self-talk, imagery, and role playing. See appendix A for helpful references to learn more about developing your mental skills.

Psychology of Hitting

Let's apply these mental skills to your hitting technique. You now know that to hit your best you want to be in flow but that flow can be elusive. Our brains function as two parts: The left side is the analyzer, and the right side is the integrator. Flow occurs when the right side is dominant; it's the side that lets you execute your motor program to hit the ball. When the analytical side takes charge it disrupts flow, but you need this side, too, to make plans and correct mistakes. Knowing when to turn on the analyzer and when to let the integrator take over, and being able to switch back and forth, is a difficult but important skill that great athletes master.

ANALYZER AND INTEGRATOR

Use your analyzer in batting practice and after you've hit the ball during games. When you're in the on-deck circle preparing to bat, you want to loosen up not only physically but also mentally. Use your analyzer to size up the game situation and determine the correct offensive tactic for that situation. That situation may change based on what the batter in front of you does, so you'll need to analyze that again just before you step into the batter's box.

While you're in the on-deck circle, rehearse in your mind any keys that you use to remind yourself what you want to do. State these keys in positive terms—for example, keep my head still, wait for the ball, keep my hands loose, swing through the ball. If you find yourself starting to think negatively, fearing that you'll make an out and let the team and yourself down, then begin to work on controlling those thoughts. The analyzer has its grip on you, and you need to turn off those thoughts. (See the suggestions for doing so earlier in this chapter.) Now is the time to turn on the integrator—quieting the mind, relaxing the muscles, anticipating the joy of hitting. If the analyzer is in charge when you're batting, you'll not only find flow elusive but also may experience paralysis by analysis, a condition in which you're unable to execute a coordinated swing because you're overwhelmed by negative thoughts.

Approach batting this way. As you walk to the batter's box you quickly determine the game situation and what offensive tactic you want to execute. With your plan in mind, you turn off the analyzer and focus your attention totally on the task of hitting the softball. Alert yet relaxed, focused but not stressed, and motivated but not pressing. You're now ready to hit.

(continued)

MENTAL BATTING PRACTICE

You don't expect just to walk up and hit the ball well without physically practicing, and you shouldn't expect to be mentally prepared to hit without practicing. So how do you practice hitting mentally?

First, when you are taking batting practice, spend part of the time imagining various game situations and hitting in them. See yourself in your mind's eye batting in the bottom of the seventh with the opportunity to win the game. Try to feel the emotions and then see yourself in control, confident, and focused on hitting the ball. Imagery can help you hit better because vivid imagery affects the nervous system almost exactly as the actual experience does. The next step is to use imagery when you're in the on-deck circle in games to create the positive mind-set for hitting.

Many athletes have found it useful to develop a routine to prepare themselves physically and mentally. When batting, your routine may begin with putting on your batting glove, grabbing your bat, and performing the activities that you do in the on-deck circle. The routine may then continue as you step into the batter's box. Routines help keep the mind focused on the task at hand, making it less likely that the analyzer will rear its ugly head.

ATTENTION AND CONCENTRATION

In softball there are times when your attention or focus should be broad, and at other times it should be narrow. Sometimes you want the focus to be external (e.g., what's going on in the game), and other times your focus should be internal (e.g., to attend to how your body is feeling or what your mind is saying to you).

Before you step into the batter's box, for a quick moment you want your attention to be broad and external, focusing on the game situation as you decide on your hitting plan. Then when you're ready to hit, your attention should be narrow and external, focusing on the pitched ball.

Concentration refers to your ability to sustain attention on the task at hand, or what is sometimes called attention span. Concentration, similar to flow, is elusive. It's not staring hard at the ball when hitting. It's not trying to concentrate directly. It's an effortless effort to focus on the ball because you're absorbed in the challenge of hitting it. Fortunately, hitting is a task that does not require long periods of concentration. The challenge is concentrating fully for the brief period when you are batting.

So what causes our concentration to wander? As your swing mechanics become automated, external events or your own negative thoughts can more easily distract you. Suddenly you find yourself not hitting as well as before. You begin changing your mechanics, which causes you to hit even more poorly. Soon it seems as if you're in a major slump, all caused by a lack of concentration. So to hit your best, for a few seconds give yourself totally to the task of hitting the pitched ball exactly as you want to hit it.

Stress is another major cause of attention and concentration problems. If you haven't been hitting well, you may sense that your teammates are displeased with your performance. You tell yourself that if you don't start hitting you'll likely lose your place in the lineup. The pressure builds, the stress grows, and your concentration when hitting is more elusive than ever. So to concentrate better, you must rid yourself of stress, which is far easier said than done, but we've given you at least a starting point on how to do so in this chapter.

To improve your attention and concentration, practice it through imagery and in batting practice. Remember that the mindless hitting of dozens of softballs without fully focusing on the physical and mental skills of hitting is not beneficial and is actually counterproductive.

REALISTIC EXPECTATIONS

So far we've considered how to establish the right mind-set for hitting and how to concentrate better. Now let's look at how you evaluate yourself after hitting, especially how you deal with failure. Consider this scenario.

You've made a couple of outs with poor swings because you didn't focus your attention well. Then you hit a line drive on the nose but right at the third baseperson for an out. Your frustration is high, so the next time you come up to bat you try extra hard, which destroys your timing, and you hit a dribbler to the pitcher. You're 0 for 4 that game, and you're in an awful slump for the rest of the tournament.

One of the major causes of slumps is having unrealistic expectations. Some players think that they should bat much better than what their abilities are. If their skill level is at about the .500 level but they expect to hit .700, they'll constantly be frustrated. Now don't get us wrong. It's good to set your goals higher than your current ability, but they shouldn't be so high that you are rarely successful in achieving them. Be realistic about your current ability by looking at what you've done in the immediate past. Then set your goal slightly higher and commit yourself to practicing to improve.

Also, remember to evaluate yourself by looking at your performance, not the outcome. When hitting, your performance is a combination of hitting the ball squarely and locating it where you want. The outcome is whether or not you get a base hit. Part of the outcome is under your control, but part of the outcome is determined by the defense. You may hit the ball well, but a defensive player makes a great catch. Or you hit the ball into the 3-4 hole, but the second baseperson guessed that you might do that and shifted over on you to get an out. Your performance was good, but the outcome wasn't.

So each time after you've hit and after each game and tournament, evaluate your hitting based on your performance, not the outcome. You may have been 4 for 4, but you know that twice you were lucky to get on because you did not hit the ball squarely. You may have been 0 for 4, but three of your hits were solid strokes. Then reward yourself for the good performances and try to determine what you did not do well in the poor performances so that you can work to improve. Then as you enter your next competition, look at the most recent past along with your longer history of hitting to set realistic goals.

And most of all remember that this sport is a game we play for fun. Don't take it all too seriously. Enjoy those precious moments on the diamond.

TEAM PSYCHOLOGY

Now let's give some thought to your being part of a team. We want to consider what you bring to the team and what you need or want from the team. How members of the team get along has a lot to do with how well you play together, so we'll recommend some guidelines for positive interpersonal relationships. And we'll again touch on communication because it's a vital part of team dynamics.

What You Bring to the Team

Of course, every member of a team hopes to contribute to the team's winning by playing well, but beyond your sports skills, what do you bring to the team?

Good communication and respect for your teammates are essential qualities of cohesive teams.

Here are some qualities that coaches and teammates appreciate in fellow players:

- Motivation not only for yourself but for the other members of the team
- Willingness to play whatever position will help the team
- Willingness to sit the bench to give others a fair turn to play
- Willingness to be coached, to be a good follower
- Willingness to lead when asked to do so
- Willingness to help your teammates play better
- Positive attitude and cooperativeness

Especially consider the last quality of being a team member. Just as your attitude and cooperativeness will influence your teammates either positively or negatively, their attitude and cooperativeness with you will influence your mental preparation. As you may have seen on teams that you've previously played with, just one sour apple on a team can ruin the barrel.

So an important element of being a good team player is having a positive attitude, or perhaps more accurately, a constructive attitude, about your team and teammates, and the sport itself. In fact, if you don't have a positive, constructive attitude about the sport, you should find another activity that you will have a positive attitude about!

What You Want From the Team

Each of us plays slowpitch softball for various reasons, and we want those reasons to be fulfilled when we play for a team. Here are common reasons why people play this sport:

- To be with friends and to develop friendships
- To challenge themselves to excellence through competition
- To win
- To demonstrate their softball skills
- To have fun
- To obtain approval and recognition

If you are unable to meet your objectives for playing, you'll likely quit or look for another team to join. So when you join a team you should keep in mind what your objectives are and that you want to play on a team that has like-minded objectives. If you want to play recreational softball in which fun and friendship are your objectives, then be sure to find a team with the same priorities. Otherwise, you're less likely to be happy.

So what type of teammate are you? Do you help to create a positive team environment or a negative one? Do you give to the team or mostly take from it? Review the preceding list of what you can bring to the team to help it play better and for all of you to enjoy playing more.

Interpersonal Relations

Team cohesiveness is a subject well studied by sport psychologists. We're sure that you won't be shocked to learn that more cohesive teams win more games. Or is it that teams that win more games are more cohesive? Actually, it's both. Teams on which the players like each other, encourage each other, and help each other play better and win more. And as they win more they become more cohesive, forming a greater bond to each other and to the team as a whole. Good leadership is a key to having a cohesive team. The leader may be the coach or a respected player, someone who provides the team with a vision of what it can

Good interpersonal relationships are the foundation on which cohesive teams develop.

be and helps guide it toward achieving that vision. You can contribute to the cohesiveness of your team by bringing to the team the attributes we listed earlier.

An important part of developing a cohesive team is getting to know your teammates and coach. To know each other, you each must be willing to disclose yourself to the other person, but when you do so you're taking a risk. The person may not like you, or may even reject you. But if you have confidence in yourself, then you'll have confidence to reveal yourself to others. As you do they will begin to trust you, and in turn they will reveal themselves to you. Meaningful relationships begin in that way.

Trust in a relationship is developed not only by appropriate self-disclosure (you can reveal too much too quickly) but also by being real—that is, by being honest, genuine, and authentic. Trust also is rooted in integrity, which means adhering to moral and ethical principles. If you speak badly about a teammate or the coach, if you try to injure others, or if you seek to cheat, you diminish your integrity.

To build relationships, you must be open not only with others but also to them. If you want others to accept and support you, you must accept and support them. Acceptance of them does not mean approval of their every action. You may disapprove of certain behaviors but still accept and care about the person.

Communication

No one needs to tell you that communication is vital to successful relationships. Here are some common communication problems that can adversely affect your relationship with your teammates and coach:

- You mostly preach when you talk, conveying that you're always right, which detracts from the respect that people have for you.
- Most of your messages are negative; people think of you as a chronic complainer, and they get tired of hearing what's wrong with the world.
- You're highly judgmental, evaluating everyone and everything. When a teammate errs, you're quick to blame. Consequently, your teammates don't trust you and thus don't reveal themselves to you.
- You're inconsistent in your messages. One day you're positive about the team; the next day you're negative. Inconsistent messages also destroy trust.
- You love to talk and are so busy talking that you fail to listen. When your teammates learn that you never listen, they'll quit listening to you, too.
- You listen, but you don't provide acknowledgment of the message by responding back verbally or nonverbally. When people talk to you they feel as if they're talking to a wall. Eventually, they will no longer bother to talk to you.

Can you see a bit of yourself in any of these six communication problems? If so, take steps to be a more effective communicator to help your team and to help yourself in all your relationships.

Acceptance of Coaching

In the mental readiness test at the beginning of this chapter, we asked you how accepting you are of coaching, and we'd like you to give that some thought now. We have found wider resistance to coaching among adults in slowpitch softball than we have in any other sport in which we've participated or coached. We observe this resistance with recreational as well as elite players. We're not sure why players are so resistant to advice on improving their individual play or adjusting their actions to fit a team strategy. With regard to improving individual play, players may believe that the person offering instructional advice, whether it's a coach or a teammate, is not qualified to do so, or they may think that they know more than they demonstrate in their play. Regardless of the reason, the lack of acceptance of coaching significantly limits teams' ability to improve their performance.

When someone suggests to you that you can improve your performance by making an adjustment, do you take it as criticism and thus quickly reject it? Do you become defensive about your play, maybe even denying a performance error that the entire team just witnessed? Or do you recognize that everyone can improve his or her performance, and that someone cared enough about your play and the team's outcome to suggest ways that you can improve your play?

Successful teams nurture a team culture whereby each player has a responsibility not only to be receptive to coaching from coaches and teammates but also to provide feedback to teammates to help them improve their game. It's part of that trust and respect in communication that is vital to success. So take a close look at how open you are to being coached and how willing you are to help improve your team by coaching.

SUMMARY

- Flow is the state of mind wherein you are totally focused on the task at hand, lose self-awareness, and feel in control. It's the state of mind that you want to achieve for optimal performance.
- Being able to control your emotions is vital to being in the state of flow. Anxiety and anger disrupt flow.
- A necessary mental skill to achieve flow and perform well is the ability to focus on or attend to the correct things during the game. Better performance comes through intense concentration.
- Being confident, not diffident or overconfident, is an important mental attribute that facilitates experiencing flow and better performance.
- To develop a realistic level of self-confidence, you want to evaluate yourself not based on winning or losing, which is not entirely under your control, but based on your individual performance, which is under your control.
- You can develop the mental skills to control your emotions, focus your attention correctly, and maintain self-confidence by using self-talk, imagery, and role-playing exercises.
- Recognize your negative self-talk and learn to replace it with more constructive messages.
- Imagery and role playing are powerful tools for practicing mental skills.
- Being a good team member involves bringing a positive attitude and cooperativeness to the team.

- When joining a team, look to match up what you want from a team with what the team has to offer.
- Cohesive teams are more successful teams and have more fun playing together. Good interpersonal relationships are the foundation on which cohesive teams develop.
- Through effective communication skills you can improve your interpersonal relationships.
- Good team players have a responsibility not only to be receptive to coaching but also to provide feedback to teammates to help them improve their game.

CHAPTER 12

Softball First Aid

Injuries are not a major problem in slowpitch softball; they do occur, of course, but they are mostly minor. In this chapter our objective is not to give you a full first-aid course, but to help you with diagnosing and treating minor injuries that you may sustain. This chapter will provide you with some basic first-aid information to help you treat your own injuries and to know when to seek additional help. You'll learn about the prevention of injuries, the use of ice and nonsteroidal anti-inflammatory drugs, and the treatment of acute and chronic injuries. We'll also look at some other common medical problems among softball players and then describe the four steps to rehabilitating injuries.

We highly recommend that you take a cardiopulmonary resuscitation (CPR) course, which often includes automatic external defibrillation (AED) training. (See appendix A for information on how to complete a CPR and AED course online easily and inexpensively.)

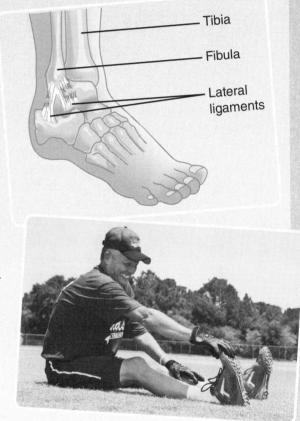

PREVENTION

The best way to deal with injuries is to avoid them, and to some extent you can. Warming up properly before practices and games is an essential part of prevention. Begin with a light jog to warm up the muscles and then stretch the major muscle groups. (See appendix A for references on proper stretching methods.)

Of course, being in excellent physical condition reduces the risk of injury. Strong bones and muscles can withstand the occasional strain on the body that comes with unexpected contact or the sudden change of direction that happens when playing slowpitch softball. Although the overall injury rate in slowpitch

Sliding is the most common cause of injury in slowpitch softball.

softball is low compared with the rate in many other sports, three groups of players have greater risk of injury and should take extra steps to reduce the risk.

- Players returning to the sport after a year or more away from the game. These players know how to play, but their muscles are not ready for the sprints on the basepaths or quick movements on the field. A good conditioning program and plenty of practice before beginning competition will help reduce the risk of injury.

- Players who are weak in fundamental skills and knowledge of the game. They may not know how to slide, possibly resulting in a sprained ankle or worse, or how to avoid collisions with fellow fielders. Sliding is the most common cause of injury in softball. In one study sliding was the cause of 27% of the injuries and in another 42%. As we've stated repeatedly in this book sliding headfirst is not recommended, and here's why. In a study, headfirst slides resulted in 20 injuries per 1,000 slides, and feetfirst slides resulted in only 10 injuries per 1,000.

- Players who have been injured and return to play without completing a full rehabilitation program. We'll describe later the four stages of a rehabilitation program that players should complete before they return to competition.

PRICE AND NSAIDS

In this section we discuss two widely self-administered treatments for a wide range of softball injuries—ice and nonsteroidal anti-inflammatory drugs (NSAIDs). The immediate first aid for many of the injuries that you may experience consists of applying ice to the injured area using the well-known PRICE principle:

- **P**—Protect the injured area by discontinuing the activity.
- **R**—Rest means not doing anything that adds to the pain and, if the injury is severe enough, immobilizing the injured body part.
- **I**—Ice immediately after the injury and up to 72 hours afterward. Compress the injured body part with an elastic wrap and then place the ice over the wrap (see figure 12.1a).
- **C**—Compress the injured area to reduce swelling and control bleeding. After you've removed the ice, apply a new elastic wrap to compress the injured area (see figure 12.1b), but be careful not to compress so tightly that you restrict blood flow. If you feel a throbbing sensation, then the wrap is probably too tight.
- **E**—Elevate the injured area to minimize internal bleeding and swelling.

Ice can be applied by placing it in a plastic bag along with a little water, a gel cold pack, chemical cold pack, or ice water bucket. Apply ice for 10 to 15 minutes and then remove it for the same period. Then repeat. Follow these cautions in applying ice:

- Do not apply ice if you lack feeling in the injured area.
- Do not apply a tight compression wrap over the ice. An elastic wrap that is applied loosely to keep the ice in place is fine. After icing, compress the injured area with a tight wrap, but not so tight that it restricts blood flow.
- Do not apply ice directly on an open wound.
- Do not ice for longer than 15 minutes.

A caution about heat: Do not apply heat to your injury if you still have swelling. Heat can increase internal bleeding.

Nonsteroidal anti-inflammatory drugs are helpful in treating acute sports injuries. Ibuprofen (Advil, Motrin, Nuprin) and naproxen (Aleve) are the drugs most widely used to reduce inflammation and relieve pain, but there are many others. Use these NSAIDs for the first 2 to 3 days after an injury and then discontinue their use. Acetaminophen (e.g., Tylenol) is not an anti-inflammatory drug but does help relieve pain.

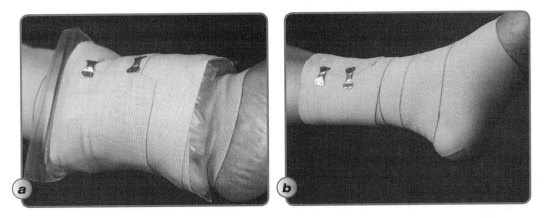

FIGURE 12.1   *(a)* First apply compression bandage and then place over wrap. *(b)* After ice is removed, apply a new compression wrap.

ACUTE INJURIES

Injuries may be categorized as acute or chronic. Acute injuries are those with a rapid onset, usually caused by trauma or sudden impact, that require immediate treatment. Chronic injuries develop slowly, often from overuse, and are persistent and long lasting. The most common acute injuries in slowpitch softball are

- abrasions,
- contusions,
- punctures and cuts,
- sprains,
- strains,
- dislocations and subluxations,
- fractures, and
- heat illness.

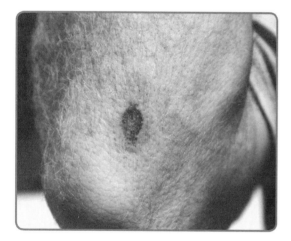

FIGURE 12.2   Abrasion.

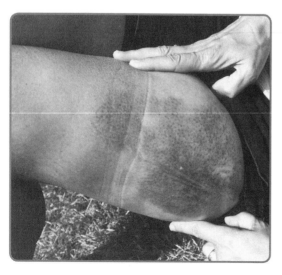

FIGURE 12.3   Contusion.

Abrasions

Injury: Scraping of the skin usually caused by sliding or diving for a ball. The most common locations for abrasions are on the hips, buttocks, knees, palms of the hands, and the inside of the elbows.

Signs and symptoms: Red patch of skin and oozing, accompanied by pain and burning sensation (see figure 12.2).

Treatment: Rinse with clean running water and use soap if necessary to remove dirt. Apply an antibiotic ointment. Cover the wound with sterile gauze if you are returning to the game or practice. Do not clean with a used, dirty towel. When you are not playing leave the wound open if possible for better healing. If the wound shows signs of infection, get medical help.

Contusions

Injury: We know these injuries as bruises caused by a direct blow to body tissue. A knee knocking into a player's quadriceps, a batted ball hitting the pitcher on the upper arm, and two outfielders colliding in pursuit of a pop-up, resulting in a bruised shoulder in one player and a contusion of the ribs in the other are all examples of this injury in softball. The impact causes tissue damage and internal bleeding.

Signs and symptoms: Pain, swelling, and discoloration are the common symptoms (see figure 12.3). If the contusion is deep, the discoloration may not be seen for 12 to 24 hours.

Treatment: Initial treatment is to ice the injured area to reduce swelling and pain. If the contusion is to muscle or bone and the pain is not severe, you can continue to play. If the contusion is to the head, ears, eyes, or kidneys and is moderate to severe, you should quit playing, ice the affected area for 5 to 10 minutes, and seek medical help.

Punctures and Cuts

Injury: Punctures in softball usually occur when coming into contact with fences that have sharp protruding wires (see figure 12.4a). Cuts can also be caused by collision with another player or a thrown ball, especially on the head. These jagged cuts are called lacerations (see figure 12.4b). Incisions are smooth cuts caused by a sharp object such as a piece of glass on the field (see figure 12.4c).

Signs and symptoms: Punctures may not bleed heavily, but cuts usually do. Both injuries carry a risk of infection from the object that caused the wound.

Treatment: Usually in softball the object making the puncture is immediately withdrawn from the body. If the puncture or cut is really deep you'll need medical help. If it is superficial, then do the following:

- Check to see that nothing is left in the wound.

- Let the wound bleed freely at first and then apply gentle pressure with a clean cloth or bandage to stop the bleeding. If the bleeding doesn't stop or the blood is squirting, you'll need medical help.

- Wash your hands and then wash the wound with running water. Use a mild soap if the wound is dirty. If you can't get all the dirt out, clean a tweezers with alcohol and remove the dirt.

- Protect the wound with an antibiotic ointment. Apply the ointment with a swab or gauze. Do not apply the ointment directly from the tube to avoid contaminating the tube. Cover the wound with a bandage if necessary.

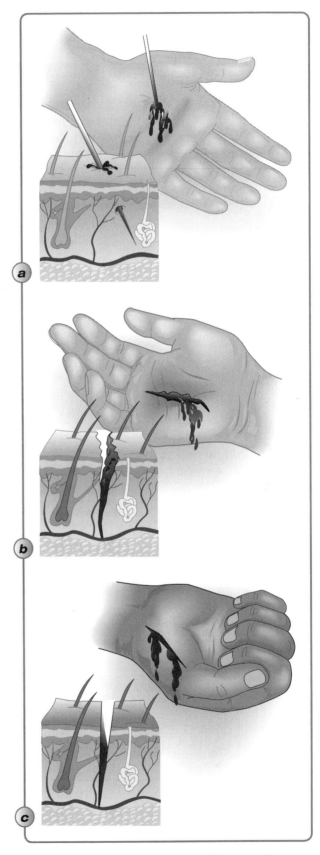

FIGURE 12.4　*(a)* Puncture, *(b)* laceration, *(c)* incision.

Reprinted, by permission, from M. Flegel, 2008, *Sport first aid*, 4th ed. (Champaign, IL: Human Kinetics), 38-39.

Sprains

Injury: When you stretch or tear a ligament, your injury is a sprain (see figure 12.5). Sprains of the ankle, knee, and wrist ligaments are common softball injuries.

Signs and symptoms: Sprains can vary from mild to severe. In mild sprains the ligament is only stretched, causing a little swelling and discomfort. In severe sprains the ligament is completely torn, creating a lot of swelling and a great deal of pain.

Treatment: For mild to severe sprains the first treatment is PRICE. After icing for 15 minutes, apply a compression wrap. For more severe sprains avoid all movement of the injured part. If you suspect any of the following, seek medical help:

- Any sign of a fracture
- Tingling and numbness, suggesting nerve compression
- Bluish areas around the injury, suggesting disrupted blood supply

With any sprain you can return to play after the pain subsides and you have full range of motion. Remember, though, that ligaments support joints by holding bones together. After they've been stretched or torn, they may not be as tight as they were before, causing some looseness or laxity in the joint. Taping or bracing may therefore be helpful in giving your joint more stability.

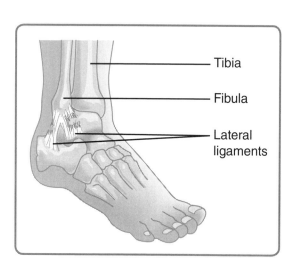

FIGURE 12.5 Ankle sprain.

Reprinted, by permission, from M. Flegel, 2008, *Sport first aid*, 4th ed. (Champaign, IL: Human Kinetics), 214.

Strains

Injury: When you stretch or tear a muscle or tendon, your injury is a strain (see figure 12.6). An explosive start, sudden stop, or quick change in direction can result in muscle or tendon being stretched or torn. These injuries are strains, not sprains, but like sprains they can vary from mild to severe.

Signs and symptoms: The signs and symptoms are identical to sprains, except for the location of the injury.

Treatment: Identical to sprains.

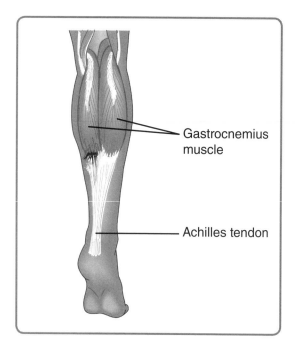

FIGURE 12.6 Calf strain.

Reprinted, by permission, from M. Flegel, 2008, *Sport first aid*, 4th ed. (Champaign, IL: Human Kinetics), 212.

Dislocations and Subluxations

Injury: Bones can move out of position from a collision of players or hard contact with a fence or the ground. When the bone stays out of position, the injury is called a dislocation (see figure 12.7). If the bone slips out of place and then pops back into place, the injury is called a subluxation. The most frequent joints affected by these injuries are the shoulders, elbow, fingers and thumb, and kneecap.

Signs and symptoms: When a bone moves out of place in a joint, injury also occurs to the soft tissues around it. These injuries are inevitably accompanied by severe pain, lack of sensation in the joint, and inability to move the joint.

Treatment: Immobilize the joint immediately. Apply ice to the injury and head for the nearest emergency room.

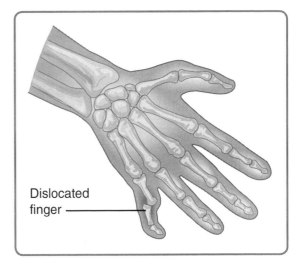

FIGURE 12.7 Finger dislocation.

Reprinted, by permission, from M. Flegel, 2008, *Sport first aid*, 4th ed. (Champaign, IL: Human Kinetics), 182.

Fractures

Injury: Bones can break from the same forces that cause sprains and strains. Although not a common injury in softball, broken ankles, leg bones, hand and wrist bones, and upper-arm and shoulder bones do occur.

Signs and symptoms: Open breaks that pierce the skin are easy but not pleasant to recognize (see figure 12.8*a*). Closed fractures may be recognized by a noticeable deformity of the body part, but some breaks are difficult to detect (see figure 12.8*b*). An avulsion fracture occurs when a ligament pulls off a piece of the bone where it is attached. Other fractures may produce hairline cracks that can be seen only by X ray or CT scan.

Treatment: Anytime you suspect that you have a fracture, you should isolate that part of your body and seek professional emergency care.

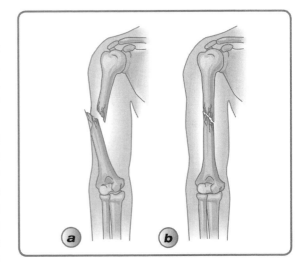

FIGURE 12.8 Fractures: *(a)* open and *(b)* closed.

Reprinted, by permission, from M. Flegel, 2008, *Sport first aid*, 4th ed. (Champaign, IL: Human Kinetics), 42.

Heat Illness

Injury: As players become increasingly dehydrated from sweating they become susceptible to heat exhaustion and heatstroke. The body goes into shock as electrolyte supplies are depleted and body temperature rises rapidly. Heat exhaustion, although not as severe as heatstroke, is a serious injury that needs immediate treatment. Heatstroke is life threatening because the brain's temperature control center is malfunctioning.

Signs and symptoms: Heat exhaustion is marked by headache, nausea, dizziness, chills, fatigue, and considerable thirst. Symptoms include pale, cool, and clammy skin; rapid, weak pulse; loss of coordination; dilated pupils; and profuse sweating. A person with heatstroke feels extremely hot, is confused or disoriented, is nauseas or vomiting, and has a headache or dizziness. Heart rate is increased, and breathing is rapid. Unlike with heat exhaustion the pupils will be restricted. Body temperature may rise above 104 °F (40 °C), and the person may have a seizure or be unresponsive.

Treatment: For heat exhaustion, move the player to a cool, shaded area and apply cool, wet towels and ice to the neck, back, and belly to cool the body. Give the player water to drink if he or she is responsive. Monitor breathing and circulation. Do not permit the player to return to activity on the same day that he or she suffered heat exhaustion.

For heatstroke, call immediately for emergency medical assistance. Remove clothing and place the player in cold water (tub or wading pool) or pack ice and cool towels around the body. Position the player in a semireclining position, monitor breathing, and apply CPR if necessary.

CHRONIC INJURIES

Slowpitch softball is played by all age groups, with large numbers of participants in their 40s, 50s, 60s, and on up. Although the game has been made safer by some of the rule modifications discussed in the introduction, players who have been playing for many years and who play often are prone to chronic injuries. These injuries are caused by repeated blows, overstretching, or just plain overuse. In this section we examine some of the most common chronic injuries of slowpitch softball players.

Bursitis

Bursas are small sacs filled with fluid that are located between bones, muscles, tendons, and other tissues that help to reduce friction between tissues. With repeated blows or irritation the bursa can become swollen and sore. When that happens you have bursitis, and it usually occurs in the elbows (see figure 12.9) or kneecap. The treatment is to rest the elbow or knee, apply ice, and take NSAIDs. If the bursitis does not subside within a week, see a physician.

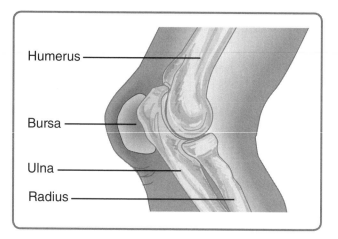

FIGURE 12.9 Elbow bursitis.

Reprinted, by permission, from M. Flegel, 2008, *Sport first aid*, 4th ed. (Champaign, IL: Human Kinetics), 43.

Tendinitis

Through overuse or over-stretching, tendons can become irritated, just as a bursa can. You'll be familiar with tennis elbow (see figure 12.10), an inflammation of the tendon where the wrist muscle attaches to the outside of the elbow joint. Where the calf muscle attaches to the heel is another common location for tendinitis, called Achilles tendinitis. The treatment is the same as for bursitis.

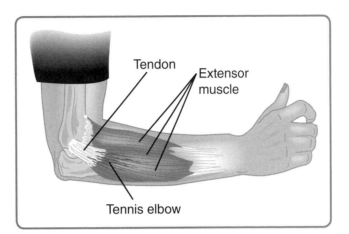

FIGURE 12.10 Tennis elbow.

Reprinted, by permission, from M. Flegel, 2008, *Sport first aid*, 4th ed. (Champaign, IL: Human Kinetics), 173.

Plantar Fasciitis

The plantar fascia are thick bands that connect your toes to your heel, and plantar fasciitis is an inflammation of those bands (see figure 12.11). The injury is not uncommon, especially among older softball players, and it is caused by flat feet, high arches, inadequate arch support, and tight calf muscles. Pain occurs under the heel and sometimes along the arch. For self-treatment, rest is always the initial recommendation, followed by slow stretching of the plantar fascia and Achilles tendon. NSAIDs may be helpful to a limited extent, but usually this problem requires medical assistance.

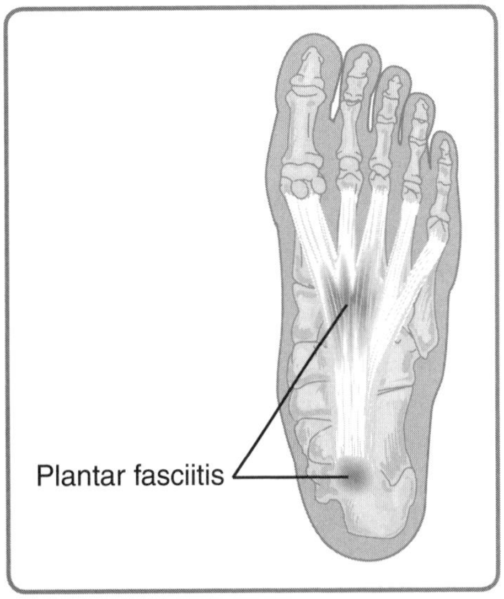

FIGURE 12.11 Plantar fasciitis.

Reprinted, by permission, from M. Flegel, 2008, *Sport first aid*, 4th ed. (Champaign, IL: Human Kinetics), 224.

Osteoarthritis

This common injury of older softball players occurs as the cartilage in the joints wears down to the point where bones rub on bones. Osteoarthritis can occur in any joint in the body, but it is most common in the knees, hips, ankles, fingers, and shoulders. There is no cure, and it usually gets worse over time. The symptoms are well known—pain, tenderness, stiffness, grating sensation in the joint, and swelling. The treatments for mild osteoarthritis include rest, exercise, use of heat and cold on the affected area, and NSAIDs.

OTHER COMMON PROBLEMS

In this section we look at several other common ailments that slowpitch softball players experience.

Blisters

If the blister is closed, leave it that way unless it is large, painful, and likely to be further irritated. If you drain it use a sterile needle and gently squeeze out the fluid. Do not remove the skin over the blister. Place a commercial callus or corn pad over the blister to protect it from further irritation (see figure 12.12). If the blister is open, clean the area with soap. Do not use iodine. Dry with sterile gauze and apply the callus or corn pad. If you see signs of infection, seek medical help.

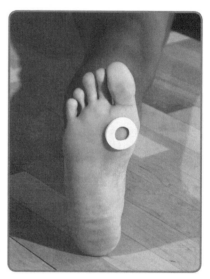

FIGURE 12.12 Blister donut pad.

Athlete's Foot and Jock Itch

These fungal infections are caused by prolonged exposure to a sweaty, hot, and poorly ventilated environment. To prevent these infections, keep your socks and jocks clean. The symptoms are burning and itching. The first aid is to change clothing frequently and keep the area clean and dry. Then apply an antifungal cream or powder.

Tooth Injury

If a tooth is knocked out of its socket, hold the tooth by the crown, not the root, and rinse it with water. Then place it in a container of milk, which will help preserve it. Keep your head bent forward, and if it is bleeding, apply pressure with gauze to the area. Seek dental help immediately. The best chance for reimplanting the tooth is within 30 minutes of the injury.

Nosebleed

When you have a nosebleed sit down and lean your head slightly forward, not backward (see figure 12.13). Use sterile gauze or a clean cloth to pinch your nostrils shut for up to 10 minutes. If the bleeding does not stop after 20 minutes of holding the nose shut, seek medical help. After the bleeding stops do not blow your nose or sneeze. Ice packs do not help. Do not stuff gauze up your nostrils.

FIGURE 12.13 Proper position for stopping a nosebleed.

Leg Cramps

Leg cramps are usually caused by muscle fatigue and dehydration and can be quite painful. The immediate treatment is to stretch the muscle for at least 30 seconds. If the spasm is in the calf, pull the toes toward the knee, keeping your knee straight (see figure 12.14). If the spasm is in the hamstring, straighten the knee. Massage the muscle until the cramp is gone. Drink, drink, drink, preferably a sports drink, because cramps are usually an early sign of heat exhaustion.

FIGURE 12.14 Stretch a cramping calf muscle by pulling the toes toward the knee.

REHABILITATION

For some injuries you're able to provide first aid and jump right back into action on the diamond, but for injuries such as serious sprains, strains, dislocations, fractures, and heat illnesses, you'll want to go through a rehabilitation process. The best approach is to do so under the guidance of a sports medicine specialist, a person who understands the rehabilitation process. But if you don't have professional guidance, we briefly describe here what you want to do. Follow this sequence:

1. **Range of motion**. When the pain and swelling have subsided you'll want to begin moving the injured limb to regain its original range of motion. When you tear tissue, the body begins healing itself by forming scar tissue, which is made of collagen and has the capacity to contract and therefore reduce flexibility. So begin your range of motion rehabilitation by icing the area for 15 minutes. Then move the limb slowly but firmly back and forth to the limits imposed by pain and swelling. Slight discomfort is fine, but don't force the limb beyond its painful limits of movement.

   For example, if you sprain your ankle, when the pain and swelling subside, put your ankle in a bucket of ice and water for 15 minutes. Remove it and exercise it by moving it forward and backward and rotating it inward and outward. Athletic trainers often have athletes spell the alphabet with their big toe to do the exercises needed.

   The exercise session can be short, 5 to 10 minutes, and repeated three times a day. You're ready to proceed to the next phase of rehabilitation when you have 80% of your normal range of motion back without pain.

2. **Endurance**. Endurance exercises use low or no weights but many repetitions. When doing endurance exercises you may feel some discomfort

but avoid strong pain. Do at least 30 to 50 repetitions of each exercise daily. You can use light weights, exercise machines, walk, swim, or cycle to perform the exercises to develop endurance in the injured muscles and other tissues in the injured limb. Add more weight or resistance when the exercises become too easy. If you've injured an arm or leg, you can easily determine when you're ready to go to the next phase of rehabilitation. Just test the opposite body part to see how many repetitions it can do. When the injured limb can do 80% of that amount, you're ready to move on.

3. **Strength**. Build up your strength by increasing the resistance of the exercises so that you can do only about 10 repetitions before the muscles tire. When you can do 3 extra repetitions increase the weight. Do three sets of these exercises with 5-minute rests between sets. If you encounter substantial pain you should stop and return to the endurance phase. When you can accomplish 80% of what the uninjured limb can do, you're ready for the skill phase.

4. **Skill development**. You've not been playing for a while, so now you want to retrain your body to perform the skills of softball. Practice hitting, fielding, throwing, and running, but begin gradually and increase the intensity of the practice as your body allows. Now you're ready to return to the game.

SUMMARY

- Prevention of injuries through proper warm-up and physical conditioning is the best medicine.

- Players more susceptible to injuries are those returning after a long absence from playing, those weak in fundamental skills (such as sliding) and knowledge of the game, and players returning from an injury.

- PRICE and NSAIDs are widely used treatments for many sports injuries.

- Acute injuries include abrasions, contusions, punctures and cuts, sprains, strains, dislocations and subluxations, fractures, and heat illnesses. Know the appropriate first aid for each.

- Chronic injuries among softball players, especially older players, include bursitis, tendinitis, plantar fasciitis, and osteoarthritis.

- Other common medical problems include blisters, athlete's foot and jock itch, tooth injuries, nosebleeds, and leg cramps.

- Players who experience serious injuries should go through a rehabilitation process of (1) improving range of motion, (2) building endurance, (3) increasing strength, and (4) practicing softball skills.

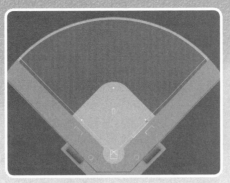

PART IV
COACHING

Slowpitch softball is mostly an adult game coached by a volunteer, often a player–coach. Recreational teams typically are composed of friends or workmates. One of the more experienced players organizes the team and serves as coach. The team has a few preseason practices, and after the season begins, practices are infrequent or nonexistent.

Competitive and tournament teams are more likely to have a diverse mix of players, some of whom are unacquainted with each other at the beginning of the season. These teams are more likely to have a nonplaying coach, but the majority of the coaches are players. Because players are often geographically separated by a considerable distance, they often get their practice by playing in a local league. They then come together on weekends to play in tournaments. Usually the only practice that these teams take together is batting practice.

If you are coaching a team that fits one of these two scenarios, you'll be coaching under less than ideal circumstances. To play any sport

well, players need to practice regularly, and to play a team sport well, players need to practice together regularly. In slowpitch softball, however, few teams do so. Recreational teams typically care not to make that much of a commitment to the game, and competitive teams simply find it impractical to practice together because of their geographical dispersion. So as a coach you do the best you can with the situation you're given.

We should make a distinction here between coaching and managing a team. Managers typically do the following:

- Select team members and see that they register to be eligible to play in the league or tournament
- Raise money and manage the team's financial affairs
- Schedule practices and games
- Organize game-day preparations to play
- Prepare the batting lineup and assign players to defensive positions

Coaches, on the other hand, fulfill two major functions:

o Provide technical and tactical instructions in practices and during games

o Make offensive and defensive tactical decisions during the game, including player substitutions

Often these functions are assigned to or fall on the same person. Although we see wide differences in the skill with which individuals manage teams, we rarely see teams that are effectively coached. Unlike some other sports in which players seem to be overcoached, slowpitch softball teams by and large are definitely undercoached.

We recognize the challenge of managing and coaching adult slowpitch softball teams. Fulfilling both functions isn't easy, and most who do have no training to coach other than having played the game. That experience may or may not be enough. (From here on we'll refer to the dual role of manager and coach as simply the coach.)

On the surface, teams win or lose because of their offensive and defensive play. But if you dig deeper, you'll find that teams' successes and failures are rooted in leadership. Players need an effective leader to become a cohesive and successful team. The coach is that assigned leader, but some coaches are unable to fill this role well, limiting their functions to the role of manager. Sometimes another player fills the leadership void on an informal basis, but often the void goes unfilled. An observer can easily recognize teams that could be far more successful with a coach who provides effective leadership.

An adult slowpitch team in which players participate voluntarily for the primary purpose of challenging themselves to execute the skills of the game and having fun is best served by a coach who uses a cooperative style of coaching rather than a dictatorial style. The cooperative style is characterized by involving the players in the decision-making when possible by listening to their views on matters of practice times, offensive and defensive lineups, and tactics. This involvement often occurs informally on and off the field. But in game situations when a decision needs to be made immediately, polling the team for a vote on what to do is, of course, not possible. The cooperative style of coaching is one in which players should have input at appropriate times. At other times, you as the coach need to make prompt decisions.

In part IV we necessarily limit our focus to helping coaches conduct effective practices (chapter 13) and making decisions on game day (chapter 14), two vital aspects of coaching. We could write an entire book on coaching, and in fact the first author has done so. If you want to gain far more insight into how to execute all the duties of a coach, we invite you to read Rainer Martens' *Successful Coaching, Third Edition*. See appendix A for more information about this book and the companion online course.

CHAPTER 13

Conducting Practices

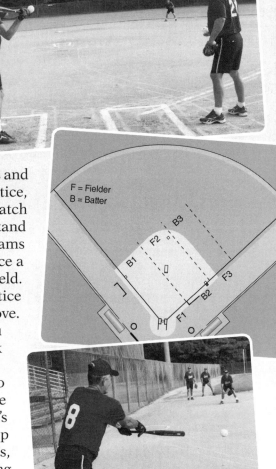

F = Fielder
B = Batter

igh school and college baseball and fastpitch softball teams as well as serious club teams practice three to five times per week. During the off-season, coaches of these teams develop season plans of the skills and tactics that will be practiced. Then during the season they prepare daily practice plans based on the season plans and how their teams are currently playing.

Coaches of recreational or competitive adult slowpitch softball teams almost never develop season plans and rarely develop a formal practice plan. When teams do practice, the session usually consists of a few minutes of playing catch before each player bats until his or her arms tire. Players stand around the field shagging the balls and mostly visiting. Teams may spend a little time on infield practice and perhaps once a year work on cutoffs and relays from the outfield to the infield.

Not only do teams seldom practice, when they do practice and play, typically there is no coaching to help players improve. The underlying assumption in such practices is that if you just keep doing the same thing, you'll get better. Now think about the logic of that approach to practice!

As we observed in the part IV opener, most people who assume the role of coach are in actuality a manager of the team, not a coach. We don't mean this in a critical way; it's simply a statement of reality. Managers are essential to help organize the team, but coaches—people who can teach skills, help correct errors, and make critical tactical decisions during games—are also needed if teams have any hope of improving their play. Throughout this chapter we'll encourage you to coach, to help players improve, and if you're not qualified to coach, we recommend that you find a player on your team or someone else who can help you with this duty. In the next section we'll share with you nine principles for practicing better and then describe specific ways to practice offense and defense more effectively. We'll then show you how to plan a practice.

NINE PRINCIPLES FOR BETTER PRACTICE

An effective slowpitch softball practice session should meet several goals:

- **Be well organized**. For whatever time your team agrees to devote to practice, you want to make the most of it. Have a place reserved for practice, make sure that everyone knows the place and time, and have the equipment ready to go. Create a strong expectation that everyone attends practice.
- **Be safe**. You want to organize activities so that players don't get hit with thrown balls or injured in other ways because of poor practice supervision.
- **Have fun**. Practices need not be long, boring sessions in which each player takes his or her turn hitting. Instead, practices can be lively sessions in which everyone is actively involved.
- **Improve skills**. The ultimate purpose of practices is for players to learn and remember the technical and tactical skills that they've been taught.

You may conduct practices in many different ways, but for players to learn the skills to improve their play, practices should follow these nine principles.

Principle 1. Practices should be short and frequent when learning a new skill or when making major modifications to a skill. Usually in adult slowpitch softball, players are not entirely new to the game, although they may be returning to the game after years of not playing or from playing baseball or fastpitch softball. When a player is working on relearning a skill or making a significant modification to a skill, such as hitting, the recommended approach is to keep the practice time relatively short, interrupt it with breaks, and then repeat practicing the skill rather than conduct the practice in one long session.

Principle 2. Practice softball skills in gamelike conditions as soon as players are able to do so. This principle seems intuitively obvious, but it is often violated. For example, when taking batting practice before games, the pitching should be identical to the pitching in games. Yet we see pitchers pitching from a distance different from that used in the game and trying to groove pitches with a relatively low arc to make it easy for batters to hit. We see batters swing at any pitch they can reach without regard to the strike zone. That type of practice is not helpful, and in fact may harm the timing of hitting pitches in the game thrown with a higher arc and from the 50- to 56-foot (15 to 17 m) distances.

Principle 2 should also be applied to defensive play. For example, what's the best way to practice fielding ground balls?

1. Initially have the batter hit the balls at a slower speed and then gradually increase the speed to gamelike conditions.
2. From the outset hit the balls at gamelike speeds.

Based on scientific evidence, the answer is number 2, with the caveat that if the player is a novice or has lost confidence in fielding, hitting the ball at a slower speed is helpful until he or she has learned the basics of the skill or regained confidence. But in general it is more beneficial to practice fielding balls hit at gamelike speeds.

Design practices to be as gamelike as possible.

Principle 3. Each player should be actively involved throughout the practice session.   The typical slowpitch batting practice session has a batter hitting 20, 30, 40, or more balls while 10 to 12 players shag balls, most of them just standing around visiting. There is a better way, but it requires more work on the part of each player and the breaking of a strong tradition in slowpitch.

What is possible to do depends considerably on the facilities available to you. Ideally, two adjacent playing fields will be available. You can hold batting practice on each and thus take half the time for this part of practice, or you can have the outfielders hitting on one field and the infielders taking infield practice on the other, and then have them switch.

If you have only one playing field available, you can have the batters hit from about where the coach's box is at first base, hitting toward right and center field. That leaves enough room on the third-base side to practice fielding ground balls and to work on double plays using the third-base bag as the second-base bag.

When outfielders are shagging balls they should work on their fielding skills, such as charging balls, going back on balls, and quickly retrieving ground balls. Then on the sidelines they can also practice fielding and throwing accurately to the cutoff or relay infielder.

Principle 4. Practice sessions should make maximum use of the available facilities and equipment.   This principle is a corollary to principle 3. With regard to equipment, players usually provide their own bats, so that's not a problem, and balls are inexpensive, so you can have plenty on hand. If the field that you practice on does not have bases, you can purchase some rubber ones or use some carpet remnants. A carpet remnant also works well as a strike mat if your league uses one.

The only other piece of equipment that we highly recommend is a pitching screen. This screen can spare your batting practice pitchers a lot of pain and potentially can be a lifesaver. See chapter 9, page 222, to learn more about portable screens.

Practicing the backhand toss among the pitcher, shortstop, and second baseperson.

Principle 5. Dedicate time to practicing skills that need to be improved. Now that principle seems obvious, but let's think about this further. Of course, everyone practices hitting because it's vital to success in the sport. But far less time is typically devoted to defensive play. Infielders may practice fielding ground balls, but how often do teams practice the following?

- Fielding fly balls hit over the heads of the outfielders and catching fly balls hit near or at the fence.
- Catching pop-ups hit over the heads of the infielders into short outfield.
- Turning double plays from the pitcher to the second baseperson or shortstop.
- Executing an out from the first baseperson to the pitcher covering first base.
- Throwing the ball in various gamelike situations, such as short throws and long throws.
- Executing rundowns of players caught between the bases.
- Making tags on players sliding.
- Executing the relay to home on balls hit deep in the outfield.
- Running the bases to be in a position to advance to the next base if an error is made in the field.

You can see that teams can work on many things in a practice session, but the coach must be organized to plan and implement practices that devote time to work on skills other than hitting, and players must be willing to expend the energy to improve.

Principle 6. Emphasize that the goal of practice is to improve performance. Yes, this principle also seems obvious, but often players come to practice and go through the motions without the intention of improving. Three things can happen to a player's performance as a result of practicing: (*a*) it can stay the same, (*b*) it can get better, or (*c*) it can get worse. Why practice if you don't want to improve? So if you see players who appear not to be putting effort into improving, you'll want to talk with them to change their mind-set. Otherwise, your team has little chance of getting better.

Principle 7. Provide feedback to help players improve. Players will improve their skills more rapidly with good instructions and feedback. If you're qualified to coach, by all means do so. If you are not qualified to provide feedback on hitting and defensive skills, then perhaps a player on the team is or you can find someone who has the ability to help your players improve. If the players are resistant to feedback, you need to change that mind-set.

Video is a wonderful way to provide feedback to your players. Video equipment is not expensive to buy or rent and is easy to use. With video, your players can see themselves hitting and fielding balls. But even with video, players may need help to identify mistakes and learn how to correct them.

Principle 8. Let your players help plan the practice sessions. At the end of each practice session or after a game and before the next practice, encourage your players to tell you what they believe they need to practice next. You can combine their suggestions with your own observations to plan the next practice. With greater involvement by your players in planning practices, you'll get greater commitment to improving skills in the practice session.

Principle 9. Make practices fun. A well-planned practice session in which everyone is active will be more fun than the typical practices that we so often see. Plan drills that have a competitive element to create interest and more enjoyment. Vary the activities in the practice and find new drills to try. (See appendix A for books and videos that describe drills for baseball and fastpitch softball that you can adapt for slowpitch softball.) Finally, an upbeat attitude on your part and that of at least a majority of your players can make practices more enjoyable.

BATTING PRACTICE

Now let's apply these principles to the batting part of a practice session. We begin by describing how to conduct batting practice as part of a dedicated practice session, and then we'll describe our recommendations for pregame batting practice.

Dedicated Practice Session

If available, use two adjacent fields so that you can have two hitting stations in action at the same time or have the infielders working on defensive skills on one field and the outfielders hitting on the other. If you have only one field, have half the team hitting and the other half working on defensive skills. Too much time is wasted with 12 to 18 players when only one batter is hitting 40 or 50 balls.

With two hitting stations, each has two batters, a pitcher pitching from behind a protective pitching screen, and a bucket person, who stands at least 75 feet (25 m) behind the pitcher. The bucket person places the balls thrown to him or her in the bucket and runs the bucket up to the pitcher when balls are needed. Having fielders throw the ball toward the pitcher and making that person retrieve balls all around him or her slows down practice and makes pitching an unfair amount of extra work.

Batting practice using one part of the field, leaving room for defensive infield practice.

We recommend a minimum of three players in the outfield to retrieve balls and throw them to the bucket person. Fielders should throw the ball to the bucket person only when he or she is looking and the ball is not being pitched. Alternatively, fielders can throw the ball on the ground as close to the bucket as possible.

Thus this station involves 7 players. If you have 14 or more players, you can have two full stations. Time devoted to batting practice will be cut in half, leaving you much more time to practice other skills that are often neglected.

Based on principle 1, that distributed practice is better than massed practice, we recommend that at least two batters take batting practice together. Batter 1 hits about 10 pitches and steps out to let batter 2 hit 10 pitches. As the coach, now is the time for you or someone else to help your players improve the mechanics of their swing. While batter 2 is hitting, the coach provides constructive feedback to batter 1. When batter 2 completes his or her 10 swings, batter 1 takes another 10 swings and the coach provides feedback to batter 2. Depending on the time available, each batter will take three or four rounds of 10 swings each. Then we recommend that you have batter 1 hit one pitch, have batter 2 hit one pitch, and repeat that five times. After the first pair of batters have finished, the next pair comes in. You should assign someone to the bucket, and if the pitcher is scheduled to hit, you need to assign another player to pitch. If you have two fields available, throughout the batting practice you may be helping players on one field and assign one of your better hitters to help batters on the other field.

As we noted in part I we often see batters swinging at almost every pitch thrown in practice. We suspect that they do so because they want to keep practice moving along, but this is a bad idea. Encourage your players to hit only strikes, to learn the strike zone well, and to avoid hitting bad pitches! Remember to make every aspect of practice as gamelike as possible.

Pregame Batting Practice

Many recreational teams and some competitive teams don't take batting practice before they play a game, but teams who are serious about their play almost always do. We recommend that you have your team bat 75 to 90 minutes before the scheduled game time. Hitting on practice fields adjacent to the softball diamonds where you will play the game is ideal, but if space is not available there, you can hit off site. If you are at an unfamiliar tournament location, scout for a place to hit the day before.

When you're preparing to play a game, you may want to use only one hitting station so that you avoid tiring out your fielders. Also, you may find it difficult to find a large space to hit. Here's a routine that you can follow:

1. When you arrive at the practice site, set up to take batting practice with the same orientation that you'll use in the game, if possible.

2. Set up the pitching screen and lay out home plate and a strike mat (if used in your league). Step off 50 feet (15 m) so that you're seeing pitches thrown the same distance that you'll see in the game.

3. If you travel by air to a tournament, have each player bring two balls for batting practice. That way no one has to carry a bucket of balls. You can designate one player to find or buy a bucket to put the balls in.

4. Begin with some light jogging and stretching and then warm up your arms by playing catch.

5. Then you're ready to hit. You may want to announce the batting lineup for the game and bat in pairs according to that lineup.

6. Rotate pitchers after four to six batters so that no one has to work too hard before the game.

7. Each player should hit five pitches and then step out for the next batter to hit five. Repeat that twice. Then each player hits one and steps out. Repeat that five times. (If a player thinks that he or she needs more batting practice, let the player hit after everyone has had a turn at bat, if time permits.)

8. After everyone hits, disassemble the screen, have each person grab two balls, roll up home plate and the strike mat, and head off to the game.

When first introducing a batting routine of this type, you may find some players resistant to it, but with some gentle nudges and reminders of how you want to conduct batting practice, they'll not only get used to it but find comfort in the routine because they know exactly what to do.

Pregame batting practice is not the best time to do any coaching on hitting technique. Coaching a player's hitting should be done in dedicated practice sessions. Pregame hitting should be devoted to warming up the muscles that execute the swing and focusing on hitting the ball as you would in the game. It's a time to encourage players when they hit the ball well.

DEFENSIVE PRACTICE

As we observed before, many slowpitch softball teams seldom practice defensive skills, and on the rare occasion that they do, they do not spend practice time optimally. In this section we'll describe how to practice defensive skills, first for a dedicated practice session and then before a game.

Dedicated Practice Session

After an efficient batting practice that takes about 45 minutes, you can devote the second half of your 90-minute practice session to defensive practice. With a carefully thought out practice plan, you can not only have the infielders practicing but also have the outfielders, pitchers, and catchers working on their defensive skills.

Pitchers and Catchers

Let's begin with pitchers and catchers. It's easy for these players to practice. Pitchers can practice on the sidelines working on varying the pitches according to the tactics discussed in chapter 5. Pitchers should also throw batting practice, working on their control and tactics. If they wish to master exceptional control, they should practice pitching at home almost every day.

Catchers have fewer defensive plays, but the few they have can be critical to the outcome of the game. The major things for catchers to practice are fielding pop-ups and, if the pop-up is in fair territory, throwing to the appropriate base. In addition, catchers should practice catching thrown balls coming home for both force and tag plays in the same way that the other infielders catch balls for these plays (remember that some leagues and tournaments use a scoring plate to avoid tag plays at home).

In any dedicated practice session we suggest that pitchers throw at least 50 pitches on the sidelines, calling out to the catcher where they intend to throw the pitch. And then they should throw batting practice to at least six batters. Pitchers should then simulate pop-ups by standing in the batter's box and throwing balls up for the catcher. The balls should be thrown at various heights and locations, and occasionally a ground ball in front of the plate should be thrown.

Pitchers and catchers should then be part of a regular infield practice, which we'll describe next.

Infielders

We recommend that in a dedicated practice session you work on the following defensive skills:

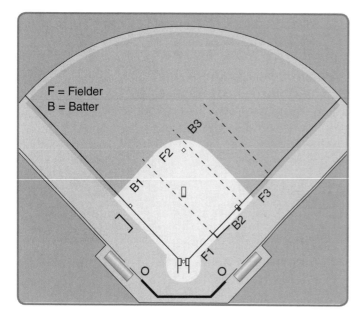

F = Fielder
B = Batter

FIGURE 13.1 Infield practice plan.

1. For a productive practice of fielding ground balls, divide the infield into three lanes as shown in figure 13.1. Have batter 1 (B1) hit 10 ground balls to fielder 1 (F1). At the same time, B2 is hitting to F2 and B3 is hitting to F3. Note that B2 is hitting in the direction opposite that B1 and B3 are hitting, a setup that reduces the chances that two fielders will collide or that a player will be hit by a ball from another lane. After fielding 10 ground balls, the batters become fielders and the fielders become batters. Repeat this at least three times so that each person fields at least 30 balls. Batters should try to hit the ball to simulate game conditions as closely as possible, hitting not only to the fielder but also to his or her right or left, but staying within the designated lane.

2. Next, have infielders work on throwing, not just the conventional throws from their positions to first or second base but all the other types of throws described in chapter 6. Pitchers and first basepersons should work on tossing the ball to each other as they cover first base. Shortstops and second basepersons should work on short and longer double-play throws to each other. The pitcher and third baseperson should join them in practicing double-play throws. You can create a variety of drills to practice these throws.

3. After throwing, it's a good time to work on the rundown play. Have the outfielders serve as runners and practice executing the rundown as described on pages 152–153 in chapter 6.

4. Infielders don't just have ground balls hit to them, so devote time to fielding pop-ups on the infield and to the short outfield. Usually it's easier to have someone throw the ball rather than hit it to practice fielding these types of hits.

5. Next have the infielders take their regular positions, including the pitcher and catcher, and conduct what most players know as a conventional infield practice. Hit balls to each position, calling out the play situation. Players practice fielding and throwing to the appropriate base for the situation. This is an especially good time to work on a variety of double plays as described on pages 150–152 in chapter 6.

Outfielders

In slowpitch the tendency is for outfielders to practice fielding only by catching balls in batting practice. We encourage you to do much more and suggest the following:

1. The toughest play for most fielders is going back to catch a ball. Practice this play by having fielders begin running away from a thrower, who then throws the ball high and over the head of the fielder but trying to lead him or her much like a quarterback throwing a pass to a receiver. The throws should be varied so that fielders have to learn how to look over their right and left shoulders. An easy drill is to set up two opposite lines as shown in figure 13.2. F1 takes off running, and F3 throws the ball. After making the catch, F1 joins the line in group B. Then F4 runs, and F6 throws the ball. After making the catch, F4 then becomes the thrower in group A, and F3 moves to the back of the line in group A. The same thing happens in group B. F1 becomes the thrower, and F6 falls into the line after F5. Each fielder should take about five or six throws with this drill.

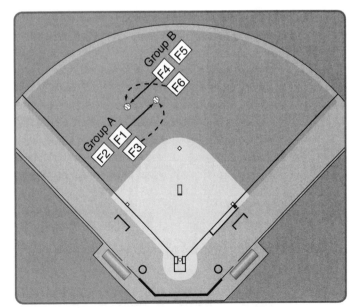

FIGURE 13.2 Outfield practice plan for catching fly balls thrown over outfielders' heads.

2. After players demonstrate proficiency in catching balls over their right and left shoulders, move this drill so that players must catch the ball at the fence, practicing how to find the fence and safely make the catch.

3. Outfielders also need to practice fielding ground balls, often in outfields that are rough. You can design a simple drill to have players practice fielding ground balls hit directly at them, to their left, and to their right. During this drill emphasize charging the ball when possible and not looking up just as they are catching it to see where they are going to throw, the cause of most missed ground balls.

4. Another useful outfield skill to practice is setting up under a high fly ball to make a long throw to a base. Fielders want to be running toward the base to which they will be throwing as they catch the ball.

5. Next you'll want to bring the outfielders together with the infielders to practice throwing to the cutoff and relay infielders. Practice throwing to second, third, and home from shallow, medium, and deep outfield positions.

Pregame Defensive Practice

If your team has a groomed softball field on which to take batting practice before the game, then you can also take a round of infield practice if you allot sufficient time. Quite often, however, you will be unable to find a vacant softball field that's groomed sufficiently well to take infield practice. Thus infield practice and additional outfield practice occur on the game field just before the start of the game.

When leading national teams move into their bench or dugout, they continue to warm up by jogging, sprinting, and playing catch. Then someone usually hits ground balls to the infielders on the sideline because often the facility management doesn't allow teams to take regular infield practice on the playing field. A suggested routine is to have a batter and a catcher hit balls to the infielders, including the pitcher. Each player catches four or five balls and then steps out to let the next fielder do the same. Try to do two rounds if time permits.

Take infield practice on the sideline before each game.

We also recommend that the outfielders do a warm-up using the drill, described in figure 13.2. About three catches for each fielder is an adequate warm-up.

Although pitchers receive warm-up pitches before each inning, they may like to take additional practice throws on the sidelines just before the game.

When playing more than one game in a day we recommend that you do the defensive warm-up before each game, but typically teams do not take batting practice between games unless they have more than 5 or 6 hours between games. You should ask the team whether they wish to have batting practice.

SAMPLE PRACTICE PLAN

Now let's put together all the parts of a dedicated practice session into a practice plan. We'll assume that you have only one softball field available for practice and 14 players. The practice session is planned for 90 minutes, 85 minutes of practice and 5 minutes for moving from one activity to the next. Take note that in the description of the practice, two activities or drills will be occurring at the same time.

Warm-Up (10 Minutes)

We recommend that you have each player spend just 10 minutes warming up before practice and games. Begin with a jog around the field or up and down the sidelines to warm the muscles. Then stretch the major muscles of the body, especially the hamstrings because they are highly susceptible to pulls. Next have players warm up their arms by throwing with each other.

Many players, young and old, don't bother to do much to warm up before playing. Consequently, they are more susceptible to muscle injuries. And even though the muscle strains may be minor when players are younger, the accumulated microtears of muscle fibers result in less elasticity and more susceptibility to major muscle tears later in life. Encourage proper warm-up.

Batting Practice Combined With Infielder and Outfielder Drills (25 Minutes)

Have all the outfielders take batting practice following the routine described on pages 281-282 earlier in the chapter. Hit from behind first base as shown in figure 13.3. When left-handers bat, move the pitching screen closer to the infield so that the batter is hitting the ball more into the playing field. When the outfielders are done, have the infielders take their turn at hitting. Expect that this simultaneous batting, infield drill, and outfield drill portion will take about 25 minutes to complete.

During the time that the outfielders are hitting, have the infielders work on their defensive skills. We recommend that infielders work on fielding ground balls at every

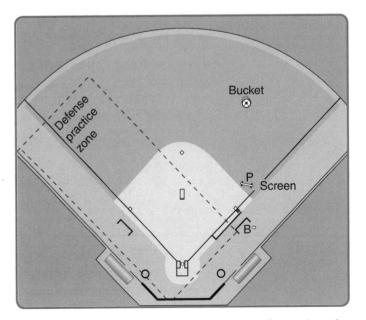

FIGURE 13.3 Batting practice portion of practice plan.

practice. Then have them work on one or two other skills that you deem need to be practiced. Don't try to practice everything in every practice session or you'll be having 3-hour practices.

When the infielders are hitting, have the outfielders move over to the defense practice zone to work on outfield skills. This is a good time for them to practice catching balls thrown over their heads and to work on fielding ground balls. When you do so, move to the grass part of the field so that the conditions are identical to those that you'll have in the game.

Infield and Outfield Practice (15 Minutes)

Have all infielders take their positions and have someone hit ground balls at game speed to practice fielding and making plays at all the bases. Teams typically have one or two rounds in which each player fields the ball and throws to first. That's usually followed by a couple of rounds to practice turning double plays. Then fielding a ball and throwing home is customary. You can add other play situations as time permits.

At the same time that infielders are practicing, outfielders can work on catching balls hit in front, behind, and to each side of them. If no one is available to hit fly balls, then have the fielders do so but rotate the task.

Outfield–Infield Relays (10 Minutes)

Now is the time to work on the relay throws and cutoffs from the outfielders to the infielders. The outfielders can work on both their fielding and throwing skills, as well as their communication with each other, as discussed in chapter 9. Infielders work on getting into the right position for relays and cutoffs, as well as their communication.

Three-Player Game (20 Minutes)

If the team is up for it, end the practice with a small-sided game. Divide players into teams of three so that you still have enough players for a full defensive team or close to it. Have each three-person team bat until they make three outs. Each hit counts as a run.

Wrap-Up (5 Minutes)

Bring the team together to comment on what went well and what needs more work. Ask for input from the players. Then agree on the next practice or time to meet for the next game. During the wrap-up encourage players to stretch as part of the cool-down.

SUMMARY

- Most slowpitch softball teams do not practice enough, and when they do practice they devote most if not all of the time to batting. Practices can accomplish far more when effectively planned and conducted.
- Practices should be short and frequent when learning a new skill or when making major modifications to a skill.

- Practice softball skills in gamelike conditions as soon as players are able to do so.
- Each player should be actively involved throughout the practice session.
- Practice sessions should make maximum use of the available facilities and equipment.
- Dedicate time to practicing skills that need to be improved and emphasize that practices are for improving.
- Provide feedback to help players improve.
- Let your players help plan the practice sessions.
- Make practices fun.
- Apply the principles of practice in planning and conducting your dedicated and pregame practice sessions.
- Schedule time to practice all the skills of the sport, not just hitting.
- Players improve their softball skills only with effective coaching and a commitment on their part to improve.

CHAPTER 14

Game-Day Coaching

It's the day you've been looking forward to, the day you've been working for. It's game day! As the team manager and coach, and most likely player–coach, you'll have a busy day. You have a number of things to take care of before the game, many decisions to make during the game, and some postgame duties as well. You can manage it all by being organized and developing what-if plans. What if a player is unable to play? What if it rains? What if the opposing team's home-run hitter comes to bat when the game is tied in the bottom of the sixth? What if we lose the game? Each of these what-ifs will require a decision from you, and making those decisions will be much easier if you've thought them through before you confront the situation. We'll help you with those decisions in this chapter by covering a variety of pregame tasks to perform, factors to consider in making a lineup and managing substitutions, and pregame routines. We'll also look at the decisions that you'll likely face during offensive and defensive play. Finally, we'll examine your postgame tasks.

PREGAME COACHING

Before game day you've informed everyone on the team of the schedule for the day. The team knows when and where batting practice will be held. They know whether you'll be playing one game or more. If you're playing in a tournament, you'll want to let them know what the tournament schedule is. If your team has more than one uniform, they should know which uniform to wear to the game. (As we noted in chapter 10, having two or three identical shirts is much simpler than having different-colored uniforms.)

If you're playing in a league or tournament for the first time, you should let the players know before traveling to the game the rule modifications for the event. It's especially important that your players know what bats are legal so that they bring

Challenge of Being a Player-Coach

Many, if not most, slowpitch softball teams are coached by a player on the team. Performing well in both roles is not easy, especially on game day. You're busy organizing the team but may fail to prepare yourself to play. Some last-minute matter comes up with the lineup or registration of the team, and then suddenly the umpire yells, "Play ball," and you have yet to warm up.

During the game your attention is divided between your own play and making tactical decisions for the team. You're concerned about getting players on the bench into the game, positioning the outfielders, inserting substitute runners, and having coaches at first and third. As you're dealing with those matters you suddenly find that it's your turn to bat and you really don't have your mind fully focused on the task of hitting. You can alleviate some of these problems by delegating some of the tasks to others and by being well organized, but even with that, your attention must be divided between tactical coaching and your own play.

bats they can use. Let players know other common rule variations, including the strike count, pitching arc, home-run limits, runner substitution rules, runs-per-inning limits, game-run-rule differences, and game time limits.

Make the Lineup

Give us 10 speedy players who hit to all fields with power and have on-base averages exceeding .800, and we'll show you the perfect way to make a lineup. Just throw the names in a hat and pull them out to create your team lineup. If all your players don't match up to our all-star team, then let's consider alternative ways to develop a productive lineup. Is making a lineup all art, or is there some science to it? Are there any rules to follow?

One logical approach would be to bat the hitter with the highest batting average first, the hitter with the second highest batting average next, and so on. The logic here is that you want your best hitters hitting more frequently and together so that they have more opportunities to bat and score runs. The downside to this approach is that you've given no consideration to where the power hitters are in the lineup, the placement of faster and slower runners, and the grouping of the weaker hitters, which increases the chances of scoreless innings.

An alternative approach is to build a lineup that considers the following factors:

- On-base batting percentages
- Power and place-hitting ability
- Baserunning speed
- Ability to hit under pressure
- Coed rules that require men and women to alternate
- Availability of substitute runners

With these factors in mind, we'll now describe how we approach the development of a lineup. Slowpitch softball teams typically bat more than the 10 defensive players, depending on league or tournament rules. Some leagues,

Announce the batting lineup prior to practice on game day.

especially recreational and senior ones, allow everyone on the team to bat in the lineup, up to a maximum of 15 or 20 players. In our example, we'll describe a batting order for 12 players. We don't suggest that this is the only way to develop a lineup, but it is one way, and you can judge the logic of our thinking.

Team Batting Lineup

- **Batter 1**—A high-percentage hitter who has excellent speed so that he or she can beat out balls hit on the infield and does not slow up runners batting later.

- **Batter 2**—Another high-percentage hitter who usually drives the ball to the outfield, thus avoiding double-play possibilities.

- **Batters 3 and 4**—Two best power hitters here. Between the two of them, they are likely to drive in the first two runners if they are on base.

- **Batters 5 and 6**—Two place hitters who can score or advance the runners on base by placing the ball, often to the right side of the field. These two hitters should bat well under pressure because they often come to bat with runners on base.

- **Batters 7 and 8**—Batters 7 and 8 have attributes similar to batters 1 and 2, although batter 7 may not have the same speed as batter 1. The same logic is used for the second half of the batting lineup as was used for the first, and the two halves should be balanced in hitting. This consideration is especially important if you are playing in a league or tournament that limits the runs per inning.

- **Batters 9 and 10**—The next best power hitters after batters 3 and 4. They often have the opportunity to score batters 5, 6, 7, and 8.

- **Batters 11 and 12**—As with batters 5 and 6, these batters are high-percentage place hitters who can score or advance the power hitters and then be on base when the top of the lineup bats again. Batters 11 and 12 ideally have good speed so that they don't slow down the leadoff batter.

Substituting Base Runners Who Are in the Batting Lineup

Here's how to calculate quickly who is safe to run and not become stranded on base when it is his or her turn to bat.

1. Begin with the current batter or the batter coming to bat when you want to make the substitution.
2. Next count the number of bases open. If a runner is on first base, then three bases remain (second, third, and home). If runners are on first and second base, two bases remain open (third and home).
3. Now add to this number the number of outs remaining. For example, if a substitute runner is needed at first base and no one is out, your total is six (three bases open and three outs). If you substitute a runner for a player on third base with another runner on first base with one out, the total is four (two bases and two outs).
4. Beginning with the current batter or the batter coming to the plate, count down the number of batters to the number that you obtained in step 3. For example, if the number is 6 and the batter at the plate is 4th in the lineup, the 9th batter in the lineup can safely run without being in jeopardy of being caught on base when it is his or her turn to bat. If the number is 4 and the current batter is 8th in the lineup and you're batting 12 players, then the 11th batter can safely run.

When developing your lineup you'll also want to consider your need for substitute runners. Some slowpitch softball leagues and tournaments only permit players not in the game to be substituted as pinch runners. Then, depending on the rules, the player who was substituted for may or may not re-enter the game. The pinch runner may run only once in a game. In senior softball, substitution for runners is much more open. Usually any player on the roster is allowed to run for any other player once per inning.

Under these generous substitution rules, you'll want to consider where you place your substitute runners in the lineup. What you must avoid is stranding a substitute runner on a base when his or her turn comes to bat. When no one is out and you want to substitute a runner for a player on first base, the substitute runner needs to be batting at least six places after the batter–runner on first base to avoid being stranded on a base and called out. See "Substituting Base Runners Who Are in the Batting Lineup" to know how to calculate the number of batters needed between the substitute runner and his or her turn to bat.

Especially when you're a player–coach, it's easier to designate before the game runners for players who *need* runners each time they get on base. Then you can focus on making tactical running substitutions throughout the game.

Plan Other Substitutions

One of the more difficult parts of coaching is making substitutions. You will need to have at least 12 or 13 reliable players. Now you need to decide how to manage substitutions. You want to play your best players, and they expect to play, yet you want to give the players on the bench the opportunity to play. Otherwise, you'll have no substitutes in the future. Almost every coach faces this dilemma. To manage substitutions, we recommend that you come to the game with a plan in mind rather than make substitutions on the fly during the game. At the same time, you want to maintain the flexibility to change those plans when game situations dictate doing so.

In recreational slowpitch softball we believe that everyone on the team should be in the hitting lineup up to the limit allowed by league or tournament rules (for example, many leagues allow teams to have 11 or 12 players in the batting order, even though only 10 are playing defense). And we recommend that each player be in the field for at least three innings. An alternative approach is not to bat extra players or everyone on the team (if the league allows) but then to substitute players so that everyone plays about an equal amount of time.

In competitive slowpitch softball, managing the playing time of each player requires tougher decisions. Because you're playing to win, and in tournaments winning permits you to play more, you want to have your best players batting and in the field. On the other hand, you'll need substitute players when players can't make it to a game, get injured, need a rest, or for some other reason can't continue to play. So how do you keep players on the bench happy? This common dilemma for coaches has no easy answers, but here are some suggestions:

- First, talk privately with each substitute player explaining what your plans are for him or her to play. Many coaches avoid doing this because they are afraid that revealing these plans will cause the player to quit. Not revealing them, however, is usually worse. Players often become disgruntled, may cause dissension on the team, and eventually quit anyway. Let substitute players know not only when you plan to play them but also what they can do to improve their play and earn a starting position on the team.

- If the rules permit, bat 12 players if you think that batters 11 and 12 will help the team. We don't like to bat more than 12 because doing so reduces the batting opportunities of our 10 starting players.

- When the substitution rules are generous, make use of them. When your team has a decided lead, play your substitutes. If there is a re-entry rule, you can re-enter your starters if the lead deteriorates. If you know that you're playing a weak team, let your substitutes start a game.

- Use substitutes to pinch run if they have the speed.

Use clear visual and auditory directions when coaching third base.

- Use substitutes to coach the bases if they know how to do so.
- Encourage the starting players to be supportive of the substitutes. They benefit by having the strongest bench possible.

When your 11th and 12th batters are close in defensive ability to your starting players, consider having them split the defensive playing time with the player in their position. One approach is to tell the two players that they'll split the playing time for that defensive position and that they can work out how they want to split it. When you play important games against excellent competition, you may want to retain control of who plays that defensive position inning by inning.

In summary, you first should determine your team goals, weighing winning versus participation. You don't have to choose one or the other entirely, but you'll need to decide where you stand on this matter. Talk privately with players who will be substitutes and let them know their status. Then come to the game with a plan for how you'll manage substitutes and do all you can to play the substitutes as often as possible.

Assign Base Coaches

Many teams let just anyone jump out and coach the bases. Don't make this mistake. Assign coaches, especially third-base coaches, who have good judgment and demonstrate good coaching abilities. You should try to have the same people coaching the bases throughout the playing season.

If you're a nonplaying coach, you most likely will want to coach third base. If you're a playing coach, you should consider assigning two players to coach the bases. Assign substitute players to coach if they are able to coach effectively as described in chapter 3. If your substitutes don't have that ability, assign two players who have excellent judgment to coach third base. Five or six players should separate them in the lineup so that they can alternate between coaching and batting. Then select two players to coach first base who are equally separated in the lineup.

Conduct Batting Practice

Game day begins with arrival at the designated practice field. After a brief warm-up, you're ready to hit. Our recommended routine for conducting game-day batting practice is described on pages 278-279 in chapter 13. Now is a good time to announce the batting lineup if you've not yet done so. Players can then hit in pairs according to the batting order.

Some coaches do not announce the starting lineup and the defensive positions until moments before the game begins. That approach creates unnecessary anxiety among some players who are uncertain about their playing status or the position that they'll likely play. Announce the lineup as soon as you are certain about the presence and health of each player.

Batting practice is a good time to watch your team members to see whether they are moving well and to talk with players one-on-one about any issues in preparation for the game. You may want to ask about players' health and their ability to run the bases. Let players know whether they will be a substitute runner for someone or whether someone will run for them in certain situations. If you've made a change in the lineup and think that a player who has been dropped in the order may not understand, you may wish to explain your reasoning for the change.

Develop a Game-Time Routine

The game preceding yours is over, the players have cleared the bench, and your team moves in. Now everyone needs to know exactly what to do because often the time between games is short. Most teams establish a routine that they follow for each game. Here's an example:

- Get equipment bags set up on the bench or dugout. Get the bats out of the bags and clip the magnetic lineup board just above the bat rack.
- Do a final warm-up consisting of light jogging, stretching, and then some short sprints that simulate running to first base.
- Throw to each other a few more times to warm up the arms again.
- Infielders field ground balls on the sidelines.
- Outfielders run a few pass routes to catch balls thrown over their heads.
- Take some practice swings (but not actually hitting a ball).
- When the umpires step onto the field, have a designated player represent the team to go over any rules and flip for home team if home team has not been previously decided. (If you're a nonplaying coach, it's customary that you represent the team.)
- The team huddles up. The coin flipper announces whether you're batting or fielding first and reviews any special rules discussed with the umpires.
- Next the coach makes any comments and invites other players to make any comments of an encouraging nature or to remind players of the opponents' attributes or playing conditions.
- Do a quick cheer, and the game begins.

Some teams have no routines, resulting in players individually doing whatever they feel they should do to get ready to play. It's not uncommon to see the coach come back from the umpire meeting and then tell the team to take the field, yelling out the positions that players are to take. Or the coach may announce that the team is hitting first and then call out the lineup. We believe that this lack of preparation leaves teams less prepared to play their best. Just a small amount of planning allows your team to be much better organized, and your players will appreciate knowing where they will bat in the lineup, what defensive position they are going to play, and what they should do in the pregame routine.

A nonplaying coach or designated player will meet with umpires before the game.

GAME COACHING

More than anyone else, as the coach you must keep your head in the game. In other words, you should know the game situation at all times. Whether your team is batting or fielding, you want to know the score, the inning, the number of outs, the location of runners on the bases, and the time remaining to play if a time limit is in effect. Of course, knowing the game situation at all times is important, but when you both play and coach, you can easily lose concentration on the game. People talking with you, either friends or teammates, can also disrupt your focus on the game. In this section we'll review the offensive and defensive coaching decisions that you may encounter. We'll also discuss how to manage your team's mental outlook and negotiate with umpires.

Coaching During Offensive Play

Here is a list of tasks and decisions that you'll confront when your team is batting:

- Instructing batters how you want them to hit. Most of the time you'll want to let batters hit as they wish, but here are a few examples of situations in which you may want to direct their hitting:
  - Instructing a batter to try to hit a home run or not based on the game situation, distance of the fences, wind, home-run limit rules, and the batter's history of success in hitting home runs under similar conditions.
  - Instructing a batter to hit a sacrifice fly to score a run from third base rather than risk a line drive or ground ball caught by an infielder that does not score the run.
  - Instructing a batter to hit to right field to increase the chances of scoring runners on second and third base.
- Substituting a faster runner for a slower runner at an important time in the game.
- Reminding the base coaches what they should be reminding the base runners to do for various possible plays.
- Informing base coaches or base runners when you want to take extra risk in running.
- Keeping upcoming batters aware of the game situation.

Coaching During Defensive Play

Your coaching decisions continue when your team takes the field to play defense. Here is a list of tasks and decisions that you'll want to consider:

- Deciding how you want to pitch to various batters based on the pitching tactics discussed in chapter 5
- Choosing to walk a batter intentionally
- Positioning players based on what you know about the hitters or adjusting the spacing between players if they are too close together or too far apart
- Deciding whether the infielders should play back to get one out or move into double-play position

- With the bases loaded, deciding where infielders should throw the ball if it is hit to them
- Reminding infielders about who will cover the bases in various play situations
- Substituting players to strengthen your defense

Next we consider two of the more common and difficult coaching decisions to make—when to walk a batter intentionally and when to change the pitcher.

Intentional Walks

Your goal when playing defense is to keep batters off the basepaths and from scoring, but sometimes in the tactics of the game you give a little to gain a little or a lot. Walking a batter intentionally is such a decision. In chapter 5, "Pitching," we gave three reasons to walk a batter intentionally:

A good coach will adjust outfielder positions to correct spacing problems.

1. To avoid letting a particular batter hit
2. To create a force-out situation for the defense
3. To get an out on a substitute runner who is due to bat

It's the bottom of the seventh, the tying run is on first base, and there are two outs. The batter is Mr. Homerun King, who has hit a line-drive triple against the left-field fence and two towering home runs. The batter behind him is a good hitter, but not a home-run hitter. Do you walk Mr. King or let him bat? In making your decision you consider that you'll be moving the tying run to second base, which means that a single could possibly score that runner. On the other hand, if Mr. King hits another home run, the game is over. The decision is not an easy one to make, but you will often confront such situations.

You must weigh the potential damage that the batter will do versus the consequence of walking the batter. In making that judgment you'll consider the inning and score, the runners on base and their locations, and the hitting ability of the following batter.

The decision to walk a batter is made easier when first base is unoccupied and when by walking the batter you create a force-out situation at second base and possibly at third base. If Mr. King is batting with the tying run on second base and first base unoccupied, intentionally walking him is a no-brainer. If the winning run or inning-ending run is on third base with less than two outs, you would want to consider walking the next two batters to set up a force play at home and the possibility of a double play.

Seldom do you want to walk a batter intentionally that moves the runners up a base and makes it easier for the opposition to score. But if the batter is a high-probability home-run hitter, the tactic may be a good one to employ, even if you walk in a run when doing so.

Changing Pitchers

The most common defensive substitution decision that coaches must make is when to change the pitcher. You may want to change pitchers for either of two reasons:

1. The offensive team is having a rally.
2. The pitcher is walking batters unintentionally.

Let's consider each of these reasons. Hitting seems to be contagious, perhaps for two reasons. First, with each hit in a rally the confidence to hit safely builds in each following batter, and with an extended rally pitchers may lose their concentration and begin to throw fat pitches that are easy to hit. These offensive rallies often are a result of not just good hitting but also some defensive errors along with a lucky hit or two.

As a coach you should be able to sense this offensive momentum, and you want to find a way to stop it. Your first tactic may be to stop the game and discuss with your pitcher what's happening and how you would like him or her to pitch to the next couple of hitters. Causing a break in the game and encouraging the pitcher to refocus may stem the offensive momentum. Consider this tactic whenever the opposing team has scored three or four runs.

Should a break in the game not stop the carnage, then you should consider changing the pitcher, if you have another pitcher available. Many competitive teams have one or more relief pitchers, often someone who is already in the lineup. In this way, if your starting pitcher is also a good hitter, you can bring in the relief pitcher without taking the starting pitcher out of the batting lineup.

We recommend that you consider changing the pitcher whenever the opposing team has scored five or six runs. Although we have no empirical data, our experience is that the change in pitchers frequently extinguishes the offensive rally. Pitchers sometimes resent being removed in a game, especially when part of the offensive rally was the result of defensive errors. You may need to remind pitchers that you are making a change not because they did not pitch well, but because you're trying to break the offensive momentum.

You also want to change pitchers when they are walking batters unintentionally. Walks are errors by the pitcher, and they not only lead to runs but also damage the psyche of the other defensive players. All pitchers walk batters occasionally, but when a pitcher walks more than two or three batters in a game, you should consider a change.

Managing Team Psychology

Changing pitchers to stop an offensive rally is as much about managing the psychology of the game as it is about executing pitching tactics. So let's consider further your coaching role with regard to team psychology.

It's about confidence! Your biggest task is managing team confidence. Research has shown that when teams get a large lead and become too confident (overconfident), their play may deteriorate, giving opposing teams an opportunity to come back and gain momentum that is hard to stop. On the other hand, teams don't play as well when they are diffident (lacking confidence) either. Teams become diffident when they think that they are overmatched against a team who may have a better record and reputation.

As a coach you want to help your team be right in the middle between diffident and overconfident; that is, you want your team to be confident to the extent of their abilities and to shift the focus from how good or poor the other team is to executing what each member of the team is capable of doing. When a teammate yells from the bench, "Don't hit into a double play," you should remind the team that you want to focus on positive thoughts, not negative ones. When your team is winning by a wide margin, challenge players to work on improving their individual play rather than backing off and possibly getting into a bad habit.

Good coaches encourage players and help build team confidence.

Negotiating With Umpires

You need to be a sport psychologist not only with your players but also with the umpires. Begin by greeting them and always treating them with respect, even when you are certain that they've made a bad call. That's tough to do, but you owe it to the game and your teammates not to rant and rave at umpires.

You may want to discuss two types of issues with umpires. One is a rule violation, and the other is a judgment call. Let's consider rule violations first.

You must know the rules. If you don't know the rules, you are in a weak position to make a case for a rule violation in a game. When you believe that a rule has been violated, ask for a time-out, calmly approach the umpire, and state your case. Don't charge out on the field yelling your concern and don't let your players do so. Don't accuse the umpire of making a mistake or of being blind, out of position, lazy, stupid, or whatever else may pop into your mind. Instead, describe the situation as you saw it and the ruling that you think should apply. If the umpire is unmoved by your request for a change in the ruling, ask him or her to consult with the other umpire about the ruling. If the umpire is unwilling to consult the other umpire and you're confident of your position, you may request to protest the game and have a ruling by the umpire-in-chief or tournament director.

When you believe that an umpire has made an error in judgment (for example, you thought that the runner beat the throw to first base), you should again approach the umpire calmly and state your case. Now I've never seen an umpire reverse a call when a coach questioned a judgment call. So after you state why you think the umpires' judgment was not correct, ask politely if the umpire will consult with the other umpire, who may have had a better view of the play. Usually umpires support each other, but if the umpire's call was clearly wrong you may get a reversal on the call.

You'll want to use discretion in questioning judgment calls. On very close plays you should recognize that your judgment might also be wrong. So question only judgment calls that are obvious enough that you have a chance to get a reversal.

Remember to thank umpires for their work after the game if they've done a good job of being in position to make calls. You may see those umpires in another game, and you certainly don't want to alienate them.

You have a right to expect umpires to know the rules and to follow correct umpiring mechanics so that they are in proper position to make calls. You have a right to expect umpires to treat all players with respect and to receive your questions about rule violations and judgment calls with the same respect that you extend to them. If you do not receive that, you should share your evaluation of the umpire with the appropriate league or tournament officials.

POSTGAME COACHING

Incorporate the following tasks into your postgame routine:

- Congratulate or thank the opposing team for their play and sportsmanship.
- Gather your equipment, clean up the bench area from any drinking containers or other rubbish, and collect your batting lineup card.
- Meet with the team immediately afterward, preferably in the shade if it is a hot day and where players can sit down. Getting this meeting organized is often difficult because players begin visiting with family and friends, go to the restroom, or get something to eat or drink. Let them know beforehand that you'll always have a postgame meeting. At this meeting invite players to acknowledge those who played well offensively and defensively and add your comments as well. Also, identify mistakes and discuss how you want to correct them. Doing so is more difficult, and you don't want to embarrass players, but teams are less likely to improve unless they recognize their mistakes and know how to correct them. Close the meeting with an announcement about when and where the team will practice or play again. Make this meeting short and to the point and encourage player participation.
- Check with players to see whether any injuries have occurred. If so, encourage them to seek appropriate treatment.
- If you've finished playing in a tournament and have won an award, keep the team together to accept the team award, to recognize any outstanding players such as all-tournament team selections and most valuable player, and to take a team photograph.
- Win or lose, celebrate with teammates the joy of playing slowpitch softball.
- And at last you're done!

SUMMARY

- If you're a player–coach, meet the demands of coaching by being well organized and delegating tasks to other members of your team.
- Coaches have many duties before the game, including conducting batting practice, preparing the lineup, planning for substitutions, and assigning base coaches.
- Establish a pregame routine so that every player knows what to do to prepare for the game.
- When developing your lineup take into account your hitters' on-base batting percentage, their power- and place-hitting ability, their baserunning speed, and their ability to hit under pressure.
- Plan for substitute runners who are in the batting lineup so that they are not stranded on the bases when it is their turn to bat.
- Coaches have many offensive and defensive responsibilities during the game that require them to be constantly aware of the game situation.
- One of the major tactical decisions that coaches make is when to walk a batter intentionally.
- Another important decision is when to replace a pitcher because of a rally by the opposing team or unintentional walks.
- Coaches should be alert that players don't become overconfident when leading or diffident when behind. The objective is to help the team play with confidence.
- Approach umpires in a civil way when you believe that they have misapplied a rule or made an error in judgment.
- Your day is not done when the game is over. You have a number of postgame tasks to perform to address events of the day and prepare for the next practice or game.

APPENDIX A

Additional Resources

The additional resources listed here, all published by Human Kinetics, will help you play slowpitch softball better and live a healthier life. Check with your local bookstore or order online at www.humankinetics.com or by calling Human Kinetics at 800-747-4457. Visit www.HumanKinetics.com for a more comprehensive list of resources in the physical activity field.

Coaching

Curran, Mike, and Newhan, Ross, *Coaching Baseball Successfully*, 2007.

Martens, Rainer, *Successful Coaching*, third edition, 2004.

Veroni, Kathy, and Brazier, Roanna, *Coaching Fastpitch Softball Successfully*, second edition, 2006.

Wrisberg, Craig, *Sport Skill Instruction for Coaches*, 2007.

Conditioning

American College of Sports Medicine, *ACSM Fitness Book*, third edition, 2003.

Gambetta, Vern, *Athletic Development: The Art and Science of Functional Sports Conditioning*, 2007.

Sharkey, Brian J., and Gaskill, Steven E., *Fitness and Health*, sixth edition, 2007.

Tamborra, Steve, *Complete Conditioning for Baseball* (with DVD), 2008.

Drills and Skills From Baseball and Fastpitch Softball

American Baseball Coaches Association, *Baseball Skills and Drills*, 2001.

American Sport Education Program, *Coaching Softball: Technical and Tactical Skills*, 2009.

Garman, Judi, *Softball Skills and Drills* (book and DVD package), 2001.

O'Connell, Tom, *Play Ball: 100 Baseball Practice Games*, 2010.

Walker, Kirk, editor, *The Softball Drill Book*, 2007.

First Aid and CPR

Human Kinetics offers a CPR–AED course that can be completed online. Go to www.EmergencyCareEducationCenter.com. Titled *Complete Emergency Care*, the online course and text are available for US$35.

Flegel, Melinda, *Sport First Aid*, fourth edition, 2008.

Gotlin, Robert, *Sports Injuries Guidebook*, 2008.

Perrin, David H., *Athletic Taping and Bracing*, second edition (book and DVD package), 2005.

Mental Training

Burton, Damon, and Raedeke, Thomas, *Sport psychology for coaches*, 2008.

Halden-Brown, Susan, *Mistakes Worth Making*, 2003.

Jackson, Susan, and Csikszentmihalyi, Mihaly, *Flow in Sports*, 1999.

Murphy, Shane, *The Sport Psych Handbook*, 2005.

Orlick,Terry, *In Pursuit of Excellence*, fourth edition, 2008.

Porter, Kay, *The Mental Athlete*, 2003.

Nutrition

Bonci, Leslie, *Sport Nutrition for Coaches*, 2009.

Clark, Nancy, *Nancy Clark's Sports Nutrition Guidebook*, fourth edition, 2008.

Dunford, Marie, *Fundamentals of Sport and Exercise Nutrition*, 2010.

For more information on supplements, see Martens, Rainer, *Successful Coaching*, third edition, 2004, pp. 368–372.

Speed Training

Brown, Lee, and Ferrigno, Vance, *Training for Speed, Agility, and Quickness*, second edition, 2005.

Cissik, John, *Speed for Sports Performance DVD*, 2007 (56 minutes).

Dintiman, George, and Ward, Bob, *Sports Speed*, third edition, 2003.

Strength and Power Training

Baechle, Thomas R., *Weight Training: Steps to Success*, third edition, 2006.

Bishop, Tim, and Shiner, Jay, *Power for Sports Performance DVD*, 2006 (37 minutes).

Delavier, Frédéric, *Women's Strength Training Anatomy*, 2003.

Delavier, Frédéric, *Strength Training Anatomy*, second edition, 2006.

Hedrick, Allen, *Strength for Sports Performance DVD*, 2007 (25 minutes).

Incledon, Lori, *Strength Training for Women*, 2005.

Shepard, Greg, *Bigger, Faster, Stronger*, second edition, 2009.

Westcott, Wayne, and Baechle, Thomas, *Strength Training Past 50*, second edition, 2007.

Stretching

Frederick, Ann, and Frederick, Christopher, *Stretch to Win*, 2006.

Frederick, Ann, and Frederick, Christopher, *Flexibility for Sports Performance DVD*, 2007 (57 minutes).

McAtee, Robert, and Charland, Jeff, *Facilitated Stretching*, third edition, (book and DVD package), 2007.

Nelson, Arnold G., and Kokkonen, Jouko, *Stretching Anatomy*, 2007.

Vision Training

Wilson, Thomas, and Falkel, Jeff, *SportsVision*, 2004.

Contact Information for National and International Slowpitch Softball Associations

Organization	Address	Phone and fax numbers	Web site	Quick facts
Amateur Softball Association (ASA)	2801 NE 50th Street Oklahoma City, OK 73111	405-424-5266; 405-424-3855 (fax)	www.asasoftball.com	The national governing body of softball as appointed by the USOC. Offers slowpitch competition for men, women, seniors, and coed.
Huntsman World Senior Games (HWSG)	1070 West 1600 South, A-103 St. George, UT 84770	800-562-1268; 435-674-0550; 435-674-0589 (fax)	www.seniorgames.net	In addition to slowpitch softball for senior men and women, HWSG hosts 25 different sports competitions each October for seniors.
Independent Softball Association (ISA)	680 E. Main Street Suite 101 Bartow, FL 33830	863-519-7127	www.isasoftball.com	Uses unique rules including the use of a "base burglar" and stealing bases. Offers competition in all age groups and competition levels in slowpitch plus girls' youth fastpitch and men's modified fastpitch.
International Senior Softball Association (ISSA)	9401 East Street Manassas, VA 20110	703-368-1188; 703-361-0344 (fax)	www.seniorsoftball.org	Runs national and international tournaments for women 40 and over and men 35 and over with competition in all skill divisions.
International Softball Federation (ISF)	1900 S. Park Road Plant City, FL 33563	813-864-0100; 813-864-0105 (fax)	www.internationalsoftball.com	The international governing body of softball as recognized by the International Olympic Committee (IOC) and the General Association of International Sports Federations (GAISF). The ISF senior slowpitch World Cup is conducted yearly in Virginia, offering competition for women over 45 and men over 50.

(continued)

CONTACT INFORMATION *(continued)*

Organization	Address	Phone and fax numbers	Web site	Quick facts
National Softball Association (NSA)	P.O. Box 7 Nicholasville, KY 40340	859-887-4114; 859-887-4874 (fax)	www.playnsa.com	Offers slowpitch and fastpitch competition at all levels for youth and adults.
North American Senior Circuit Softball (NASCS) – also referred to as Senior Softball World Series	2510 Champion Way Lansing, MI 48910	517-393-0505; 517-887-1710 (fax)	www.nascs.org	Offers regional and national competition for men and women over 50.
Senior Softball World Champion-ships (SSUSA)	2701 K Street Suite 101A Sacramento, CA 95816	916-326-5303; 916-326-5304 (fax)	www.seniorsoftball.com	Conducts local, regional, and national tournaments for men and women over 40.
Softball Players Association (SPA)	925 W. State Highway 152 Mustang, OK 73064	405-376-7034; 405-376-7035 (fax)	www.softballspa.com	Conducts regional and national competition for women 35 and older and men 50 and over.
United States Specialty Sports Association (USSSA)	611 Line Drive Kissimmee, FL 34744	321-697-3636; 321-697-3647 (fax)	www.usssa.com	Runs tournaments in 13 different sports including slowpitch. Competition is offered at all age and skill levels for youth and adults, men, women, and coed.
World Softball League (WSL)	911 NE Macedonia Church Road Lee, FL 32059	229-460-7474	www.worldsoftball league.com	Offers all levels of competition for men, women, and coed.
Slo-Pitch National Softball (Canada)	63 Galaxy Blvd. Unit 4 Toronto, ON M9W 5R7, Canada	416-674-1802; 416-674-8233 (fax)	www.slo-pitch.com	Offers a Canada-wide qualify-ing tournament program in 22 divisions leading to Regional, Provincial, and National champi-onships.
Softball Canada	223 Colonnade Road, Suite 212 Ottawa, ON K2E 7K3, Canada	613-523-3386; 613-523-5761 (fax)	www.softball.ca	The national governing body for softball in Canada offers compe-tition for men, women, and coed.

Note: Page references followed by an italicized *f* or *t* indicate information contained in figures and tables, respectively.

ABOUT ASA

The Amateur Softball Association (ASA) has been the organization of choice for softball players throughout the United States for decades. As the National Governing Body of the sport in the United States, the ASA has many important responsibilities including regulating competition to ensure fairness and equal opportunity to the millions of players who annually participate in its programs.

The ASA is constantly working to offer new programs that will keep players involved in the game for years to come. Through its network of 76 local associations, the ASA sanctions competition in every state in the country and offers qualifying events that will lead teams to the ultimate National Championship.

Whether you play 10-Under Fast Pitch or 75-Over Slow Pitch, the ASA has a National Championship for you. Annually, the ASA could potentially host over 100 National Championship Finals in different divisions of play. Once you are crowned as an ASA National Champion, you have earned the right to boast you are the "Best of the Best" in your division.

As a member of the ASA you are also a part of one of the sport's most storied programs – USA Softball. As the National Governing Body, the ASA is responsible for selecting, training, equipping and promoting the four National Teams that compete in international and domestic competitions. The U.S. women have won seven consecutive world championships and three consecutive Olympic Gold Medals and have been ranked No. 1 in the world for the past two decades.

So whether you are a weekend warrior or aspire to represent your country as part of a USA Softball National Team, the ASA is the only softball organization that can give you all these opportunities.

WWW.ASASOFTBALL.COM

Not an Imitator,
the Originator!

INDEPENDENT ISA SOFTBALL ASSOCIATION

ISA offers competitive amateur softball for all ages with multiple classes and divisions to choose from.

680 E. Main Street, Suite 101
Bartow, FL 33830
863-519-7127

www.isasoftball.com

INTERNATIONAL SENIOR SOFTBALL ASSOCIATION

ISSA Executive Director, R.B. Thomas, Jr. and Keciihi Toda, President of the Japan Senior Softball Federation, shown inducting Eddie Feigner in the National Senior Softball Hall of Fame

The ISSA is a non-profit corporation established in 1994 and organized to:

- establish national and international goals for senior softball activities and encourage the attainment of those goals

- coordinate and develop amateur senior softball activity to foster productive working relationships among other senior softball and sports organizations

- promote and encourage physical fitness and public participation in senior athletic activities

- assist organizations and persons concerned with senior sports in the development of amateur athletic programs and other events that foster the special camaraderie among seniors

- provide the opportunity for any amateur athlete, coach, trainer, manager, administrator, or official to participate in senior amateur athletic competition

- foster the development of amateur athletic facilities for use by amateur athletes and assist in making existing amateur athletic facilities available for use by senior participants

- provide and coordinate technical information on physical training, equipment design, coaching, and performance analysis

- encourage and support research, development, and dissemination of information in the areas of sports medicine and sports safety

- encourage and provide assistance to organizations providing amateur athletic activities for all seniors

- provide world class competition for senior softball teams worldwide

The ISSA World Championships and other tournaments promise an exciting and competitive event for players at all skill levels. Tournament information is available on the ISSA Website, www.seniorsoftball.org.

For more information, contact:

R.B. Thomas, Jr. • ISSA Executive Director
9401 East Street • Manassas, VA 20110
703-368-1188 • Issa94@aol.com

www.seniorsoftball.org

NATIONAL SOFTBALL ASSOCIATION

The Player's Association

The NSA offers a division of play for youth through seniors throughout all 50 states.

The NSA promotes competition from local leagues and local tournaments all the way to the World Series and the Super World Series.

NSA is dedicated to offering a quality program, run by dedicated, trained, well-informed and professional directors and umpires.

For information on the NSA, contact a member of the

National Office Staff at 859-887-4114 or

e-mail NSAhdqtrs@aol.com – www.PlayNSA.com

Visit the NSA Sports Hall of Fame located at

101 NSA Way, Nicholasville, KY 40356

Monday – Friday 9:00 AM – 4:00 PM EST

North American Senior Circuit Softball
and
Senior Softball World Series

NASCS Regional Tournaments

Regional tournaments sanctioned by NASCS provide an opportunity for senior softball associations or local municipalities to raise funds to support their programs. For more details contact Greg Maas at the e-mail below.

Senior Softball World Series®

First established in 1989, the Senior Softball World Series® is the "Grand Daddy" of senior softball tournaments. The tournament brings teams from across the country to host cities for a week of competition, site seeing and fun. Since 1989, the tournament has been hosted by cities in Arizona, California, Florida, Iowa, Michigan, Minnesota, Nebraska, North Carolina and Texas.

NASCS FOUNDER
Ken Maas (1922-2004)

After "retiring" from the insurance business, Ken devoted his time to a lifelong love and hobby, softball. Ken incorporated NASCS in 1985 and held its first tournament that year hosting teams from seven states. He helped the Sporting Goods Manufacturer's Association organize the Senior Softball World Series® and shared his expertise as a member of the Technical Advisory Board for the World Senior Olympics, now known as the World Senior Games, in St. George, Utah. Ken was a true pioneer and leader in promoting senior softball.

Incorporated in 1985

For information on hosting the "Grand Daddy" of senior softball tournaments contact:

**Greg Maas,
kennascs@aol.com**

Softball Players Association

"A fun and rewarding place to play"

"Representing Senior Softball Players Nationwide"

<u>For information call:</u>

405-376-7034 – Office   405-376-7035 – FAX

Softball Players Association (S.P.A.)

925 W. Highway 152

Mustang, OK 73064

Or visit

<u>www.softballspa.com</u>

"TO GOD BE THE GLORY"